Kurt Ankeny / Salem, MA

COMICS SHORT STORIES 2014-2019

AdHouse Books / Richmond, VA

Gulls

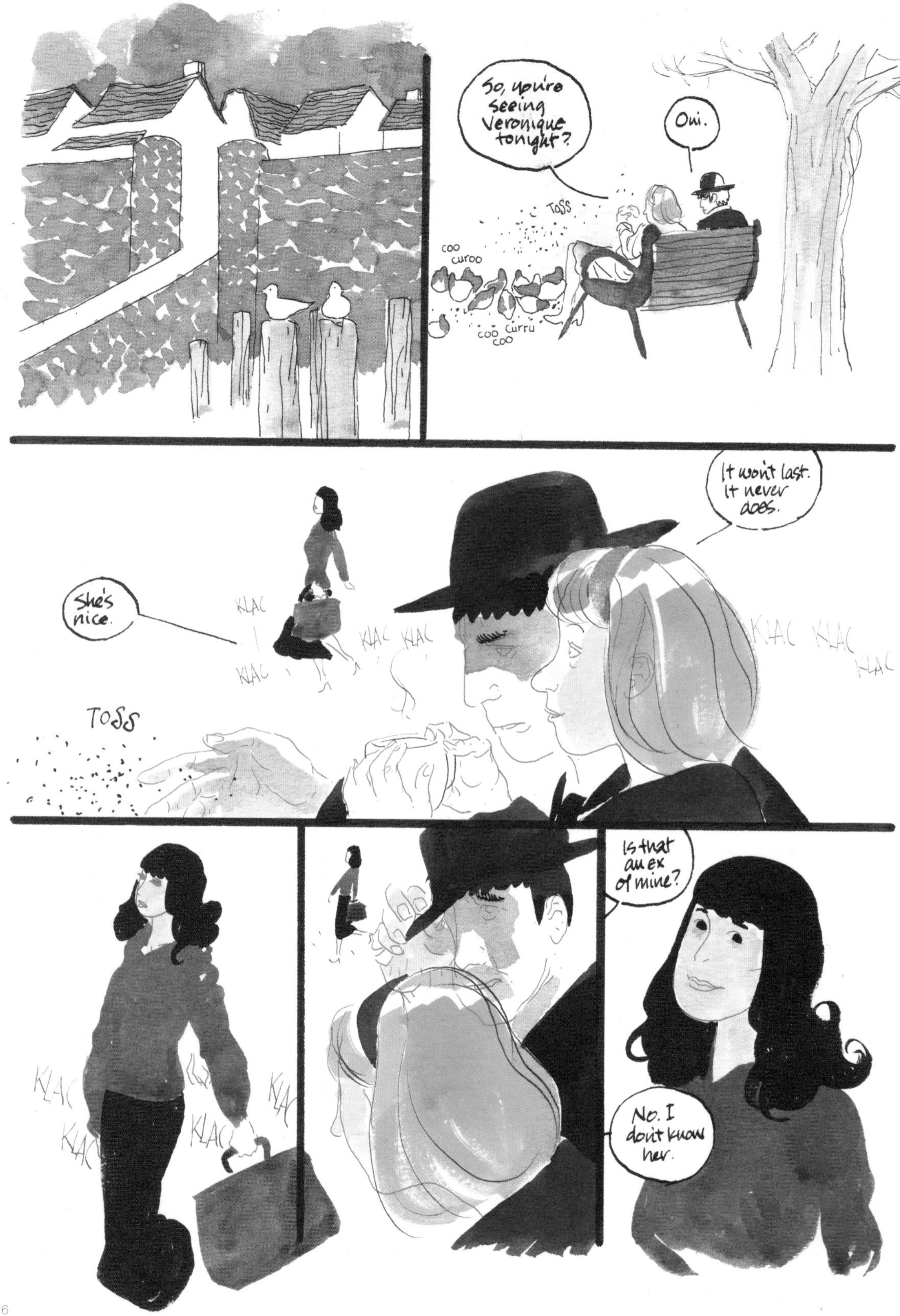
So, you're seeing Veronique tonight?
Oui.
TOSS
COO CUROO
COO COO CURRU
It won't last. It never does.
She's nice.
KLAC KLAC KLAC KLAC
KLAC KLAC KLAC
TOSS
KLAC KLAC KLAC KLAC KLAC
Is that an ex of mine?
No. I don't know her.

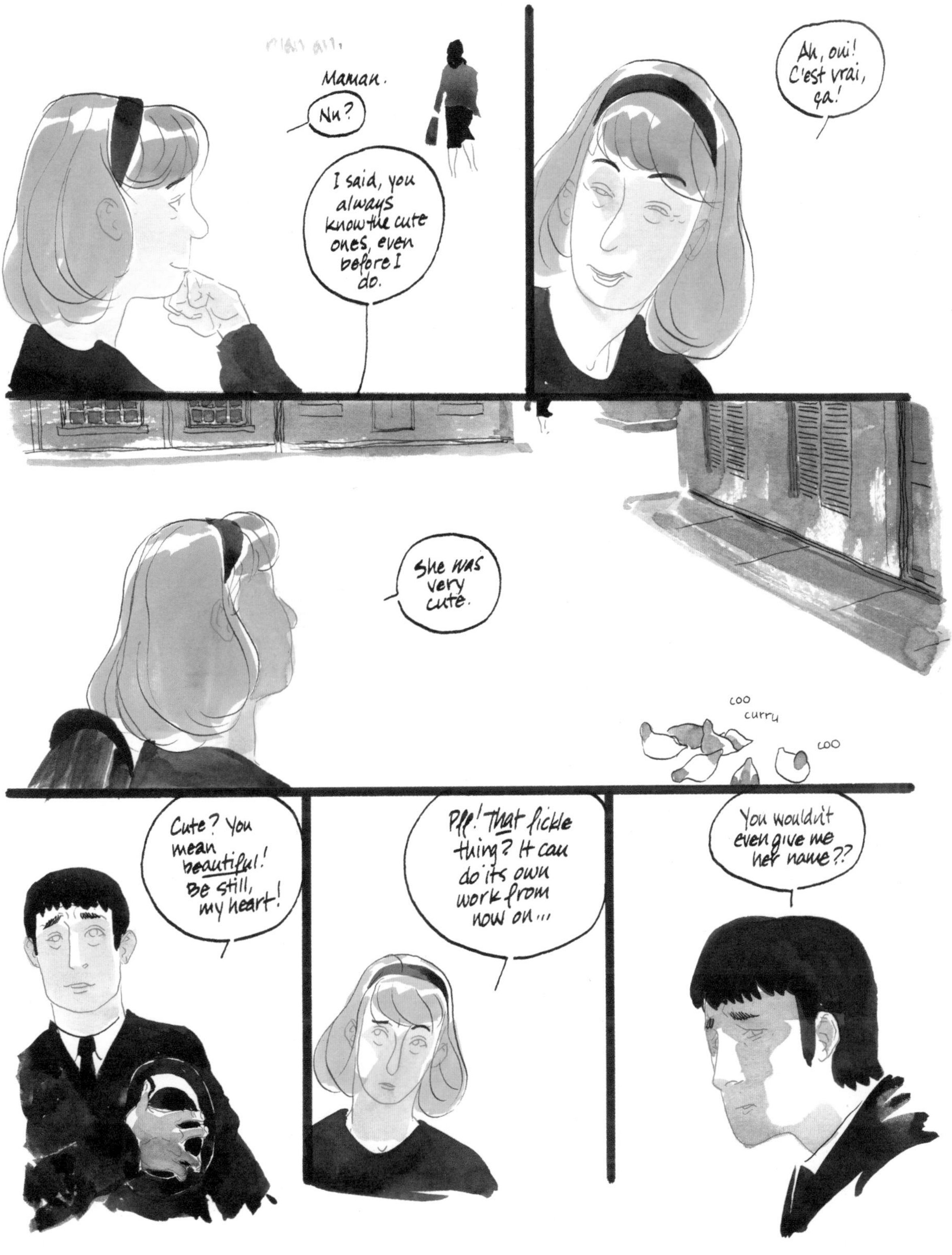
Maman.
Nu?
I said, you always know the cute ones, even before I do.
Ah, oui! C'est vrai, ça!
She was very cute.
coo
curru
coo
Cute? You mean beautiful! Be still, my heart!
Pff! That fickle thing? It can do its own work from now on...
You wouldn't even give me her name??

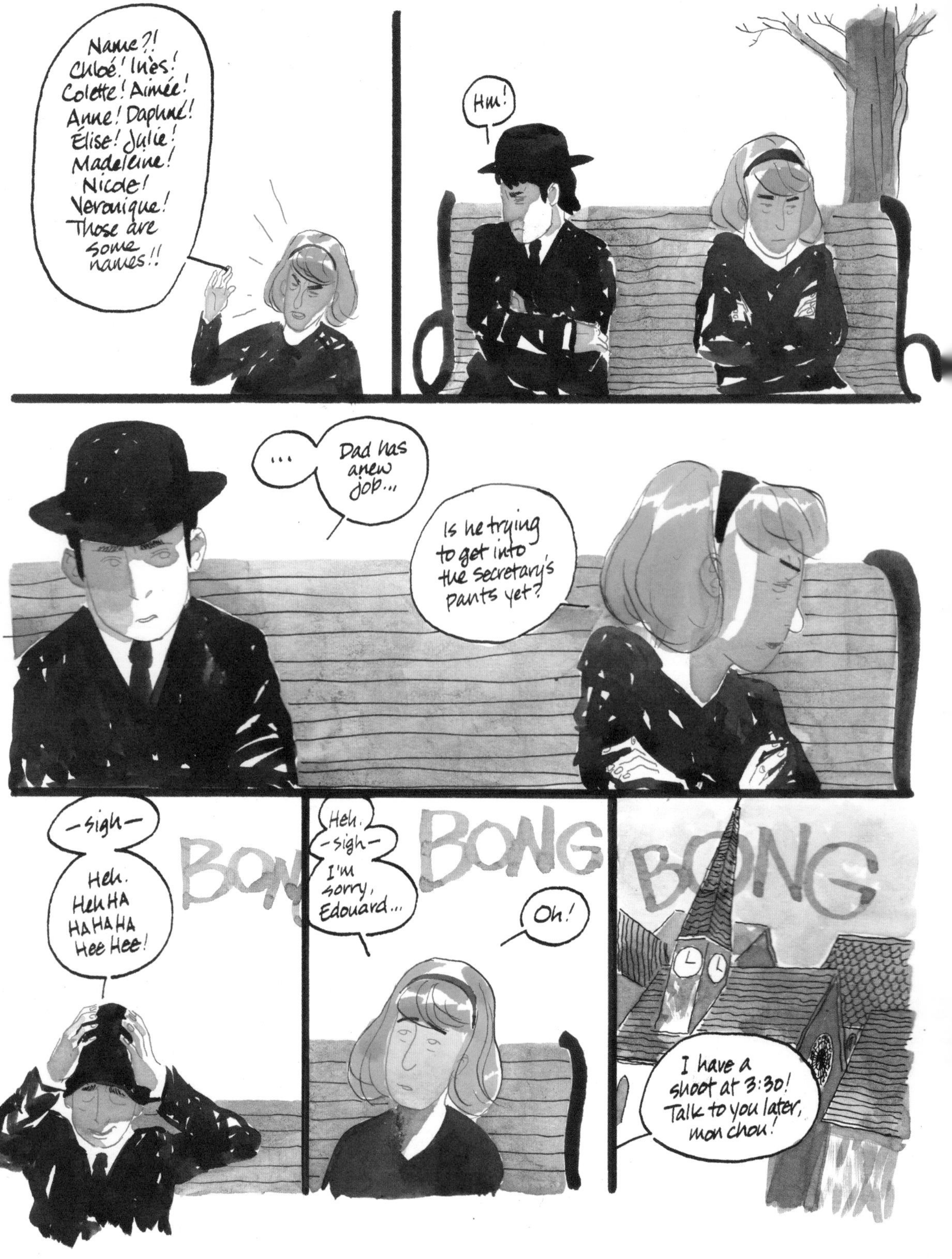
Name?! Chloé! Inès! Colette! Aimée! Anne! Daphné! Élise! Julie! Madeleine! Nicole! Veronique! Those are some names!!
Hm!
...
Dad has anew job...
Is he trying to get into the secretary's pants yet?
-sigh-
Heh. Heh HA HA HA HA Hee Hee!
BONG
Heh. -sigh- I'm sorry, Edouard...
Oh!
BONG
BONG
I have a shoot at 3:30! Talk to you later, mon chou!

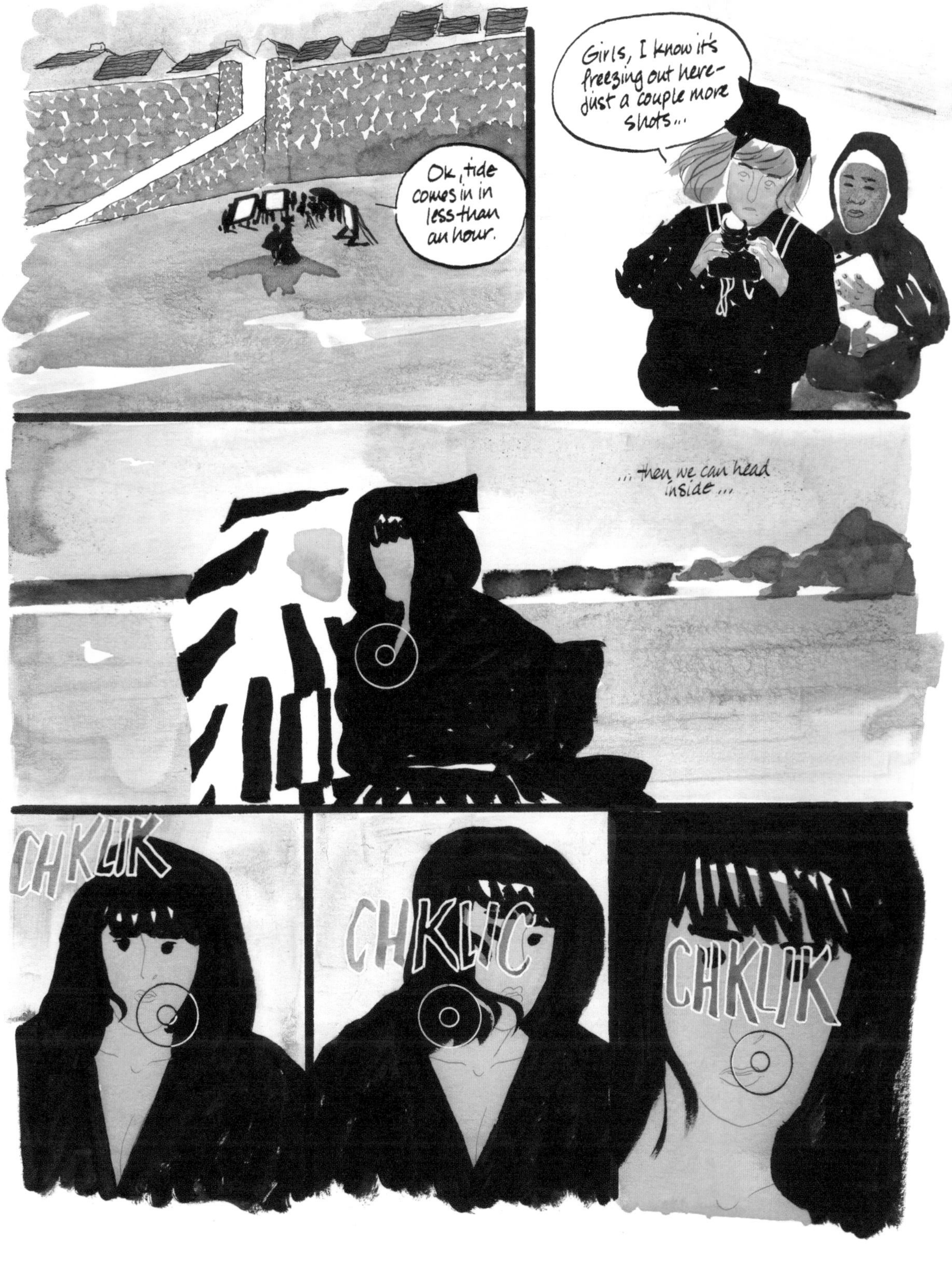
Ok, tide comes in in less than an hour.
Girls, I know it's freezing out here- just a couple more shots...
... then we can head inside ...
CHKLIK
CHKLIC
CHKLIK

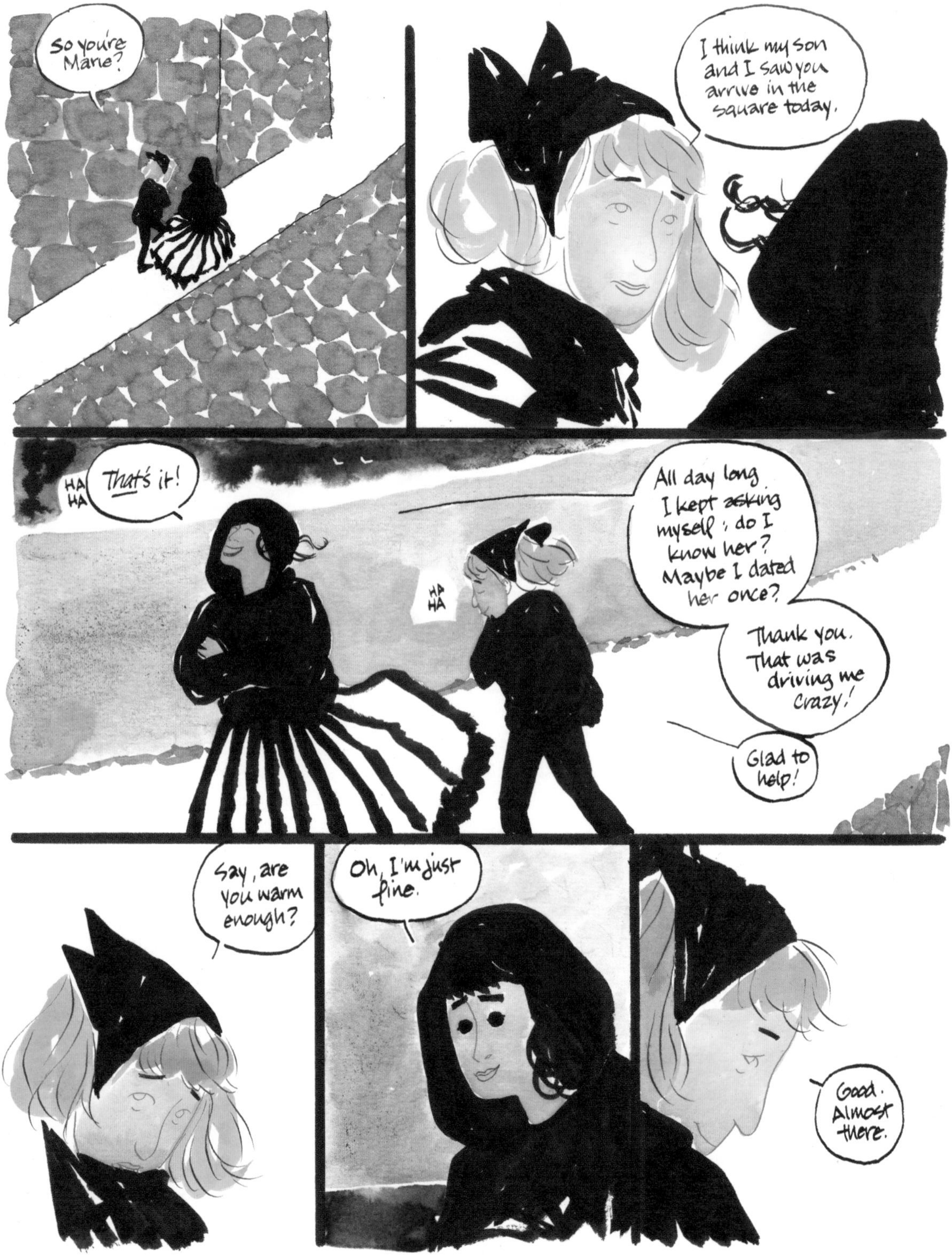
So you're Marie?
I think my son and I saw you arrive in the square today.
HA HA
That's it!
All day long I kept asking myself; do I know her? Maybe I dated her once?
HA HA
Thank you. That was driving me crazy!
Glad to help!
Say, are you warm enough?
Oh, I'm just fine.
Good. Almost there.

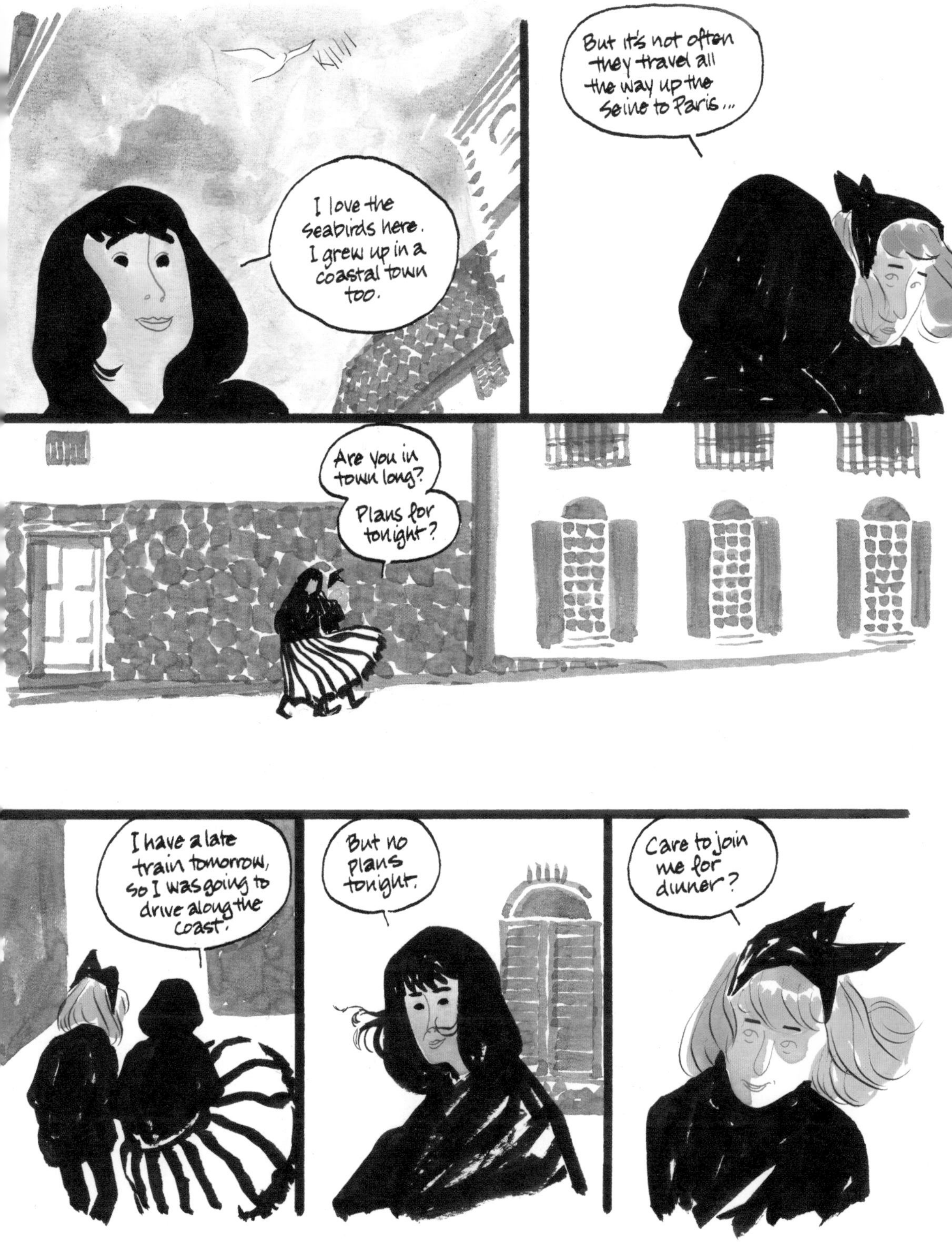
I love the seabirds here. I grew up in a coastal town too.
But it's not often they travel all the way up the Seine to Paris...
Are you in town long?
Plans for tonight?
I have a late train tomorrow, so I was going to drive along the coast.
But no plans tonight.
Care to join me for dinner?

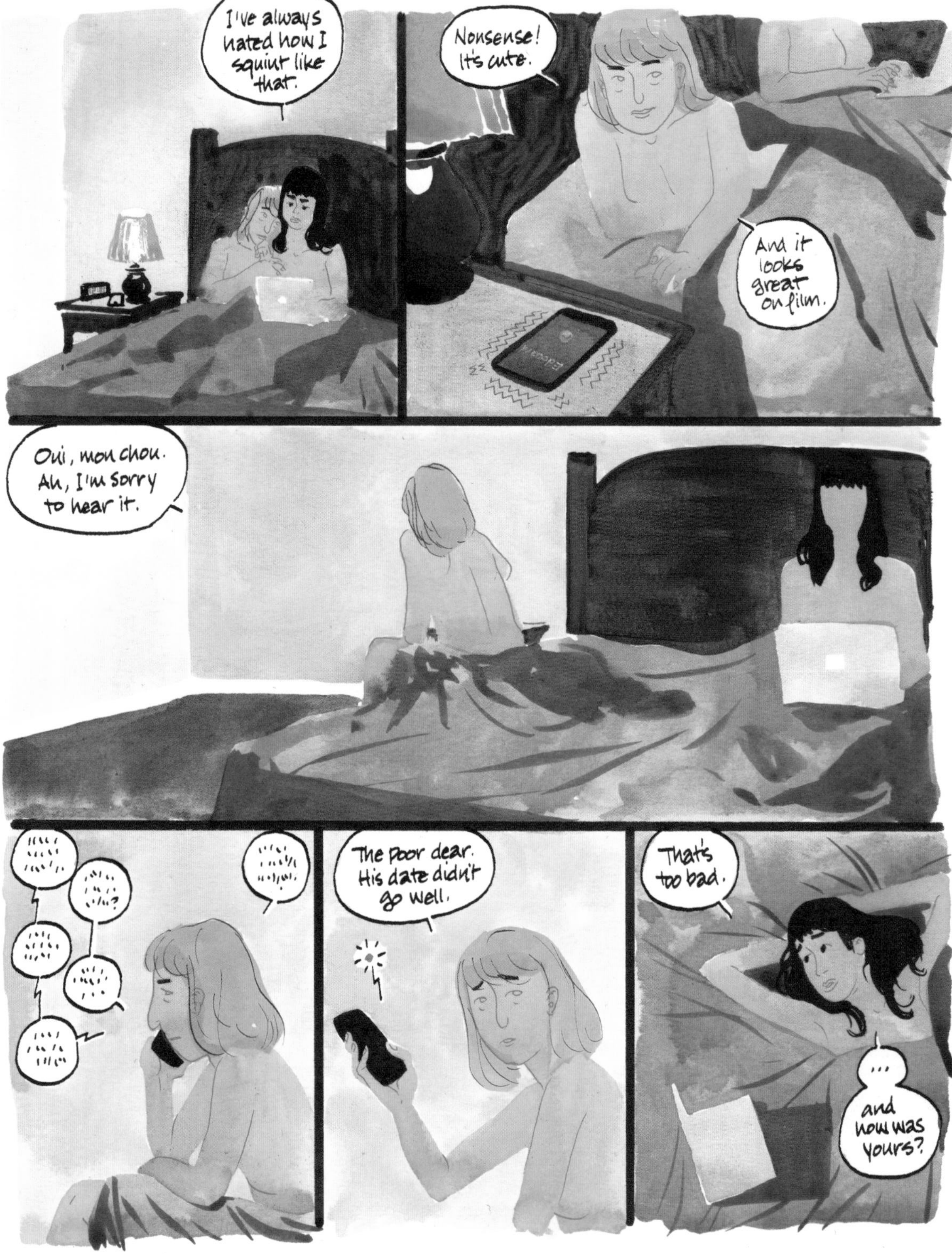
I've always hated how I squint like that.
Nonsense! It's cute.
And it looks great on film.
Oui, mon chou. Ah, I'm sorry to hear it.
The poor dear. His date didn't go well.
That's too bad.
...
and how was yours?

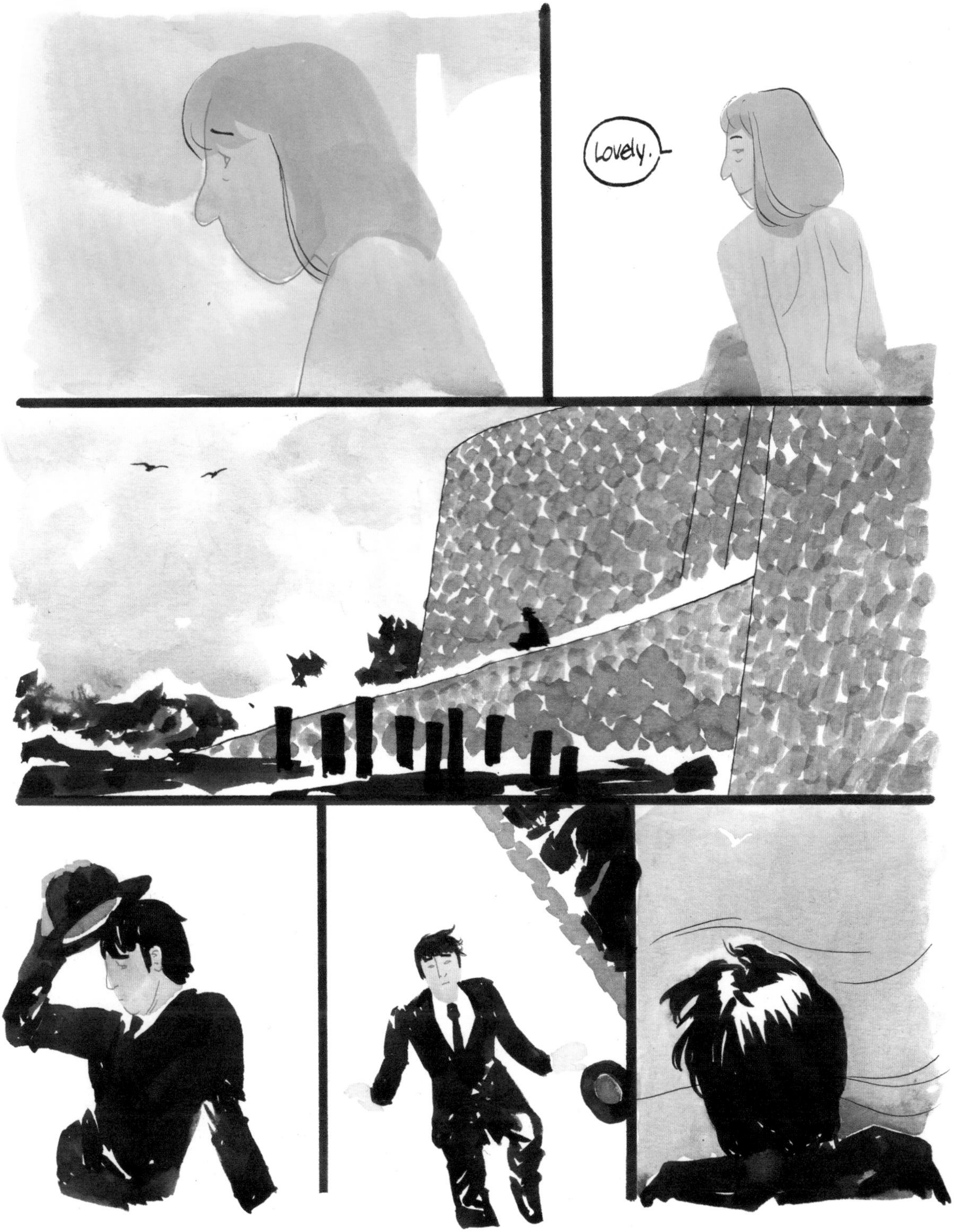
Lovely.

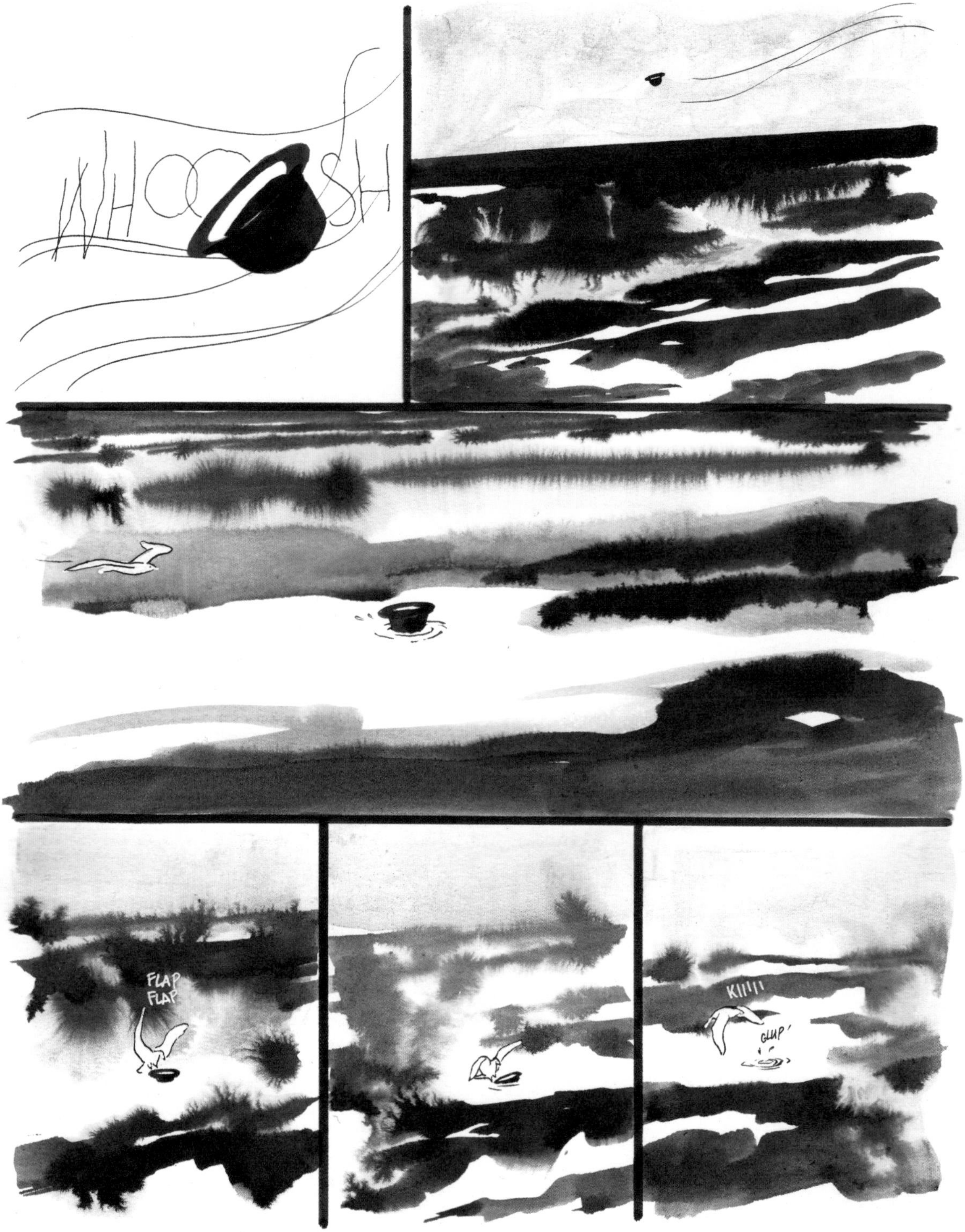
WHOOSH
FLAP FLAP
KIIII
GLUP!

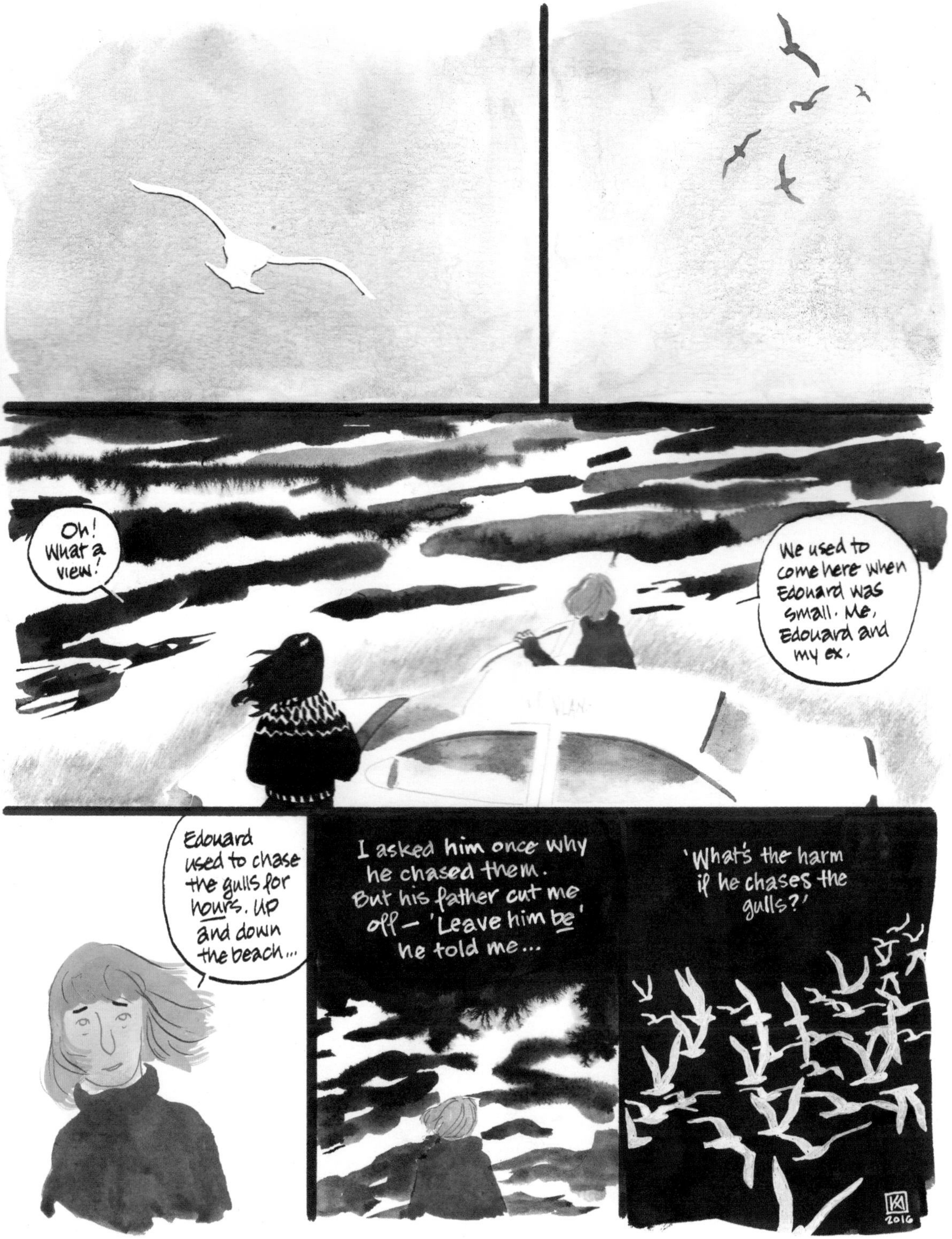

Oh! What a view!
We used to come here when Edouard was small. Me, Edouard and my ex.
Edouard used to chase the gulls for hours. Up and down the beach...
I asked him once why he chased them. But his father cut me off – 'Leave him be' he told me...
'What's the harm if he chases the gulls?'
KA 2016

Saltwater Snow

one

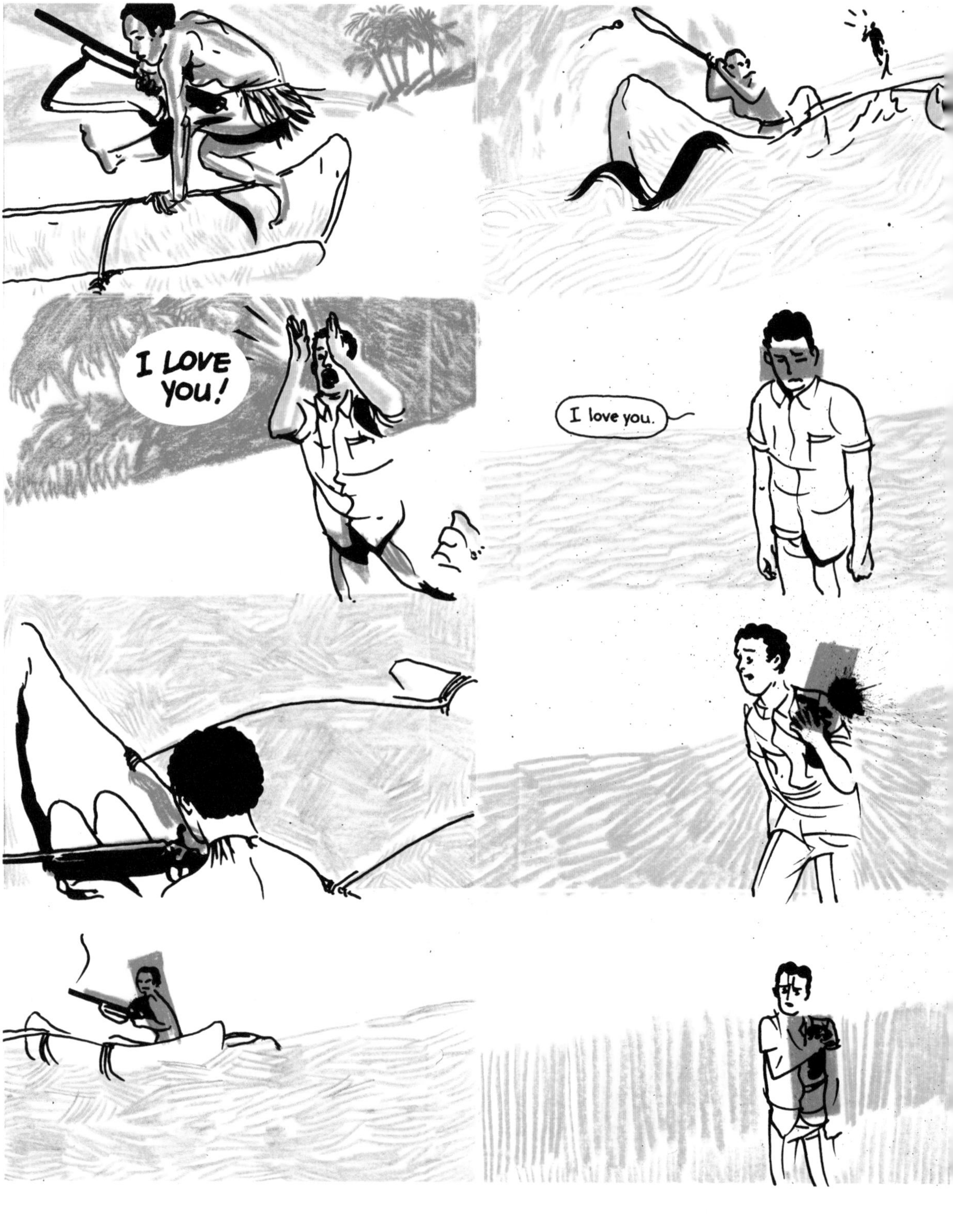
I LOVE YOU!
I love you.

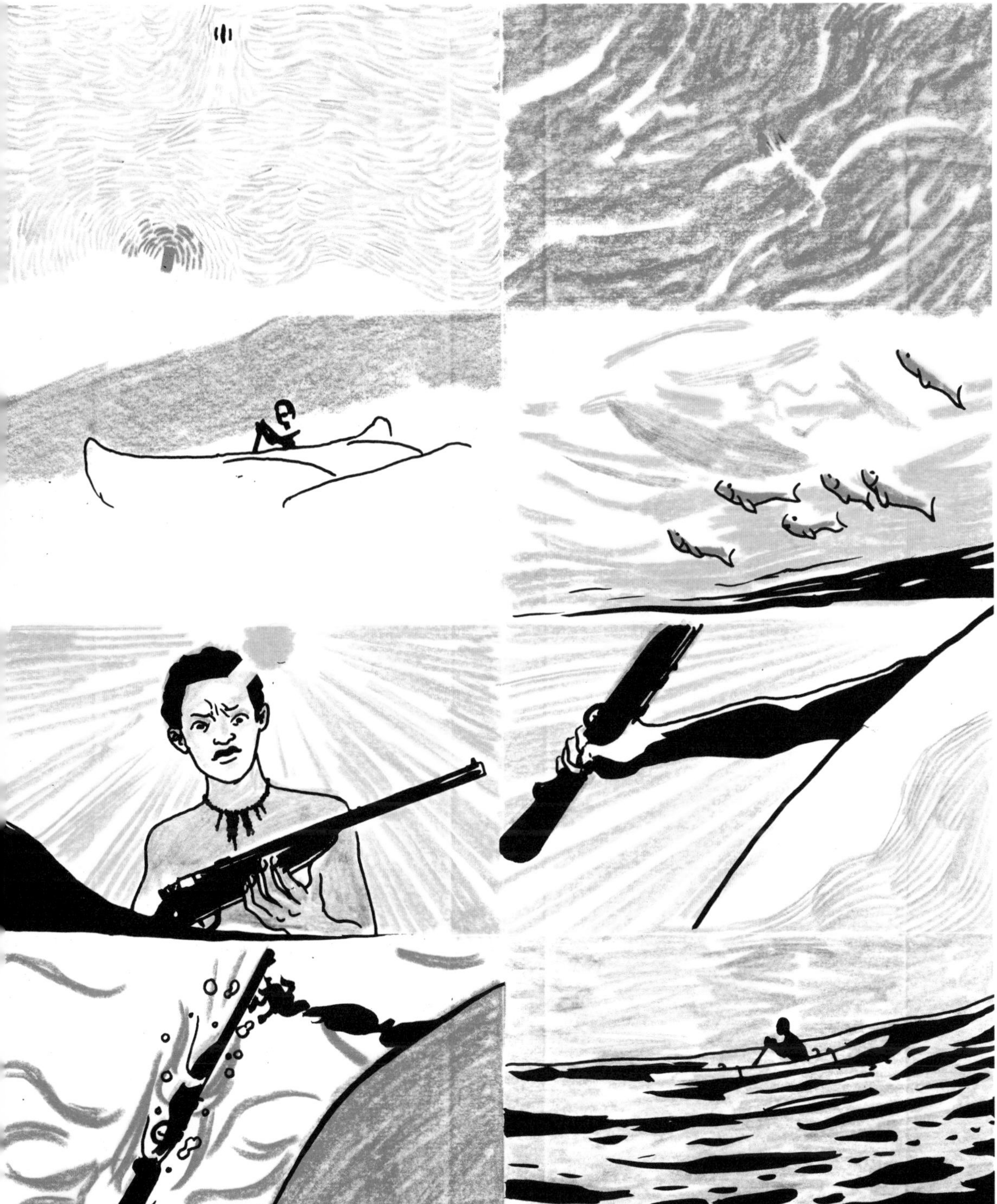

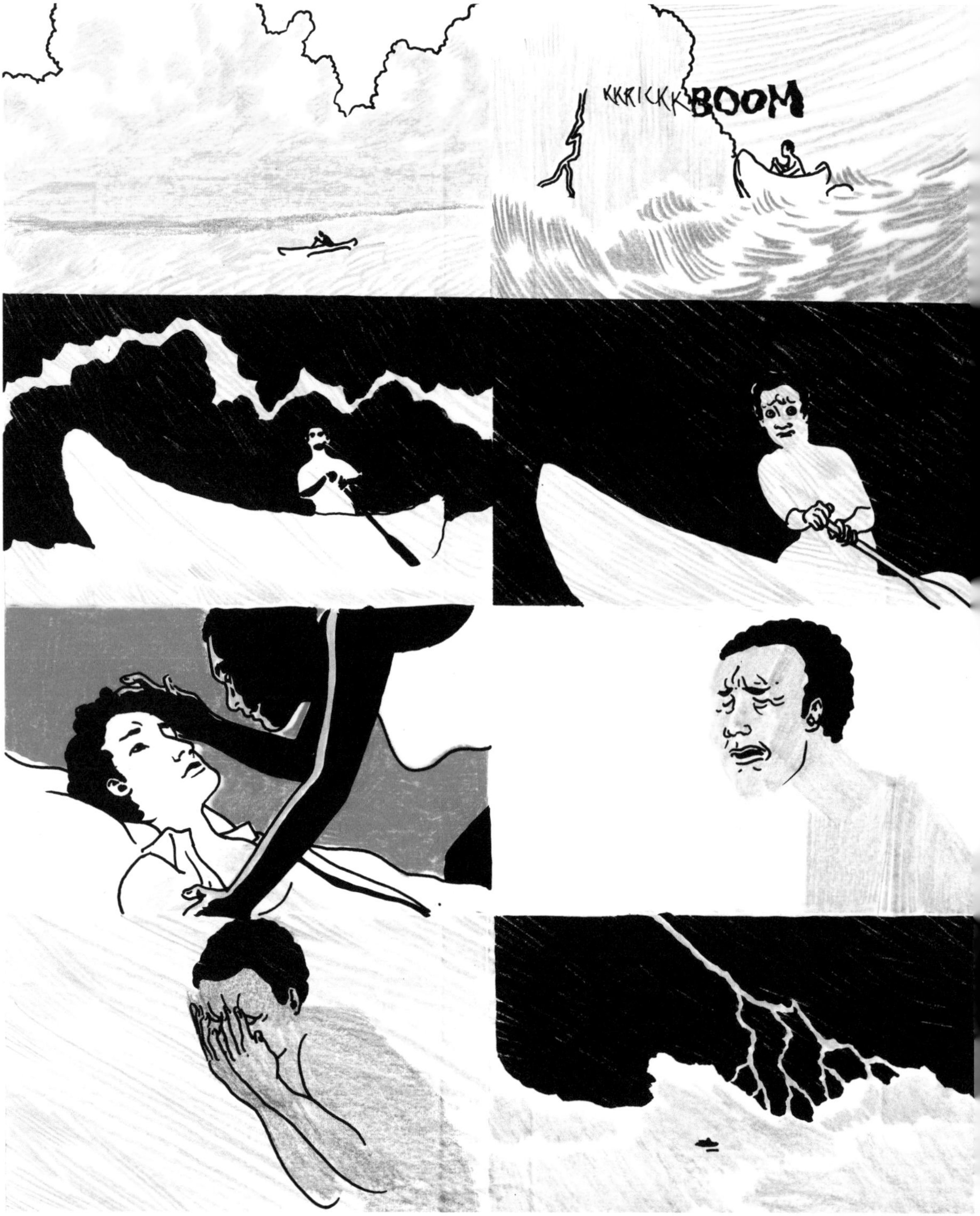
KKRICKK BOOM

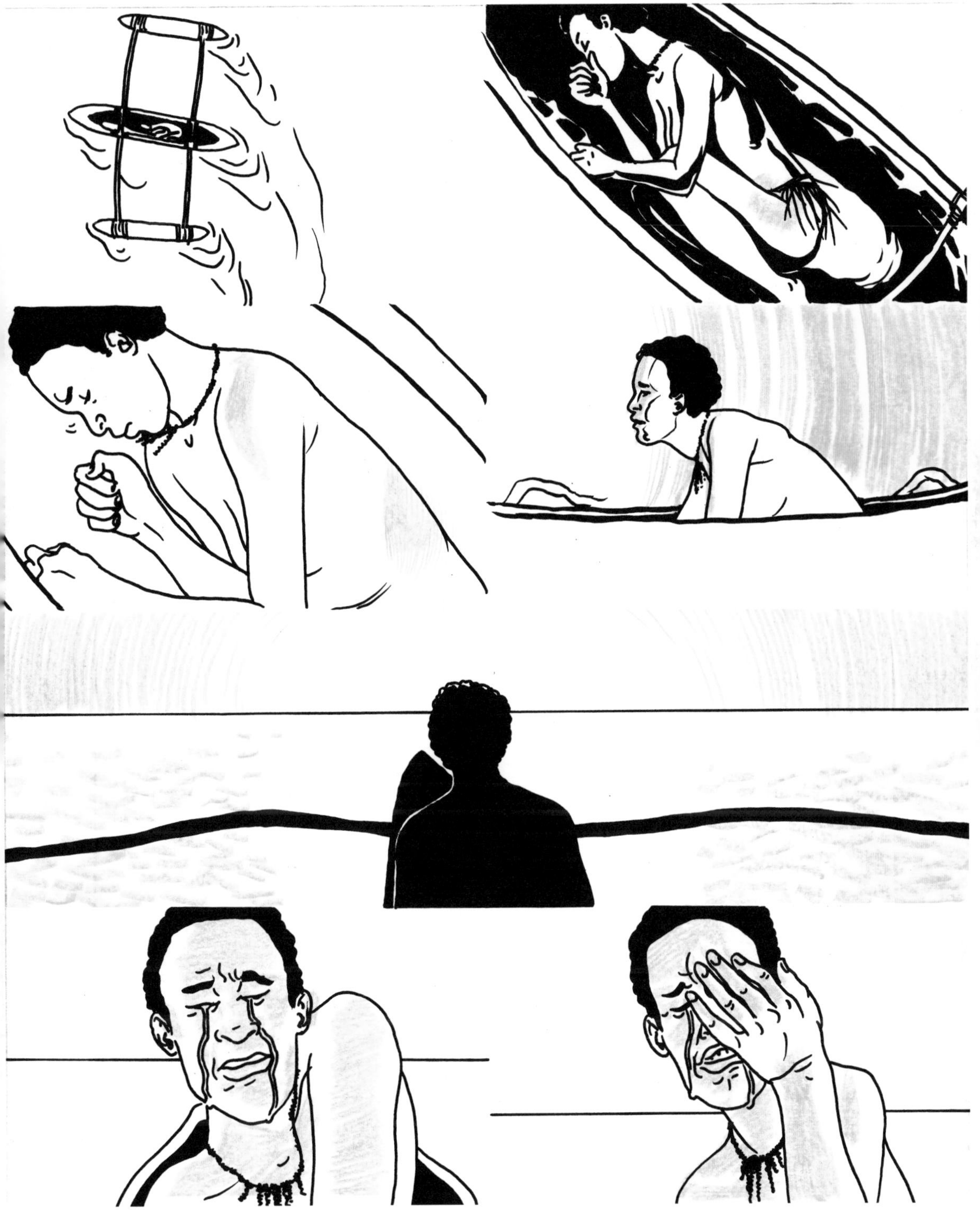

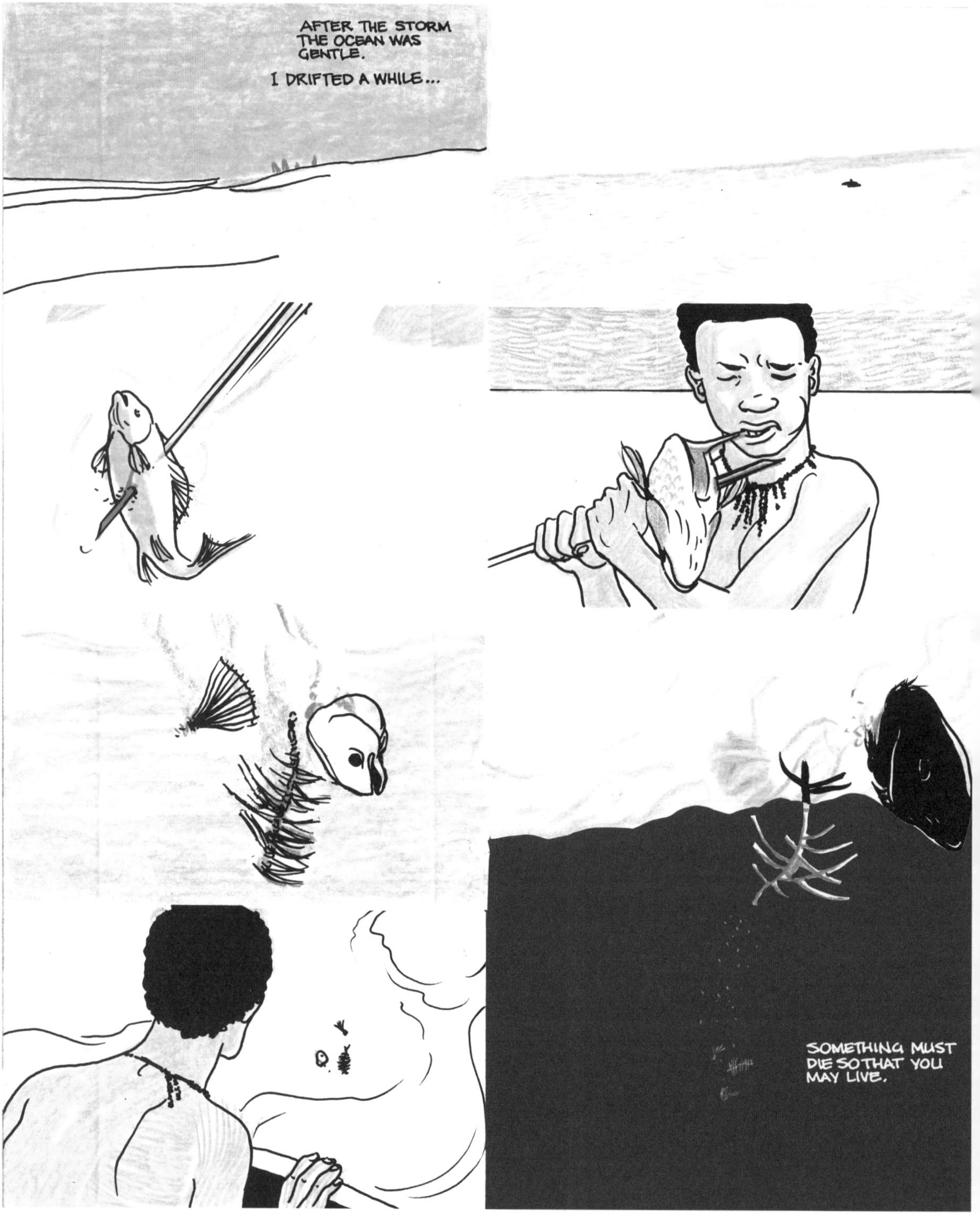
AFTER THE STORM THE OCEAN WAS GENTLE.
I DRIFTED A WHILE...
SOMETHING MUST DIE SO THAT YOU MAY LIVE.

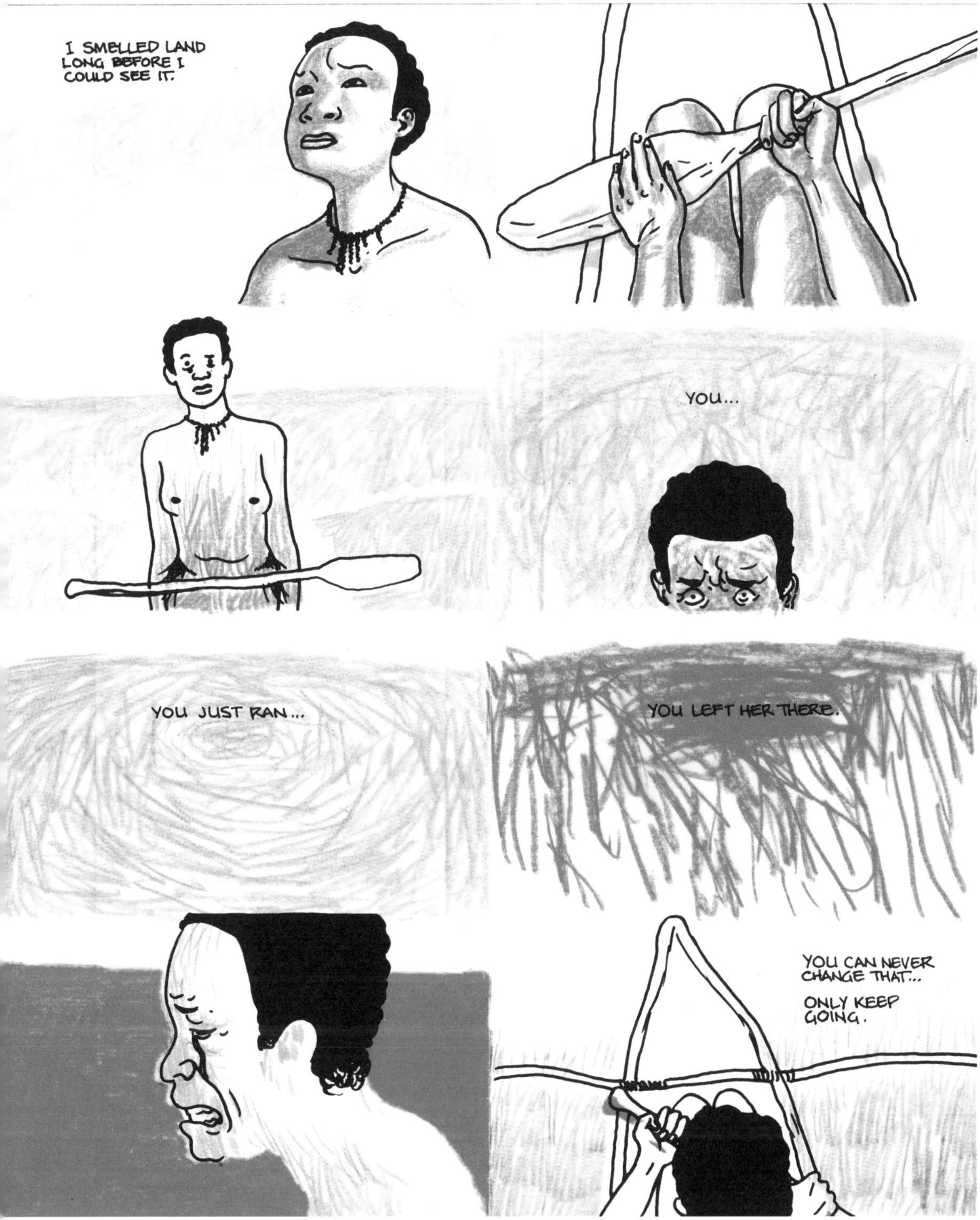
I SMELLED LAND LONG BEFORE I COULD SEE IT.
YOU...
YOU JUST RAN...
YOU LEFT HER THERE.
YOU CAN NEVER CHANGE THAT...
ONLY KEEP GOING.

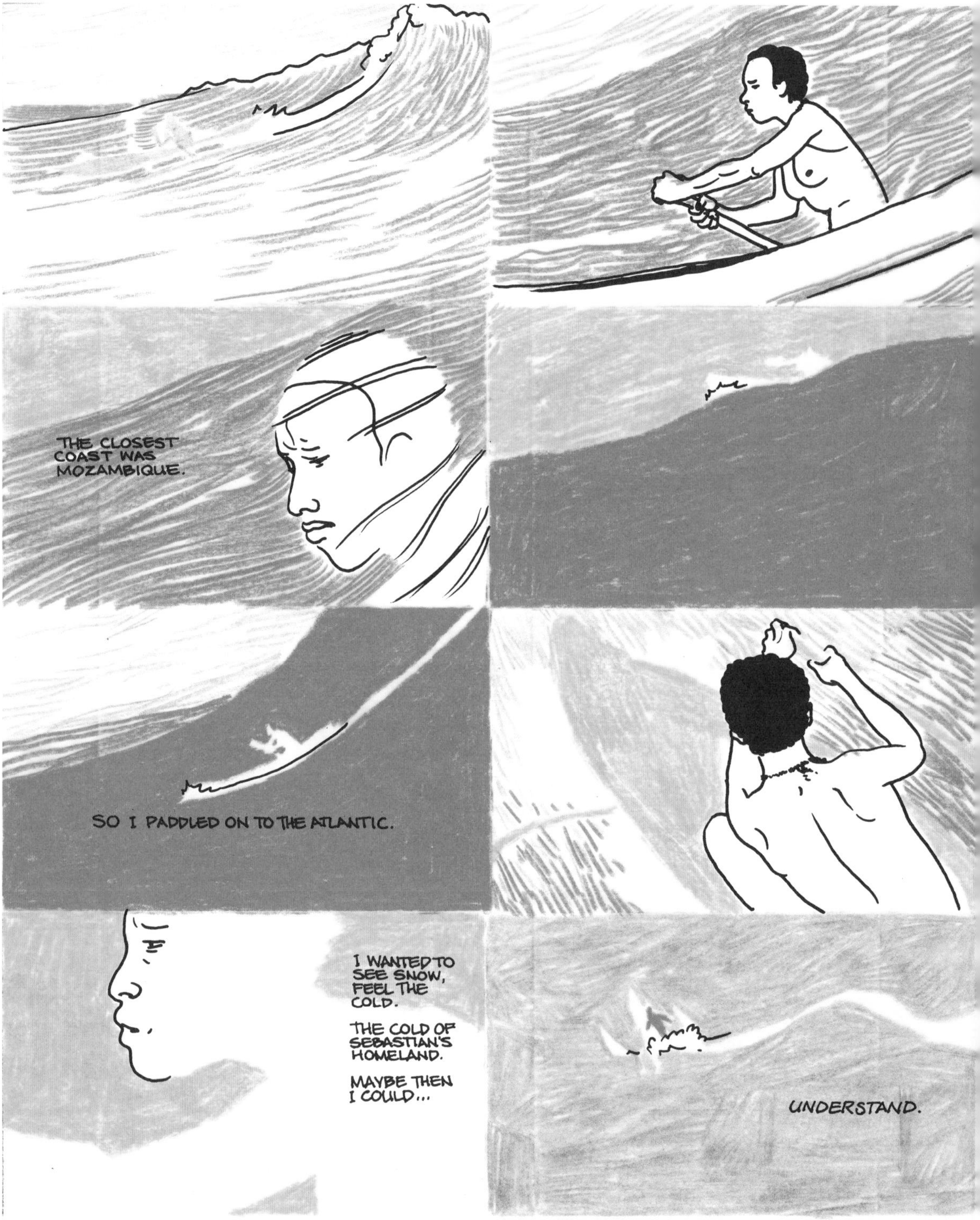
THE CLOSEST COAST WAS MOZAMBIQUE.
SO I PADDLED ON TO THE ATLANTIC.
I WANTED TO SEE SNOW, FEEL THE COLD.
THE COLD OF SEBASTIAN'S HOMELAND.
MAYBE THEN I COULD...
UNDERSTAND.

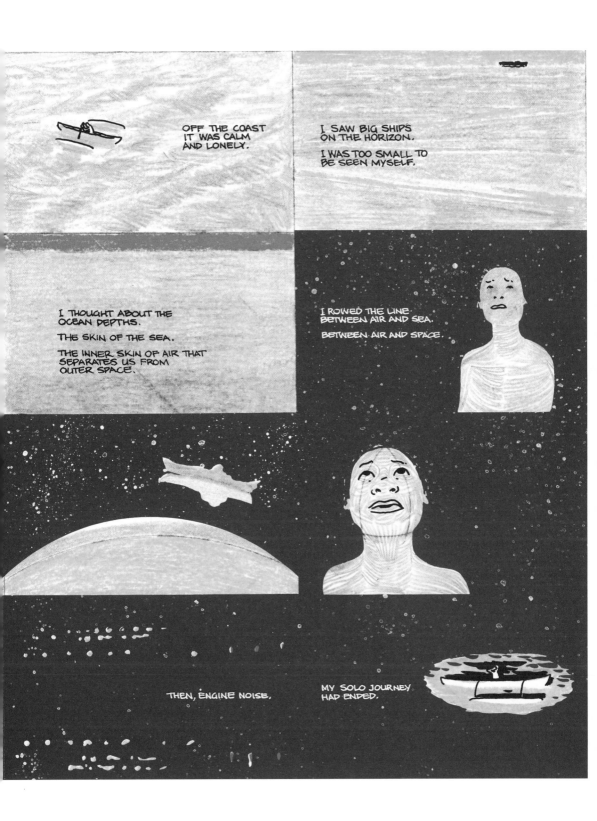

OFF THE COAST IT WAS CALM AND LONELY.

I SAW BIG SHIPS ON THE HORIZON.

I WAS TOO SMALL TO BE SEEN MYSELF.

I THOUGHT ABOUT THE OCEAN DEPTHS.

THE SKIN OF THE SEA.

THE INNER SKIN OF AIR THAT SEPARATES US FROM OUTER SPACE.

I ROWED THE LINE BETWEEN AIR AND SEA.

BETWEEN AIR AND SPACE.

THEN, ENGINE NOISE,

MY SOLO JOURNEY HAD ENDED.

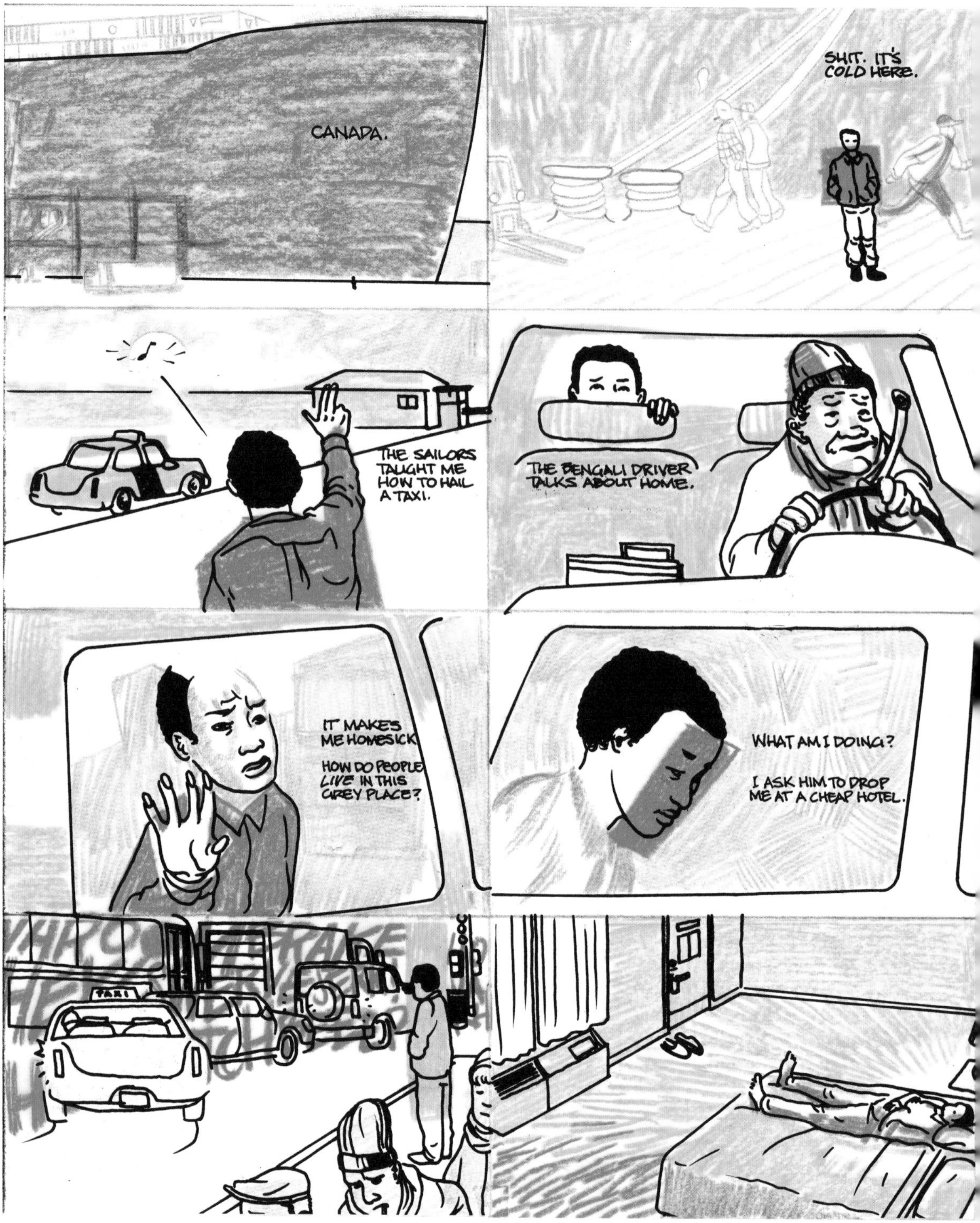
CANADA.
SHIT. IT'S COLD HERE.
THE SAILORS TAUGHT ME HOW TO HAIL A TAXI.
THE BENGALI DRIVER TALKS ABOUT HOME.
IT MAKES ME HOMESICK
HOW DO PEOPLE *LIVE* IN THIS GREY PLACE?
WHAT AM I DOING?
I ASK HIM TO DROP ME AT A CHEAP HOTEL.
TAXI

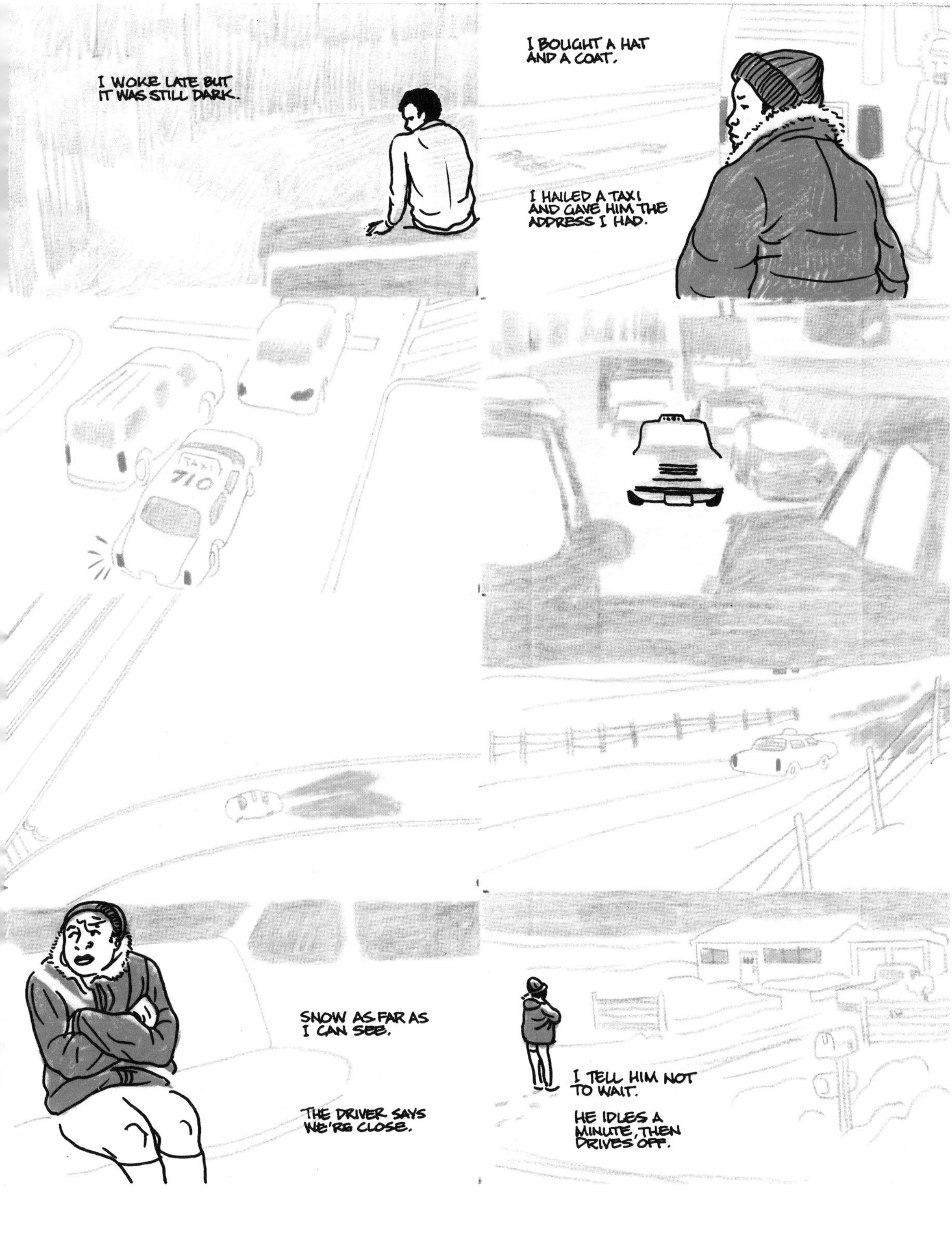
I WOKE LATE BUT IT WAS STILL DARK.
I BOUGHT A HAT AND A COAT.
I HAILED A TAXI AND GAVE HIM THE ADDRESS I HAD.
TAXI 710
SNOW AS FAR AS I CAN SEE.
THE DRIVER SAYS WE'RE CLOSE.
I TELL HIM NOT TO WAIT.
HE IDLES A MINUTE, THEN DRIVES OFF.

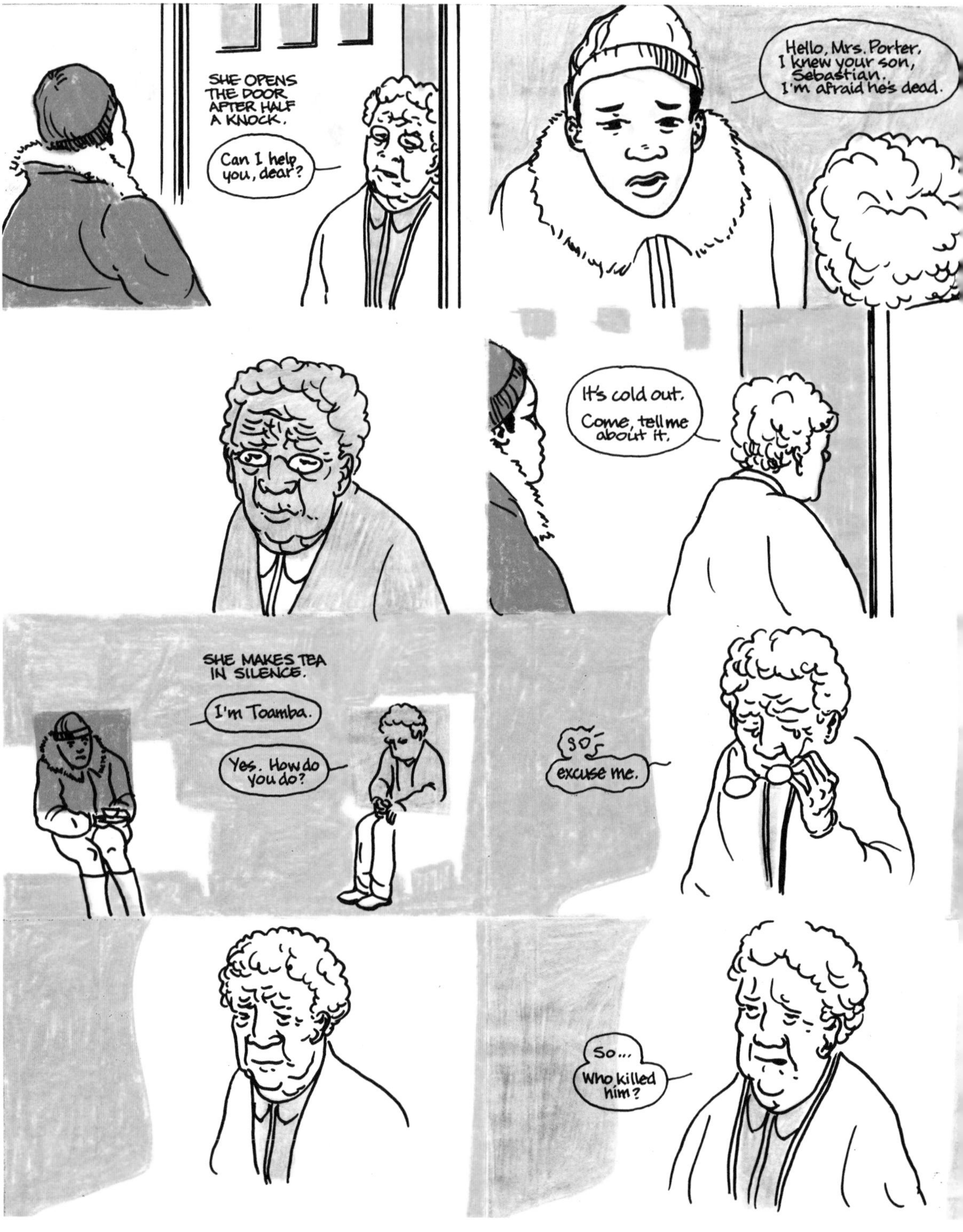

SHE OPENS THE DOOR AFTER HALF A KNOCK.
Can I help you, dear?
Hello, Mrs. Porter, I knew your son, Sebastian. I'm afraid he's dead.
It's cold out.
Come, tell me about it.
SHE MAKES TEA IN SILENCE.
I'm Toamba.
Yes. How do you do?
so
excuse me.
So...
Who killed him?

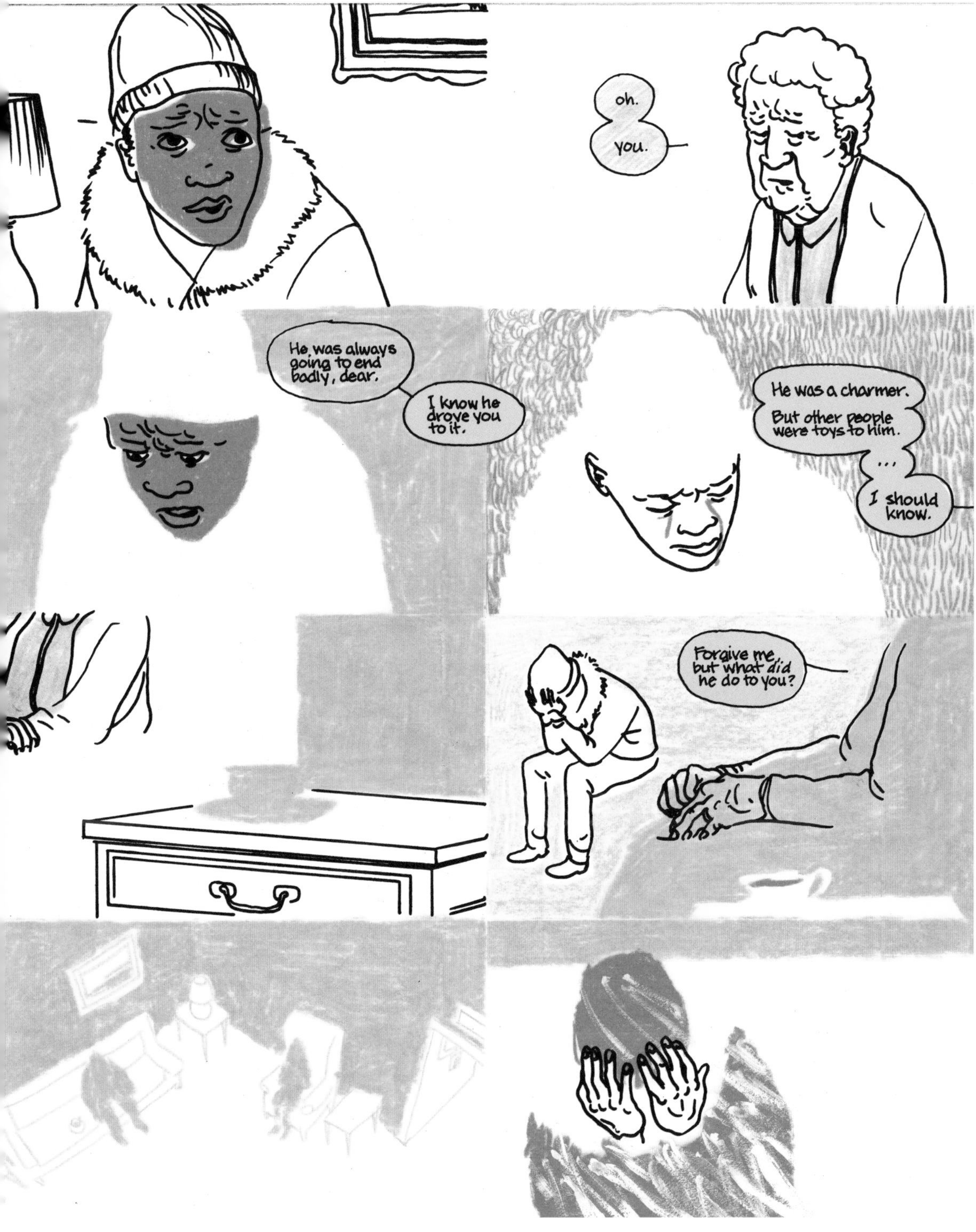
oh.
you.
He was always going to end badly, dear.
I know he drove you to it.
He was a charmer.
But other people were toys to him.
...
I should know.
Forgive me, but what *did* he do to you?

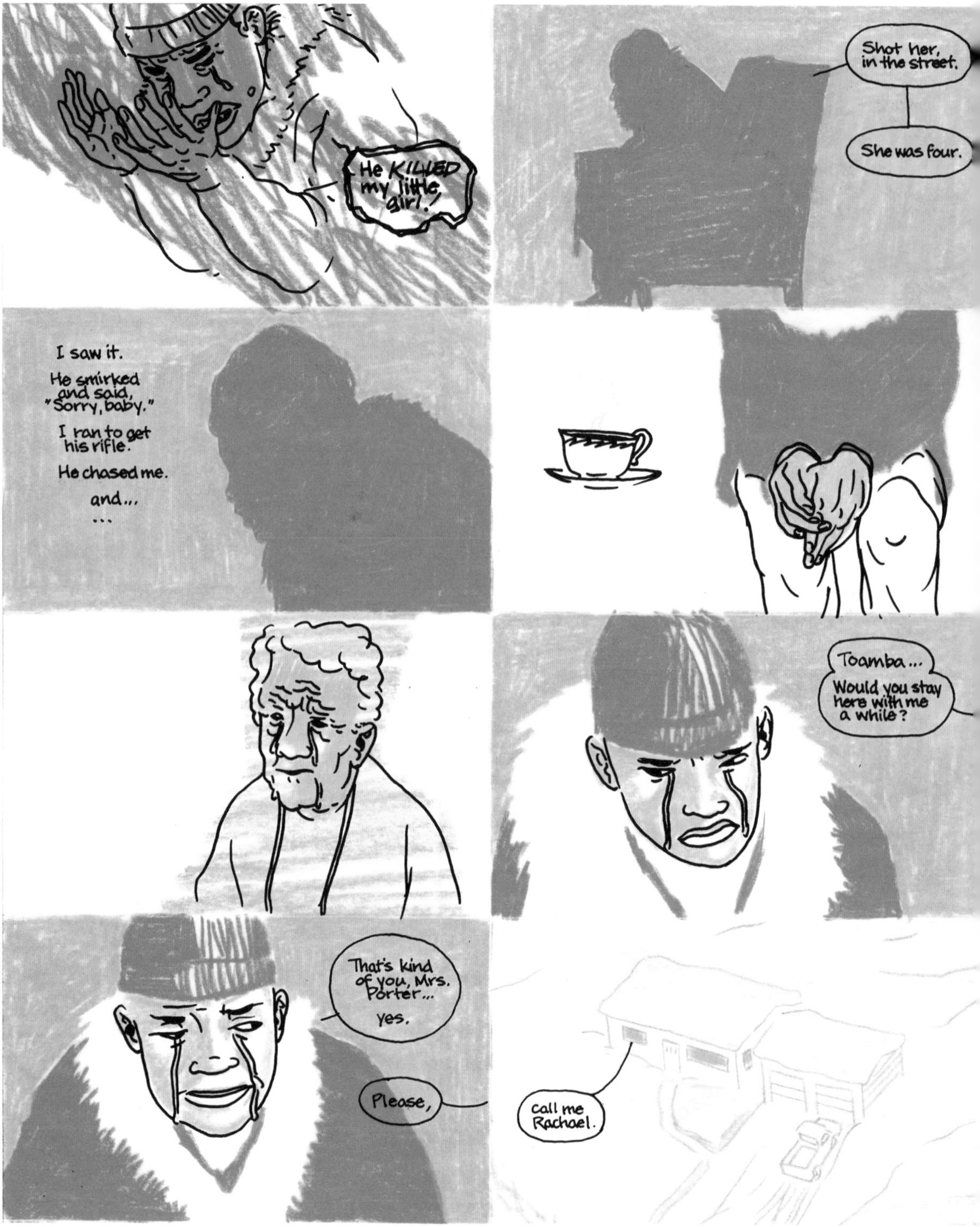
He KILLED my little girl!
Shot her, in the street.
She was four.
I saw it.
He smirked and said, "Sorry, baby."
I ran to get his rifle.
He chased me.
and...
...
Toamba...
Would you stay here with me a while?
That's kind of you, Mrs. Porter...
yes.
Please,
call me Rachael.

two

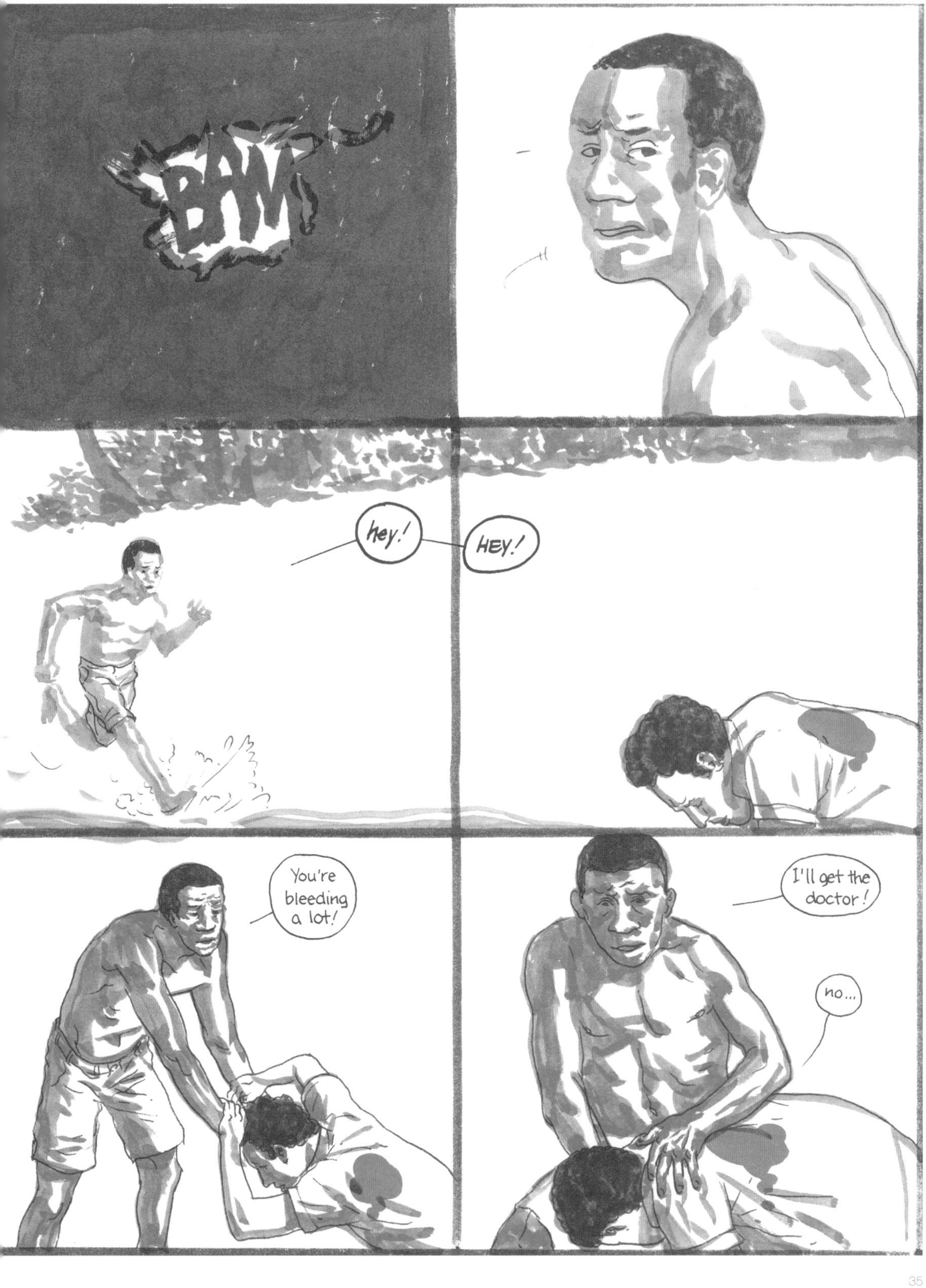
BAM
hey!
HEY!
You're bleeding a lot!
I'll get the doctor!
no...

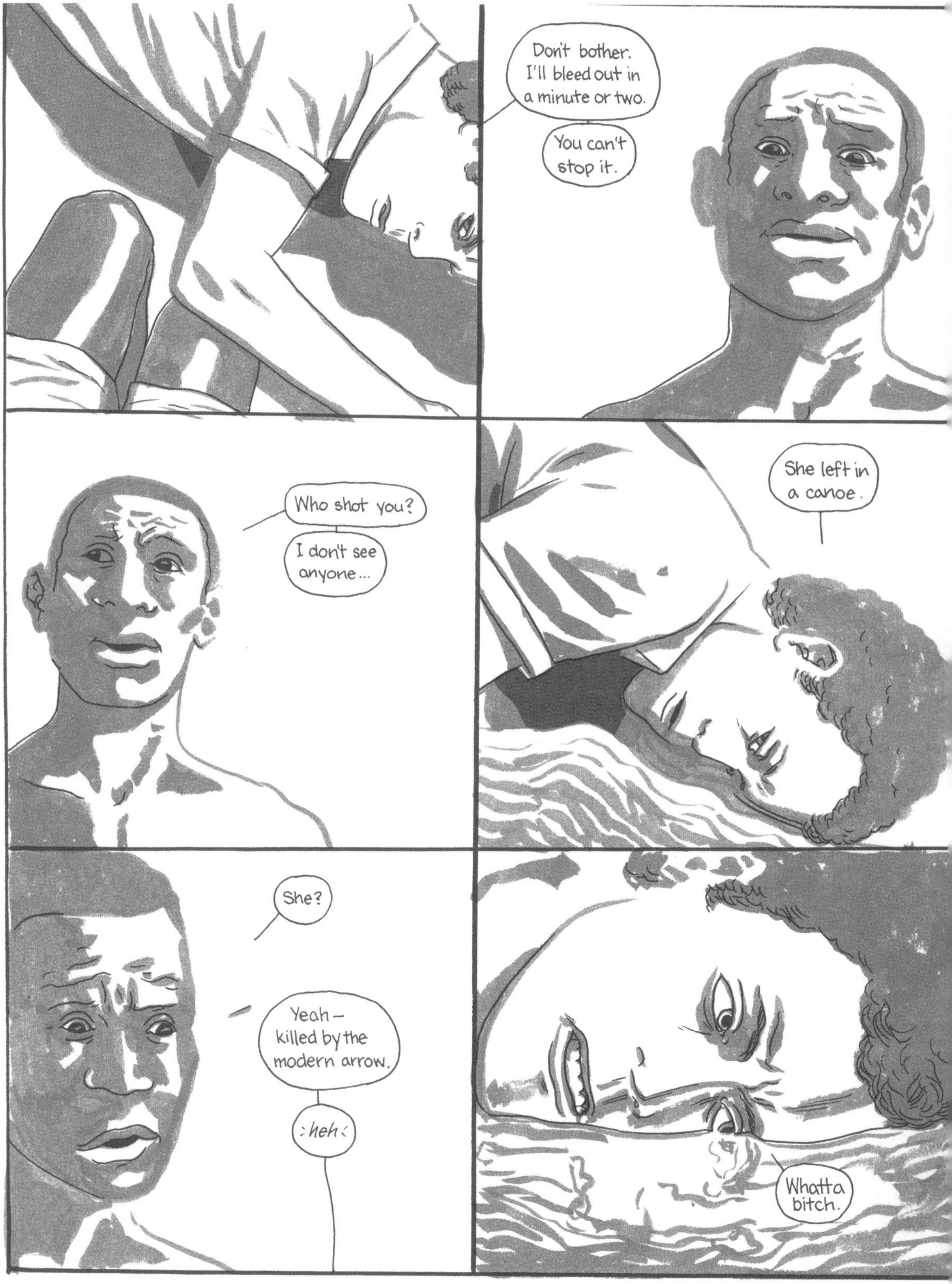
Don't bother. I'll bleed out in a minute or two.
You can't stop it.
Who shot you?
I don't see anyone...
She left in a canoe.
She?
Yeah— killed by the modern arrow.
heh
Whatta bitch.

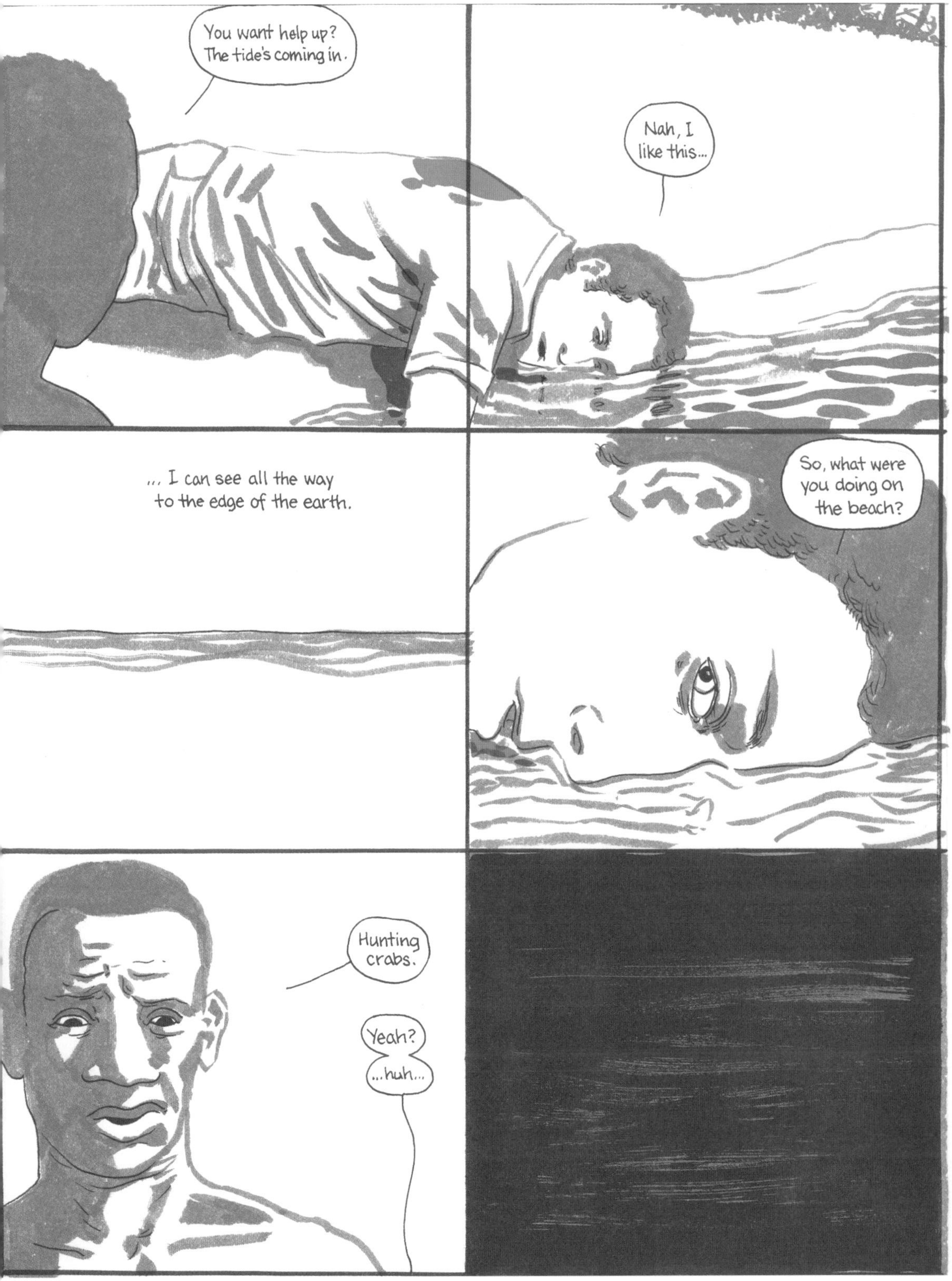
You want help up? The tide's coming in.
Nah, I like this...
... I can see all the way to the edge of the earth.
So, what were you doing on the beach?
Hunting crabs.
Yeah?
...huh...

three

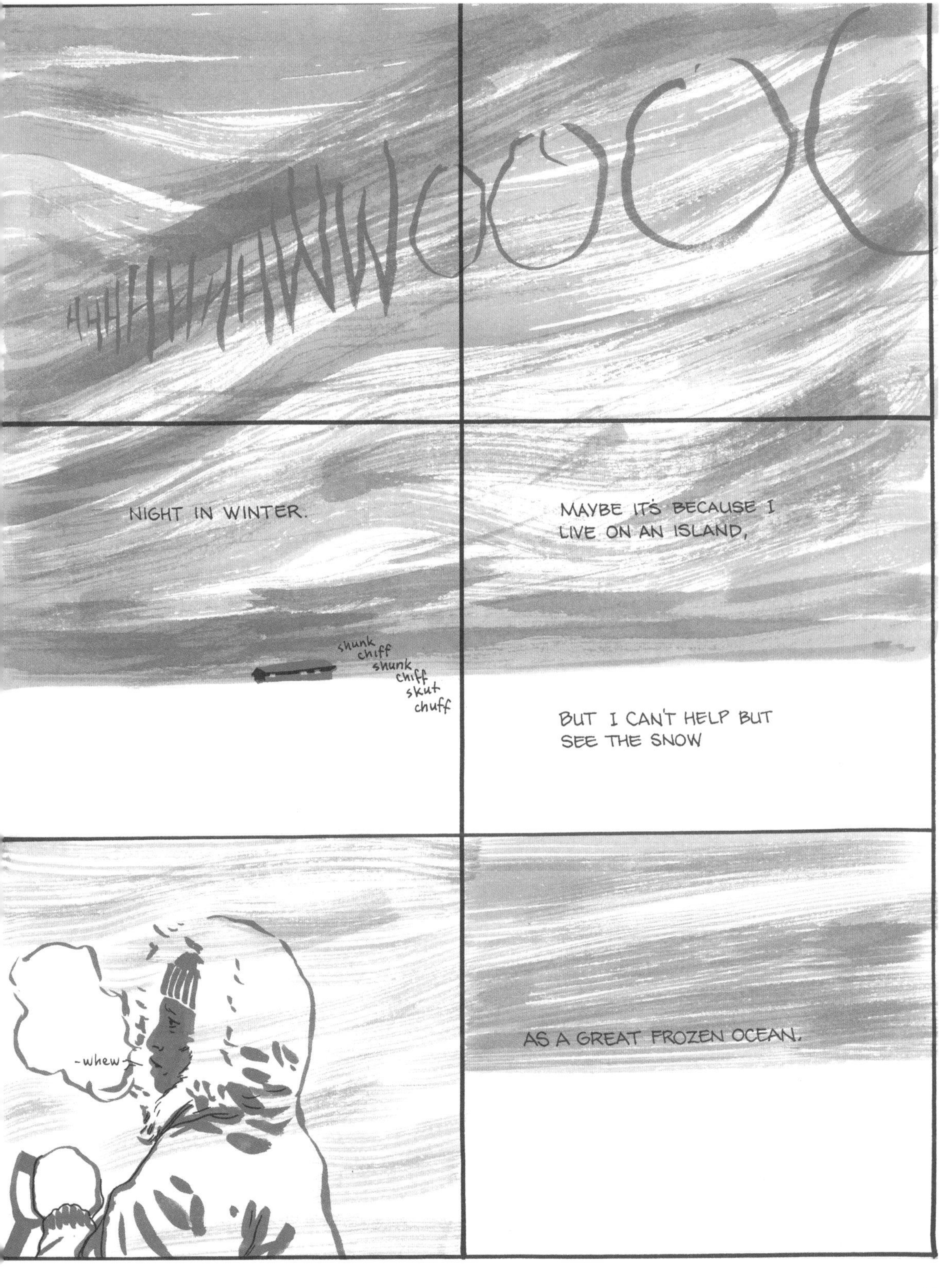

HHHHHHWWOOOOO
NIGHT IN WINTER.
shunk
chiff
shunk
chiff
skut
chuff
MAYBE IT'S BECAUSE I
LIVE ON AN ISLAND,
BUT I CAN'T HELP BUT
SEE THE SNOW
-whew-
AS A GREAT FROZEN OCEAN.

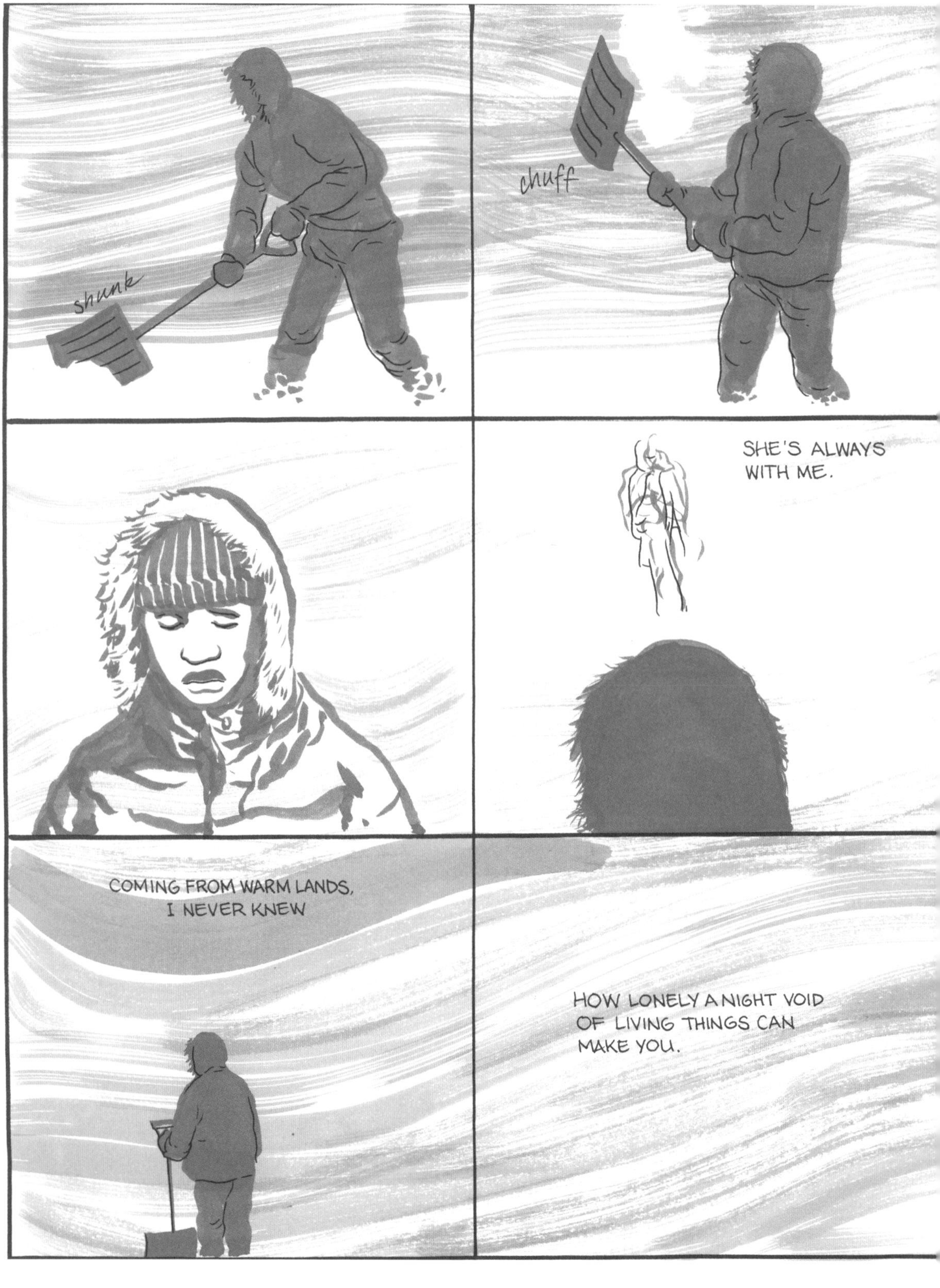
shunk
chuff
SHE'S ALWAYS WITH ME.
COMING FROM WARM LANDS, I NEVER KNEW
HOW LONELY A NIGHT VOID OF LIVING THINGS CAN MAKE YOU.

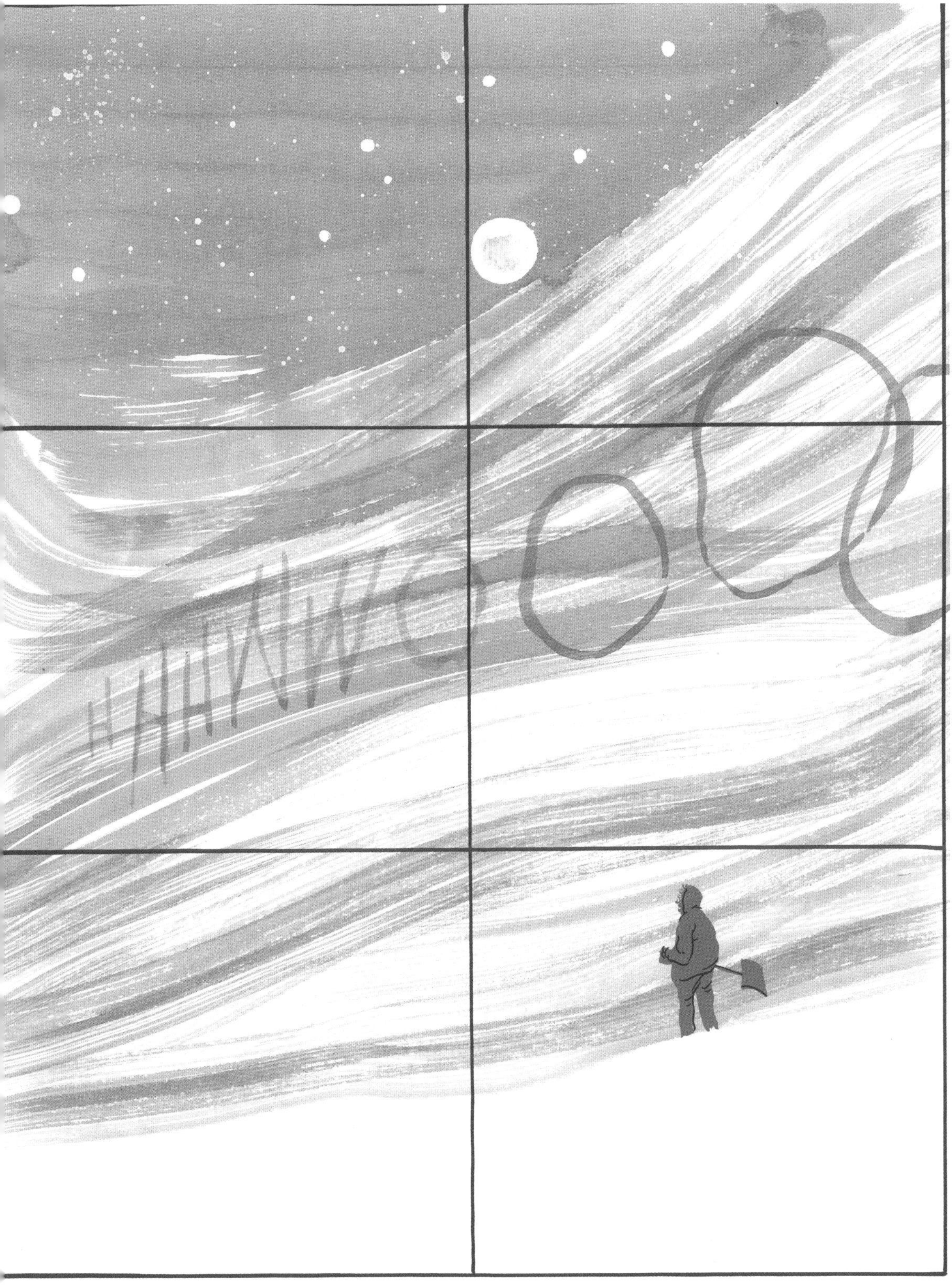

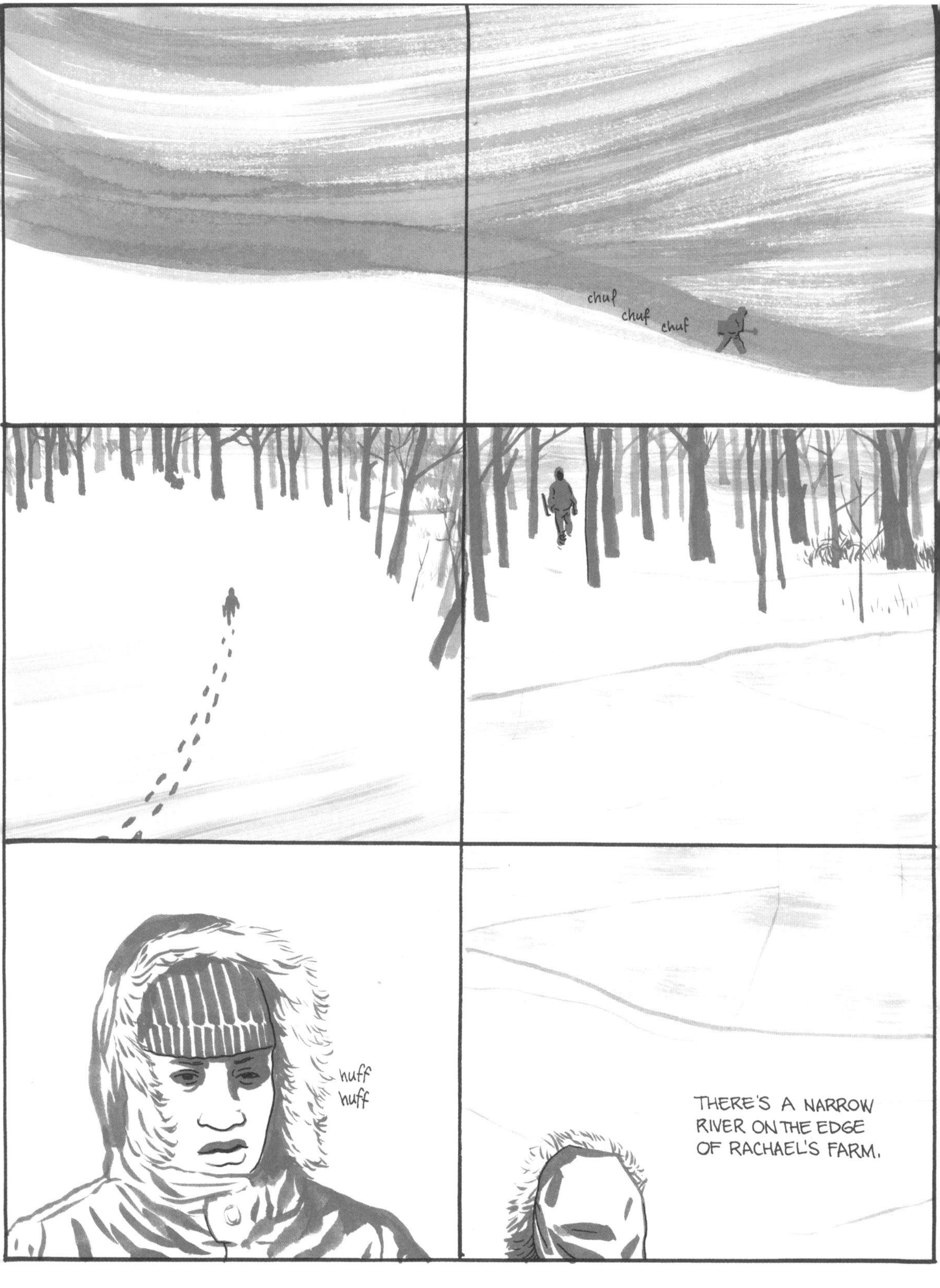
chuf
chuf
chuf
huff
huff
THERE'S A NARROW RIVER ON THE EDGE OF RACHAEL'S FARM.

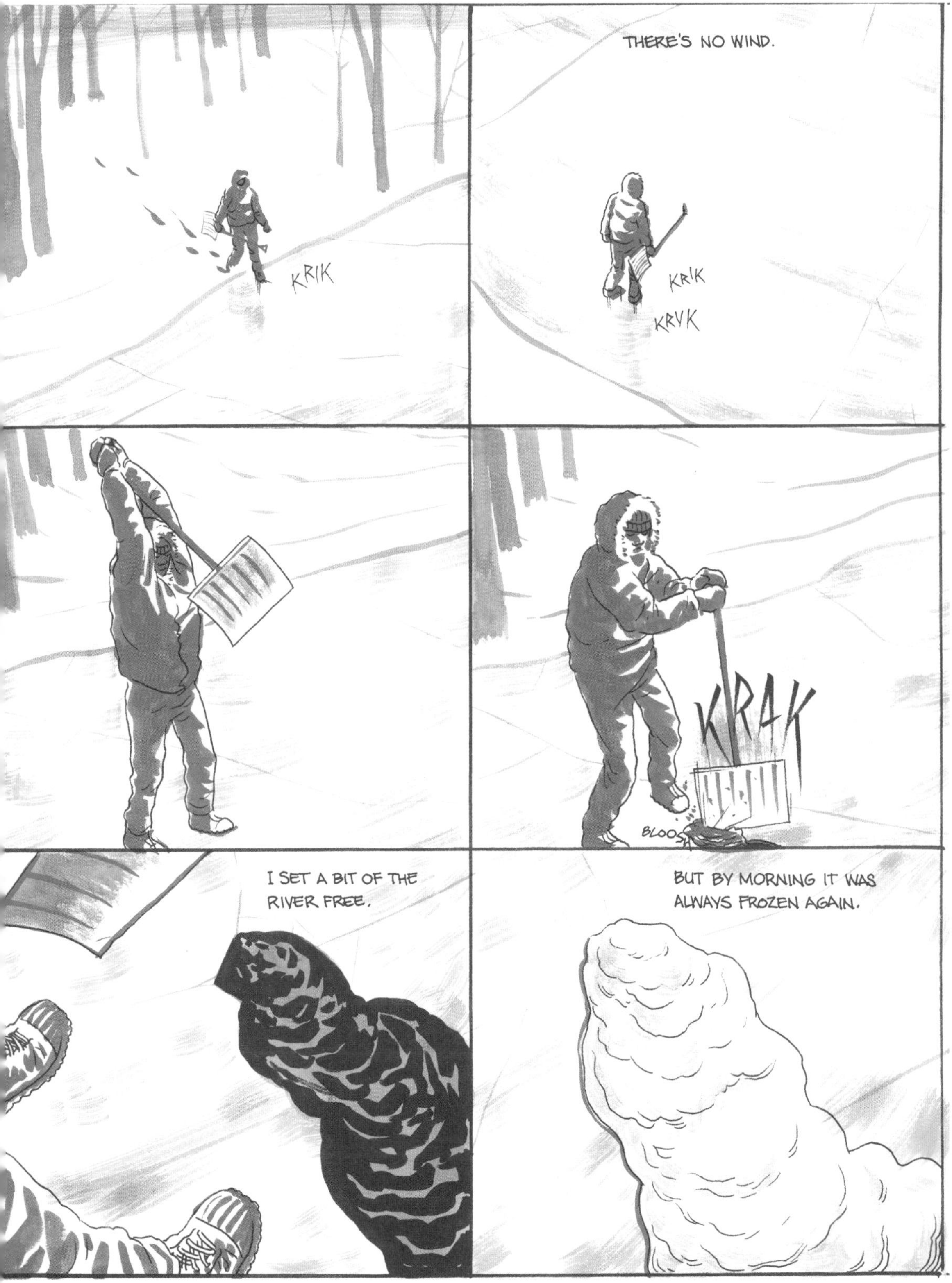
KRIK
THERE'S NO WIND.
KRIK
KRUK
KRAK
BLOOSH
I SET A BIT OF THE RIVER FREE.
BUT BY MORNING IT WAS ALWAYS FROZEN AGAIN.

four

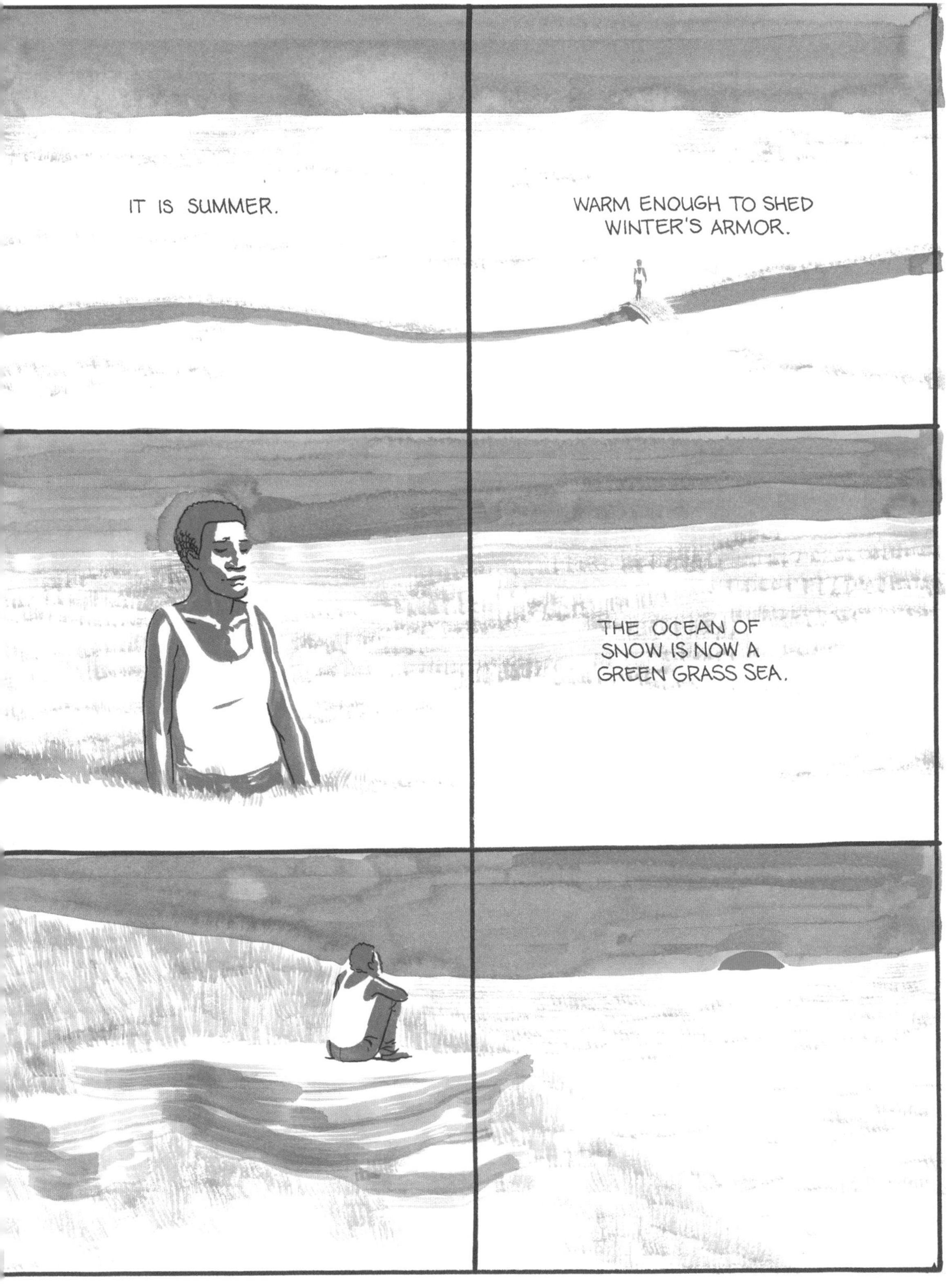
IT IS SUMMER.
WARM ENOUGH TO SHED WINTER'S ARMOR.
THE OCEAN OF SNOW IS NOW A GREEN GRASS SEA.

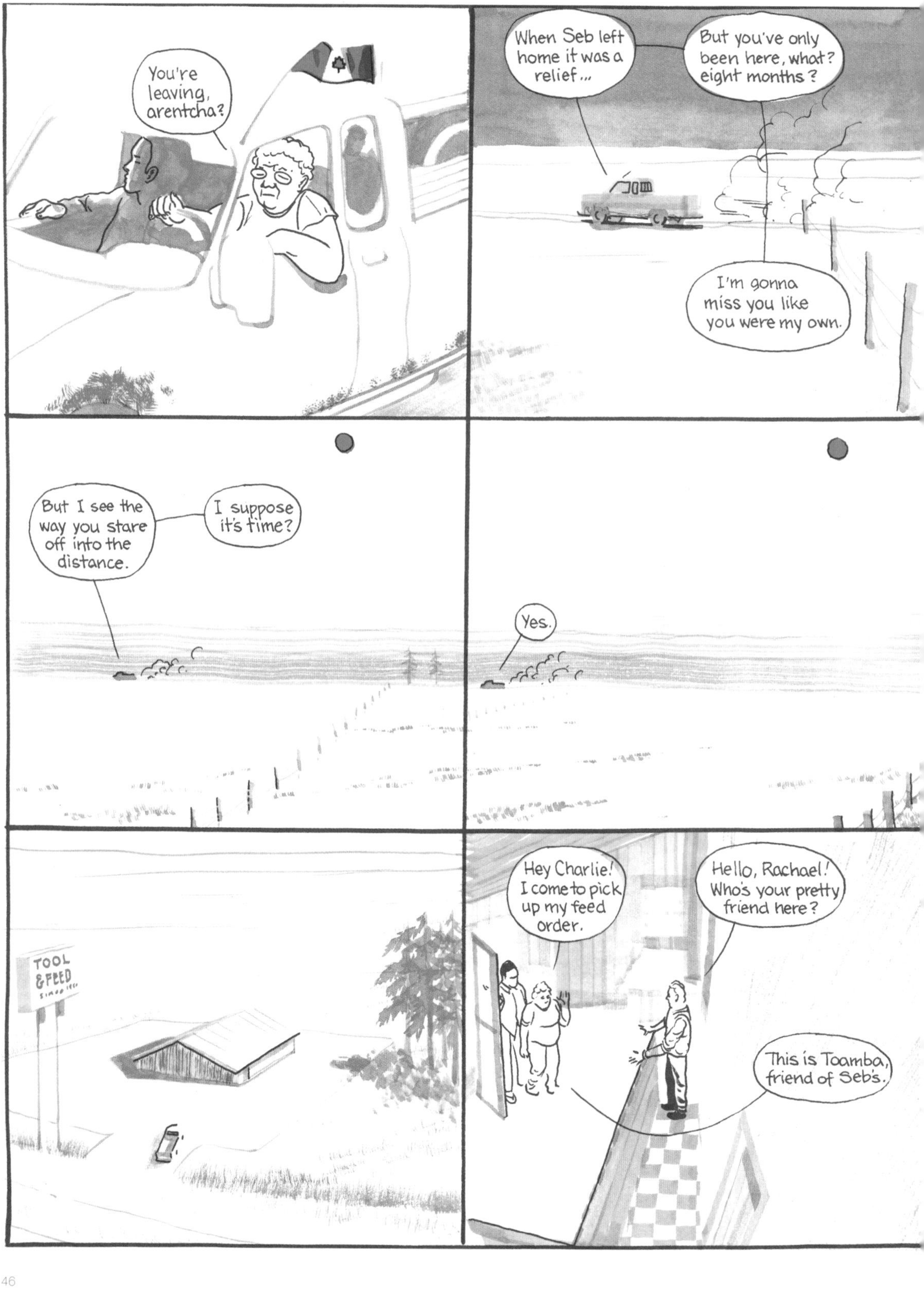
You're leaving, arentcha?
When Seb left home it was a relief...
But you've only been here, what? eight months?
I'm gonna miss you like you were my own.
But I see the way you stare off into the distance.
I suppose it's time?
Yes.
TOOL & FEED
Hey Charlie! I come to pick up my feed order.
Hello, Rachael! Who's your pretty friend here?
This is Toamba, friend of Seb's.

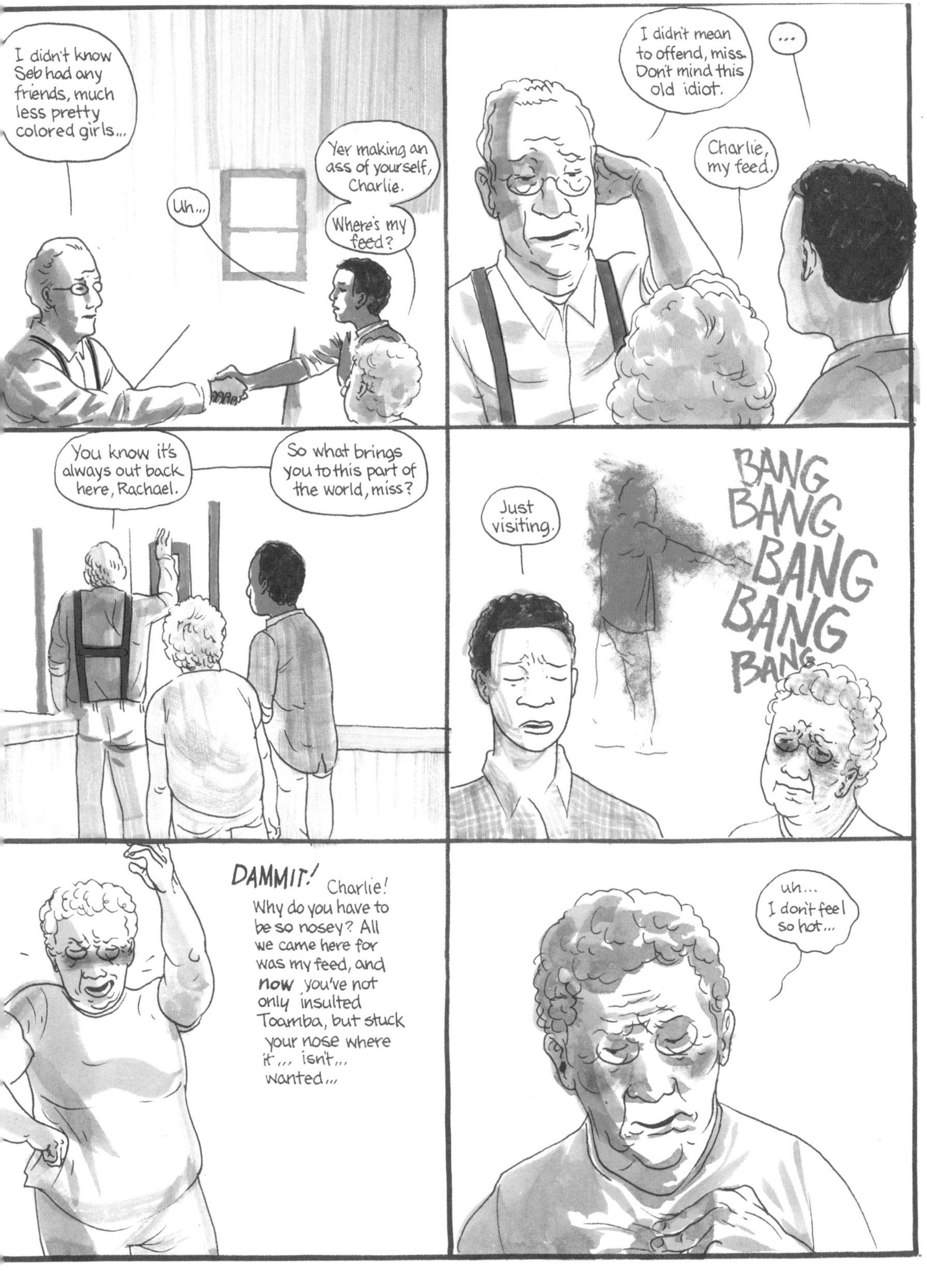

I didn't know Seb had any friends, much less pretty colored girls...
Uh...
Yer making an ass of yourself, Charlie.
Where's my feed?
I didn't mean to offend, miss. Don't mind this old idiot.
...
Charlie, my feed.
You know it's always out back here, Rachael.
So what brings you to this part of the world, miss?
Just visiting.
BANG BANG BANG BANG BANG
DAMMIT! Charlie! Why do you have to be so nosey? All we came here for was my feed, and now you've not only insulted Toamba, but stuck your nose where it... isn't... wanted...
uh... I don't feel so hot...

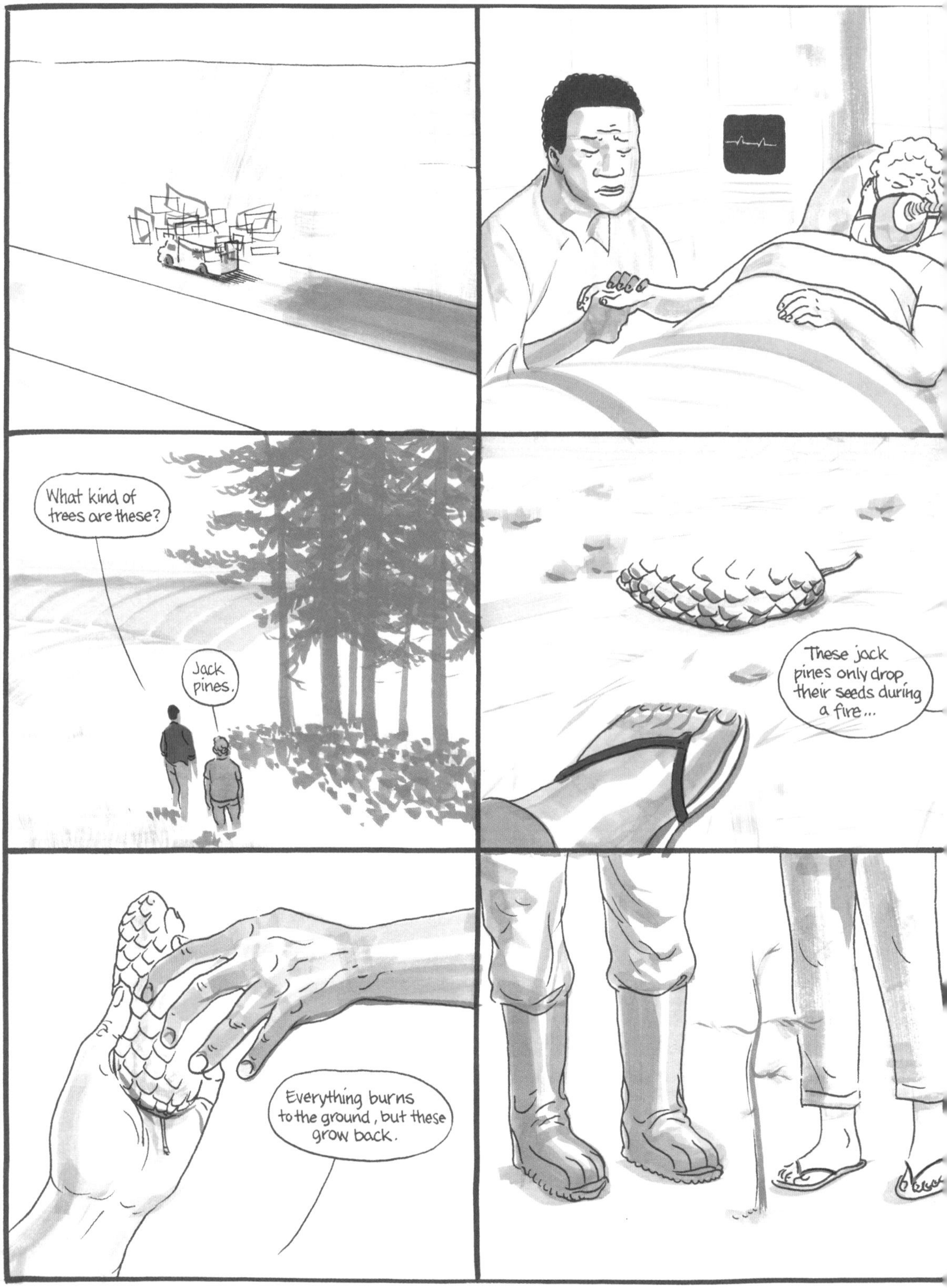
What kind of trees are these?
Jack pines.
These jack pines only drop their seeds during a fire...
Everything burns to the ground, but these grow back.

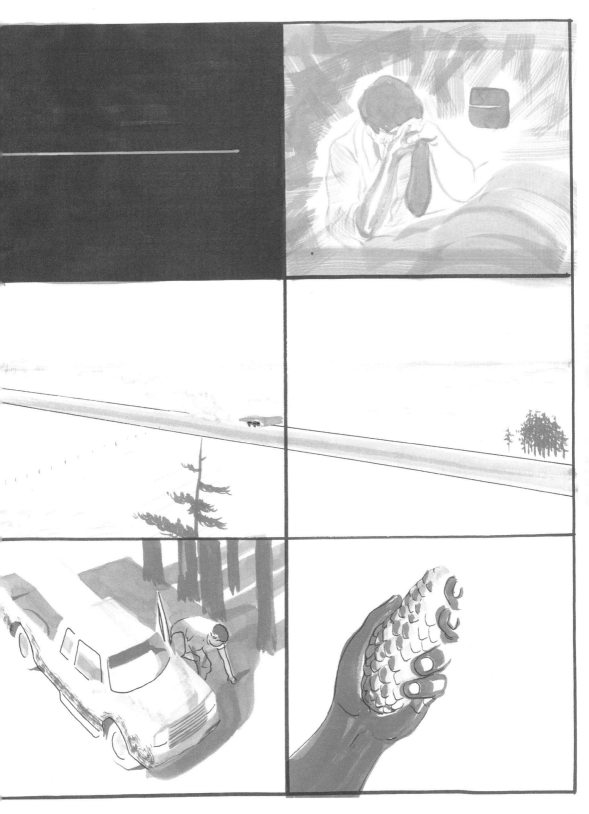

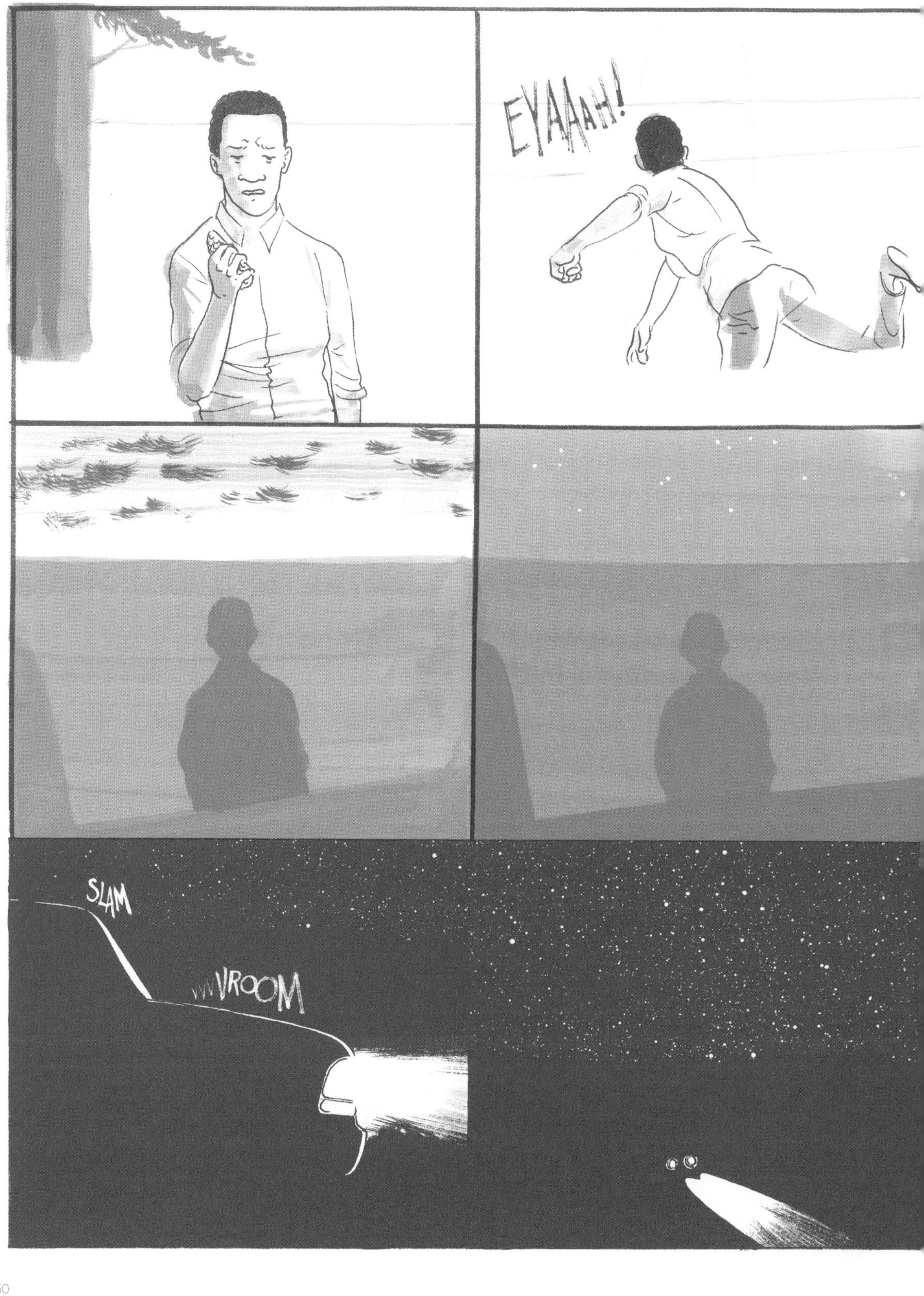
EYAAAH!
SLAM
VVVVROOM

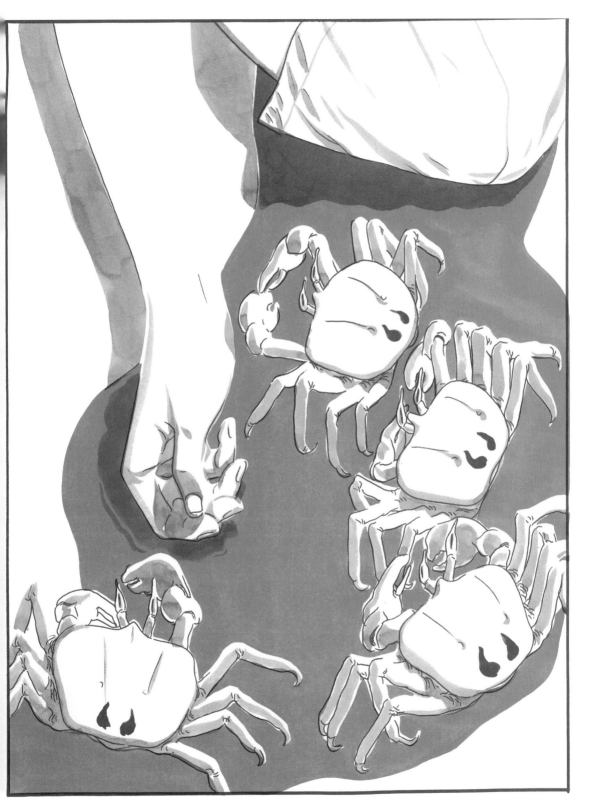

Between December and March

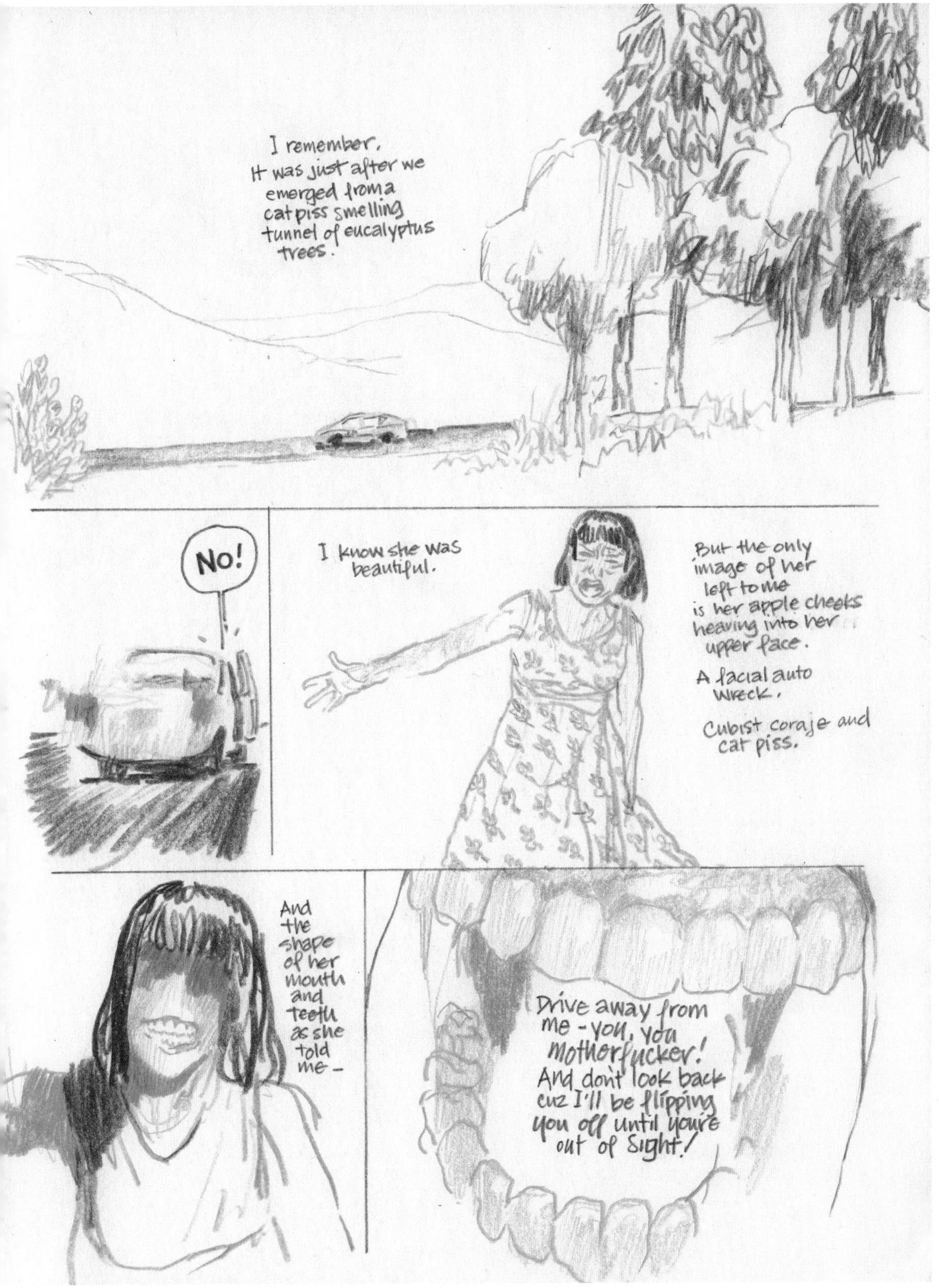

I remember.
It was just after we emerged from a cat piss smelling tunnel of eucalyptus trees.
No!
I know she was beautiful.
But the only image of her left to me is her apple cheeks heaving into her upper face.
A facial auto wreck.
Cubist coraje and cat piss.
And the shape of her mouth and teeth as she told me -
Drive away from me - you, you motherfucker! And don't look back cuz I'll be flipping you off until you're out of sight!

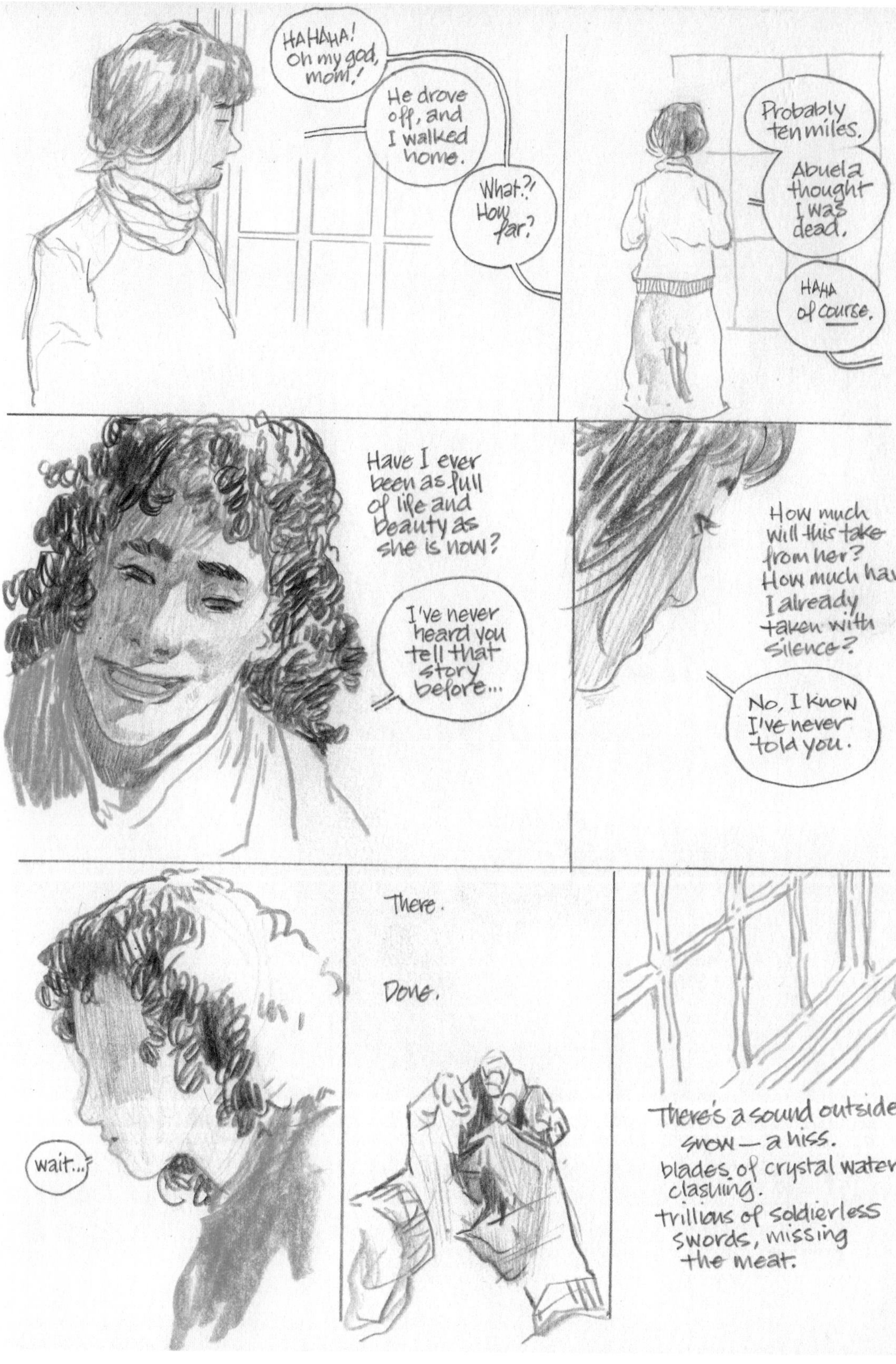
HAHAHA! Oh my god, mom!
He drove off, and I walked home.
What?! How far?
Probably ten miles.
Abuela thought I was dead.
HAHA of course.
Have I ever been as full of life and beauty as she is now?
I've never heard you tell that story before...
How much will this take from her? How much have I already taken with silence?
No, I know I've never told you.
wait...
There.
Done.
There's a sound outside.
snow — a hiss.
blades of crystal water clashing.
trillions of soldierless swords, missing the meat.

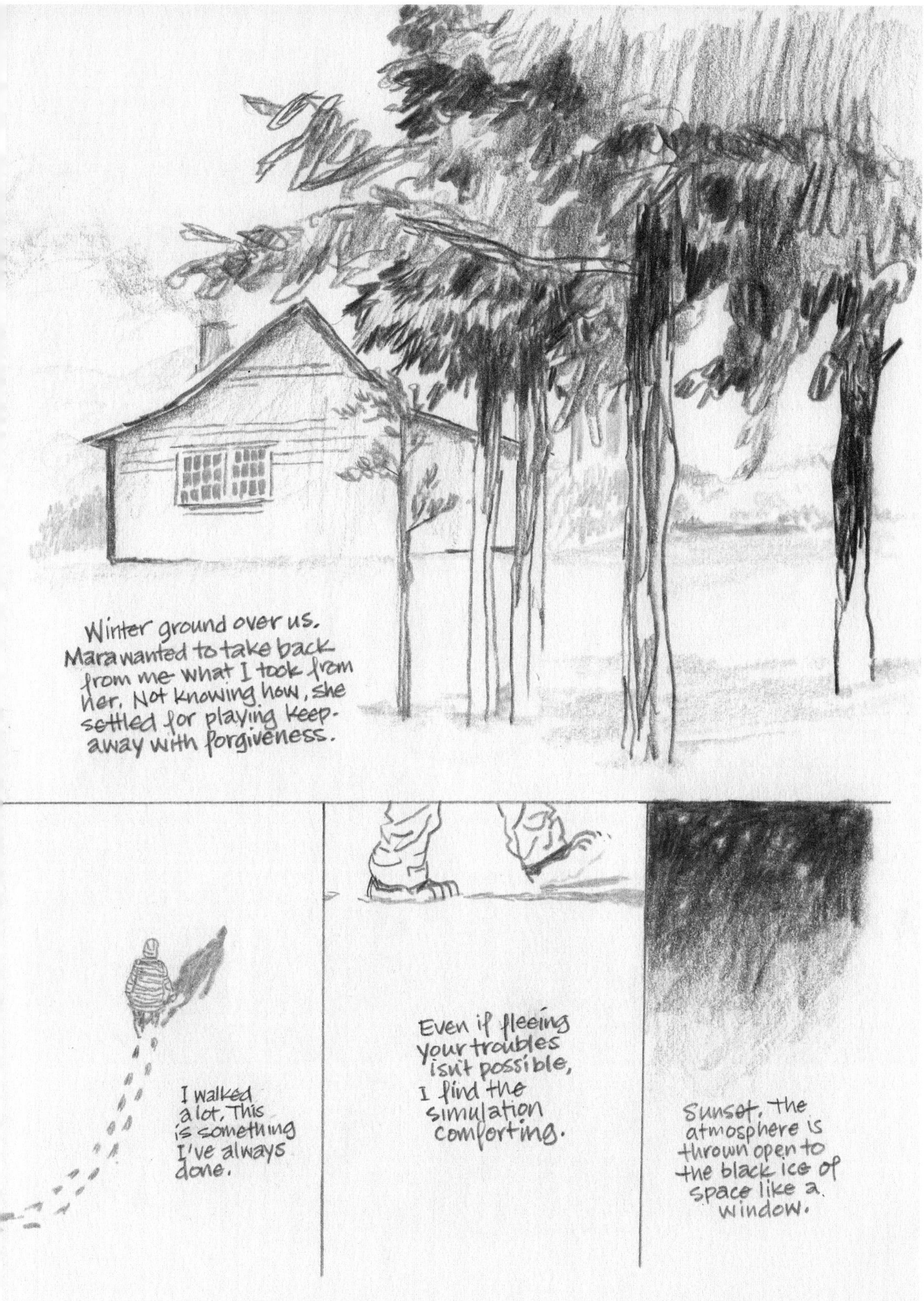
Winter ground over us. Mara wanted to take back from me what I took from her. Not knowing how, she settled for playing keep-away with forgiveness.
I walked a lot. This is something I've always done.
Even if fleeing your troubles isn't possible, I find the simulation comforting.
Sunset, the atmosphere is thrown open to the black ice of space like a window.

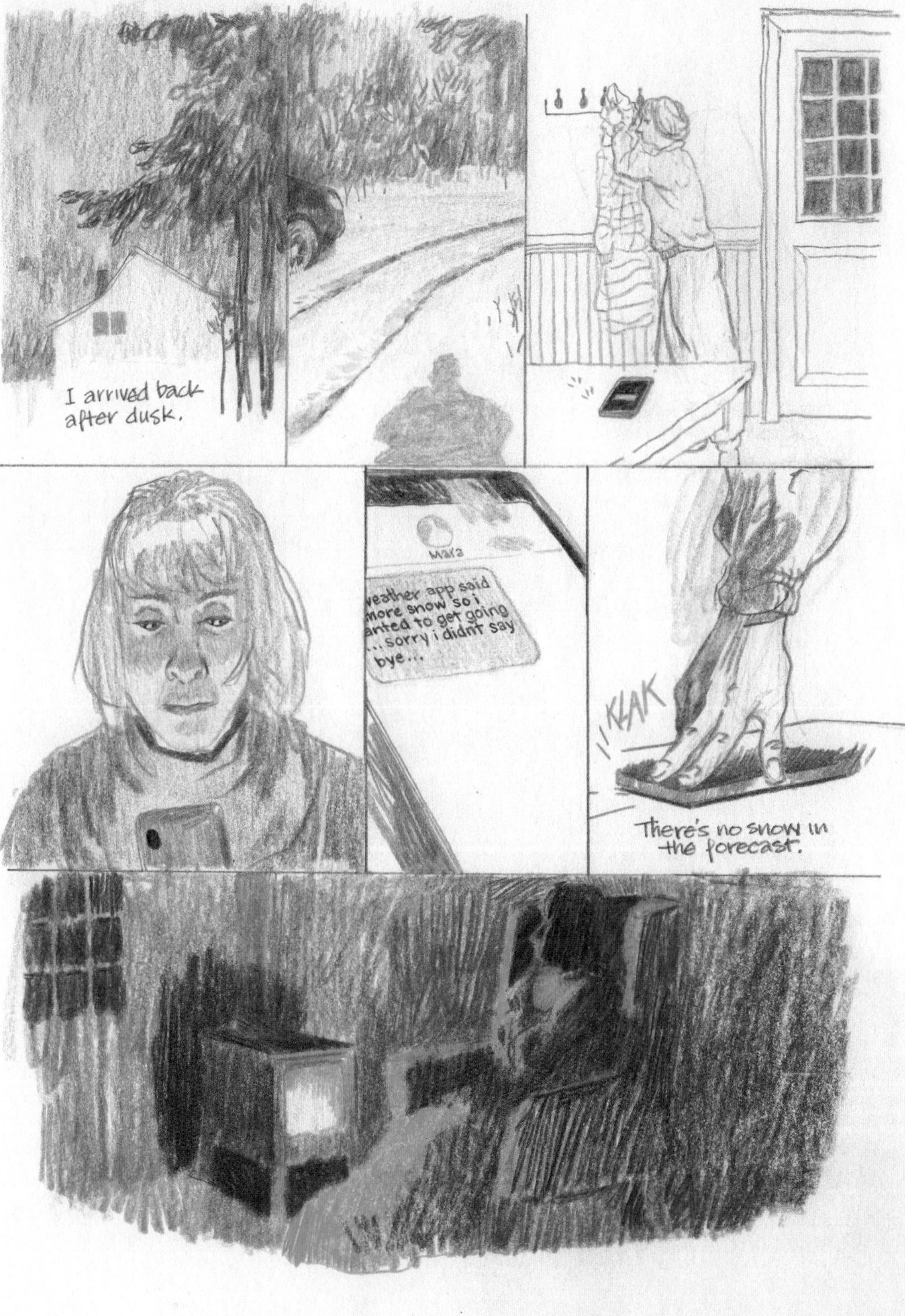
I arrived back after dusk.
Mara
weather app said
more snow so i
anted to get going
...sorry i didnt say
bye...
KLAK
There's no snow in the forecast.

My mood festered in the snowblinding days that followed.

But the sky in the west got dark. Mara texted several times and I let them stay unread.

Then the storm let loose. Maybe Mara wasn't lying. No service in the area for a week, though.

College kids aren't the only ones who get to be petty.

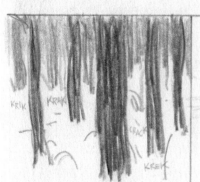

KRIK KRAK CRACK KRIK

Cold clapped through the thicket out back.

Luckily, I always liked cutting kindling.

Reminds me of my mom.

Mom once heard that saying, 'Firewood warms you twice.'

'No,' she said. 'It is violence. Violence warms you twice.'

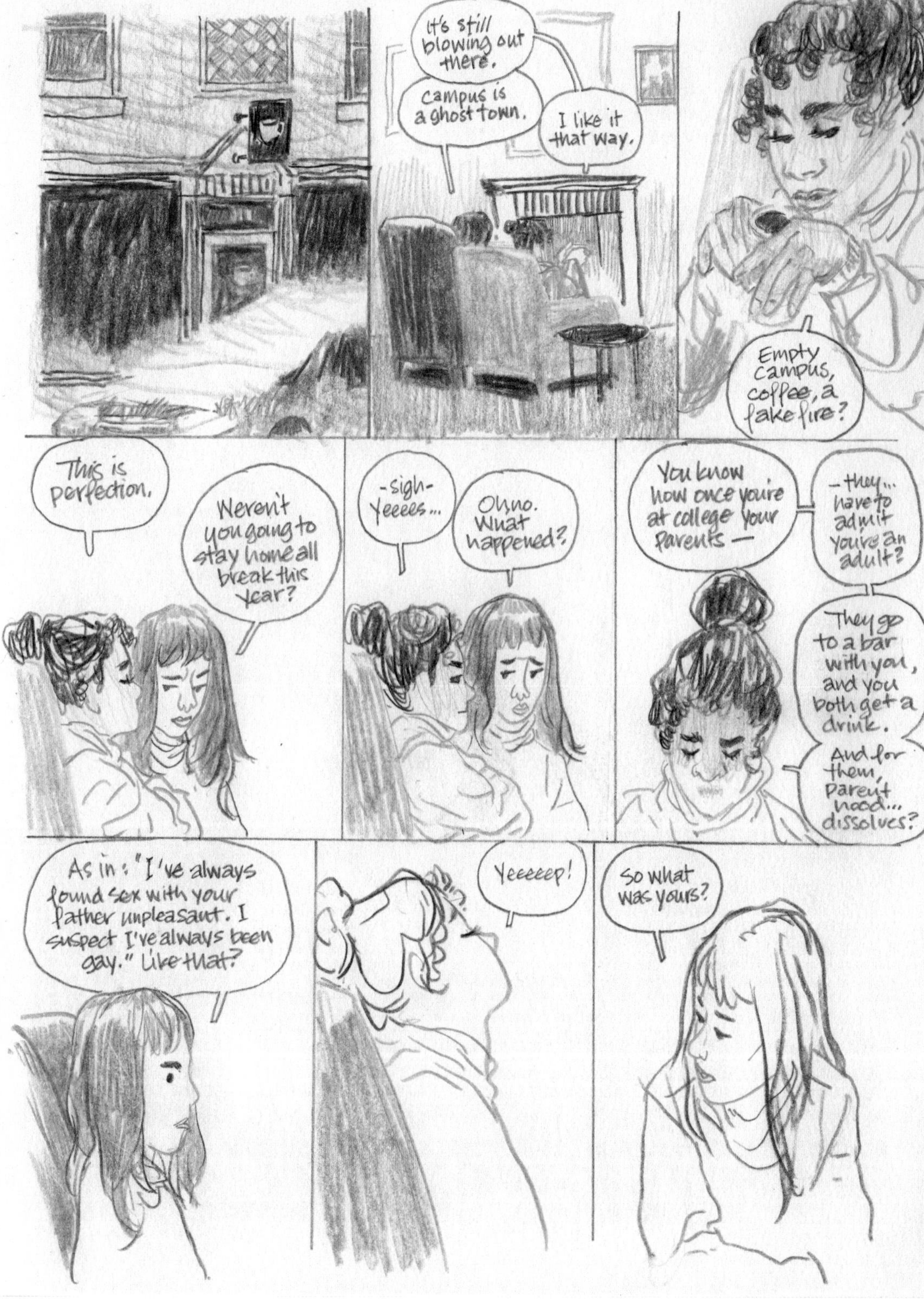
It's still blowing out there.
Campus is a ghost town.
I like it that way.
Empty campus, coffee, a fake fire?
This is perfection.
Weren't you going to stay home all break this year?
-sigh- Yeeees...
Oh no. What happened?
You know how once you're at college your parents —
— they... have to admit you're an adult?
They go to a bar with you, and you both get a drink.
And for them, parent hood... dissolves?
As in: "I've always found sex with your father unpleasant. I suspect I've always been gay." Like that?
Yeeeeep!
So what was yours?

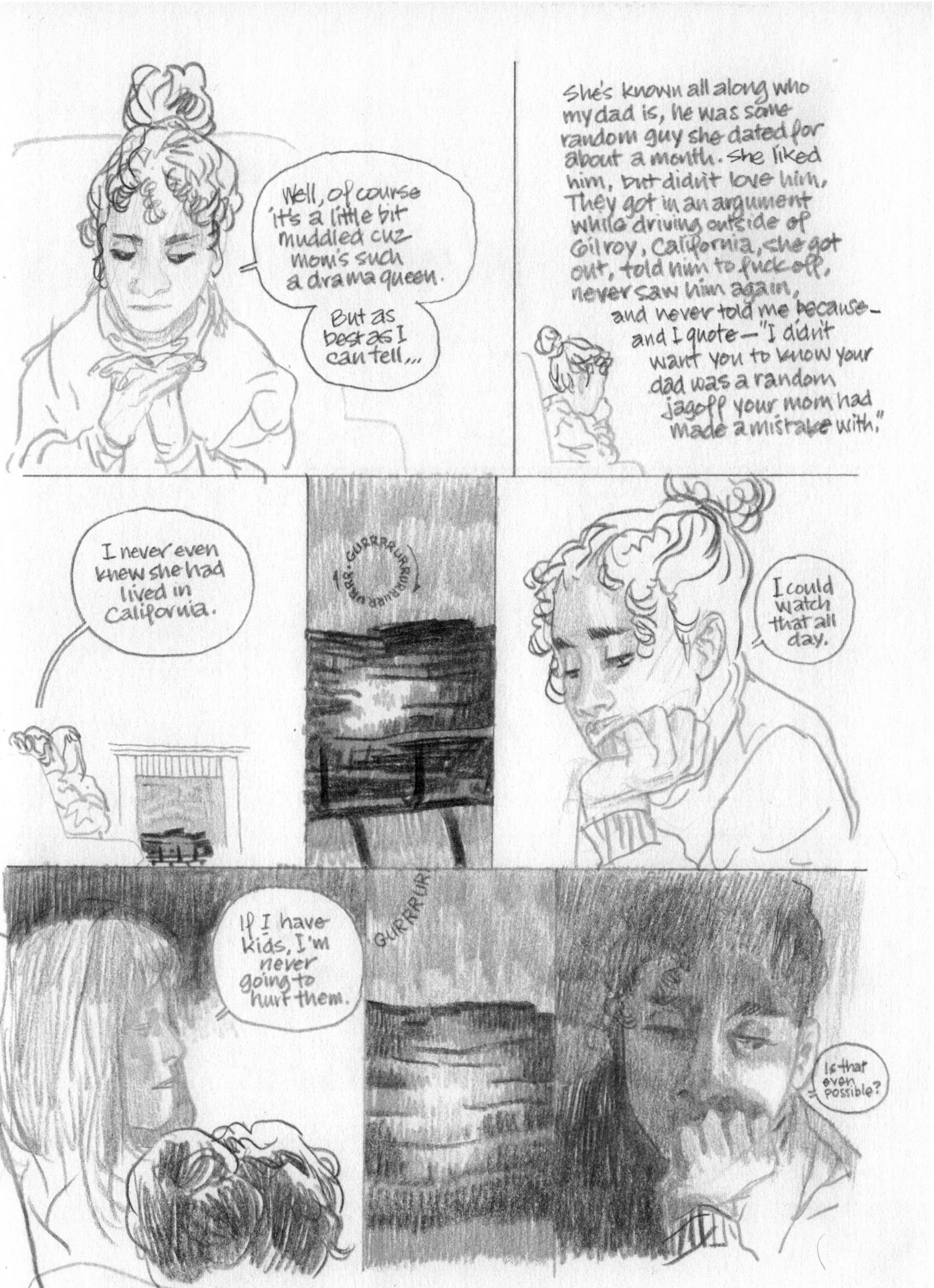
Well, of course it's a little bit muddled cuz mom's such a drama queen.
But as best as I can tell,...
She's known all along who my dad is, he was some random guy she dated for about a month. She liked him, but didn't love him. They got in an argument while driving outside of Gilroy, California, she got out, told him to fuck off, never saw him again,
and never told me because - and I quote - "I didn't want you to know your dad was a random jagoff your mom had made a mistake with."
I never even knew she had lived in California.
GURRRRURRURRURRR
I could watch that all day.
If I have kids, I'm never going to hurt them.
GURRRURR
Is that even possible?

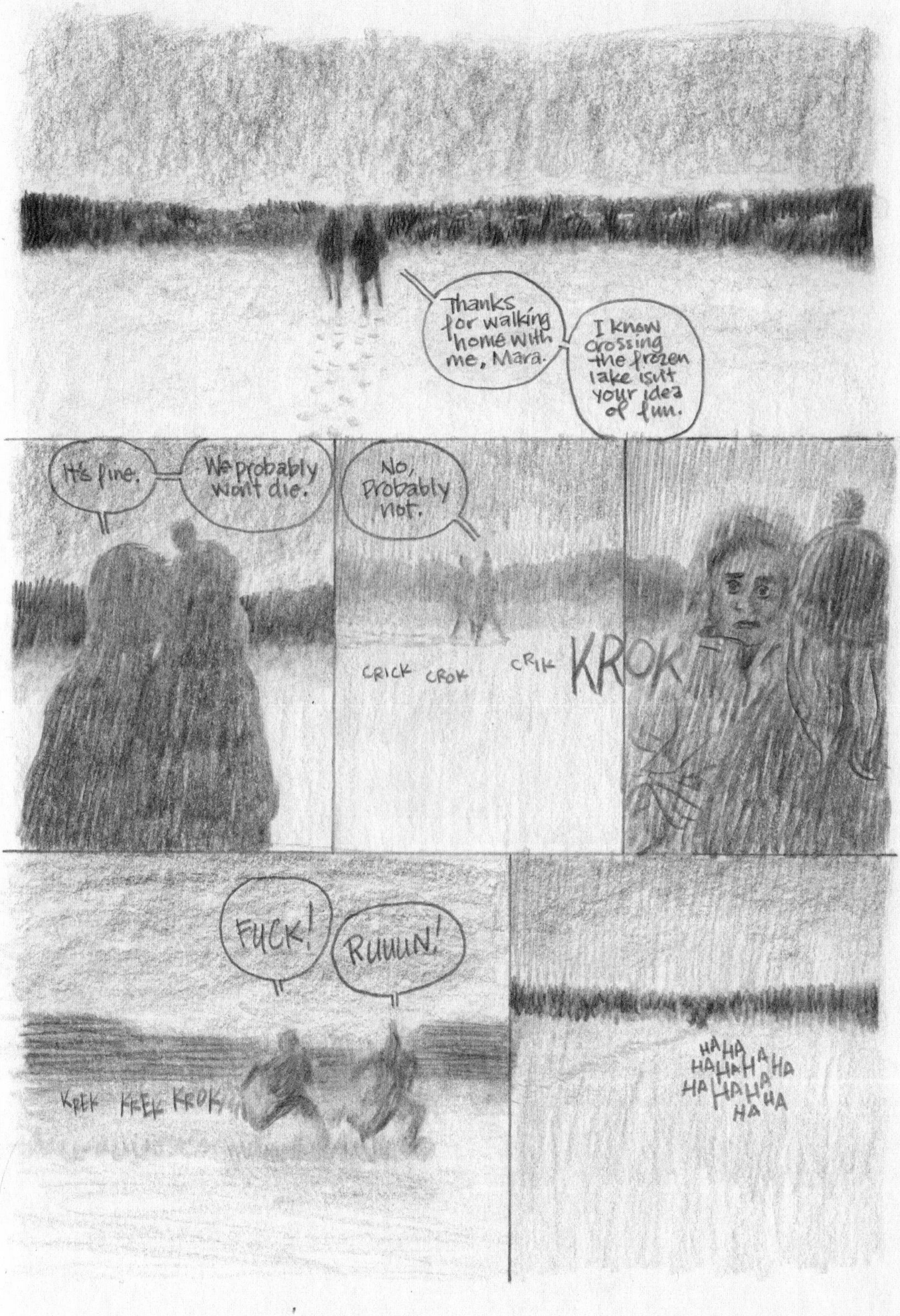
Thanks for walking home with me, Mara.
I know crossing the frozen lake isn't your idea of fun.
It's fine.
We probably won't die.
No, probably not.
CRICK CROK CRIK KROK
FUCK!
RUUUN!
KREK KREK KROK
HA HA HA HA HA HA HA HA HA HA HA HA HA

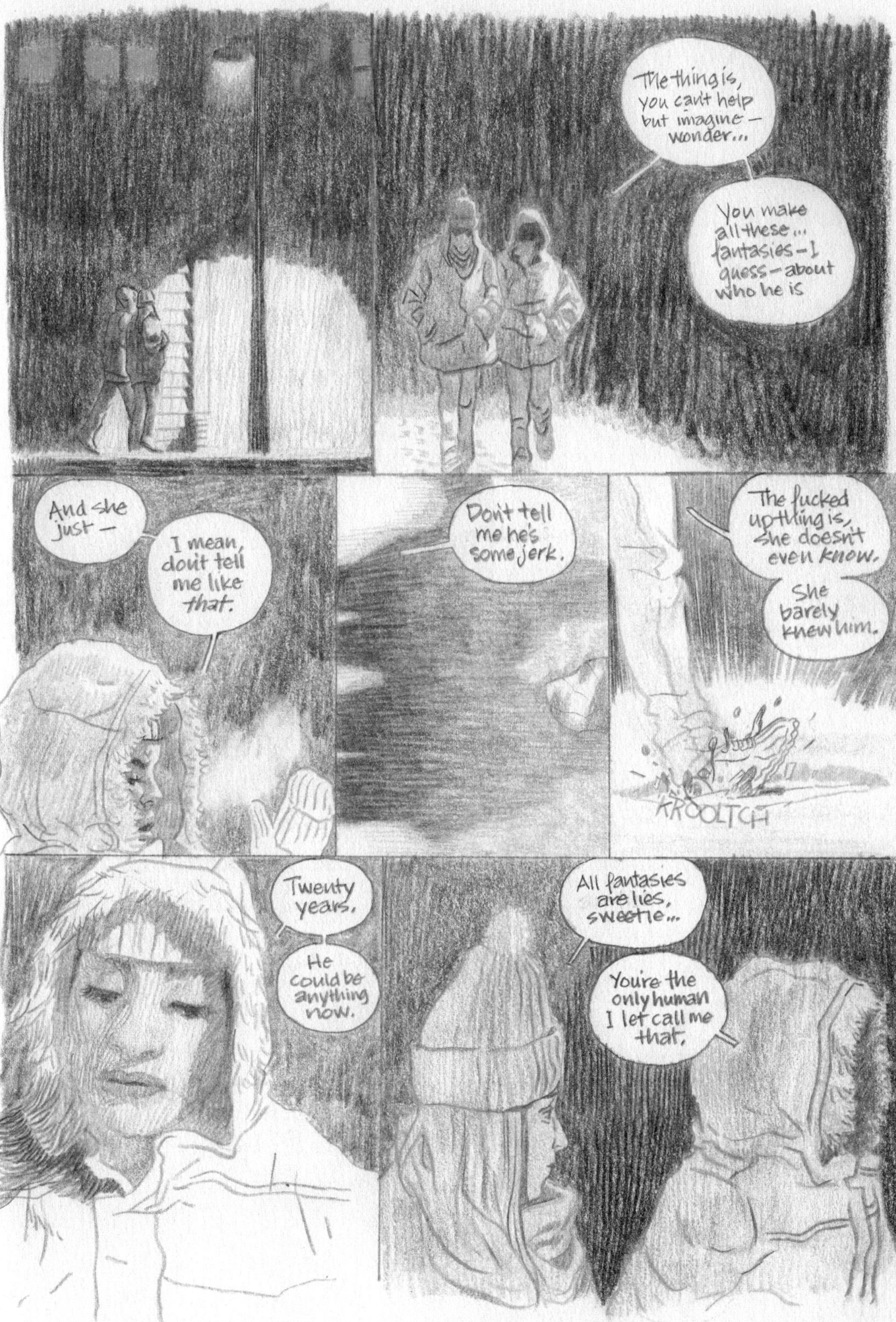
The thing is, you can't help but imagine— wonder...
You make all these... fantasies—I guess—about who he is
And she just—
I mean, don't tell me like *that*.
Don't tell me he's some jerk.
The fucked up thing is, she doesn't even *know*.
She barely knew him.
KROOLTCH
Twenty years.
He could be anything now.
All fantasies are lies, sweetie...
You're the only human I let call me that.

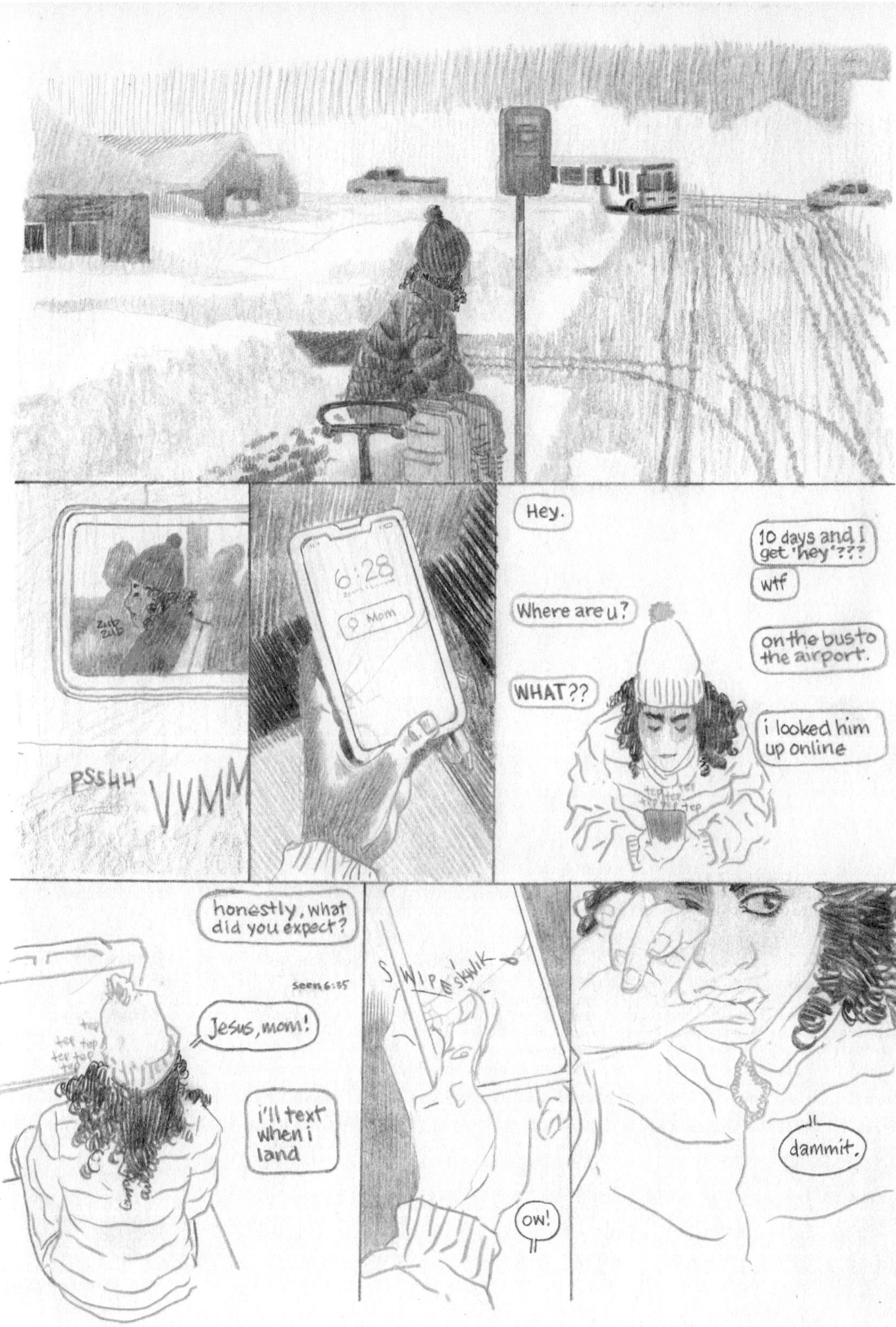
PSSHH
VVMM
6:28
Mom
Hey.
10 days and I get 'hey'???
wtf
Where are u?
on the bus to the airport.
WHAT??
i looked him up online
honestly, what did you expect?
seen 6:35
Jesus, mom!
i'll text when i land
SWIPE
OW!
dammit.

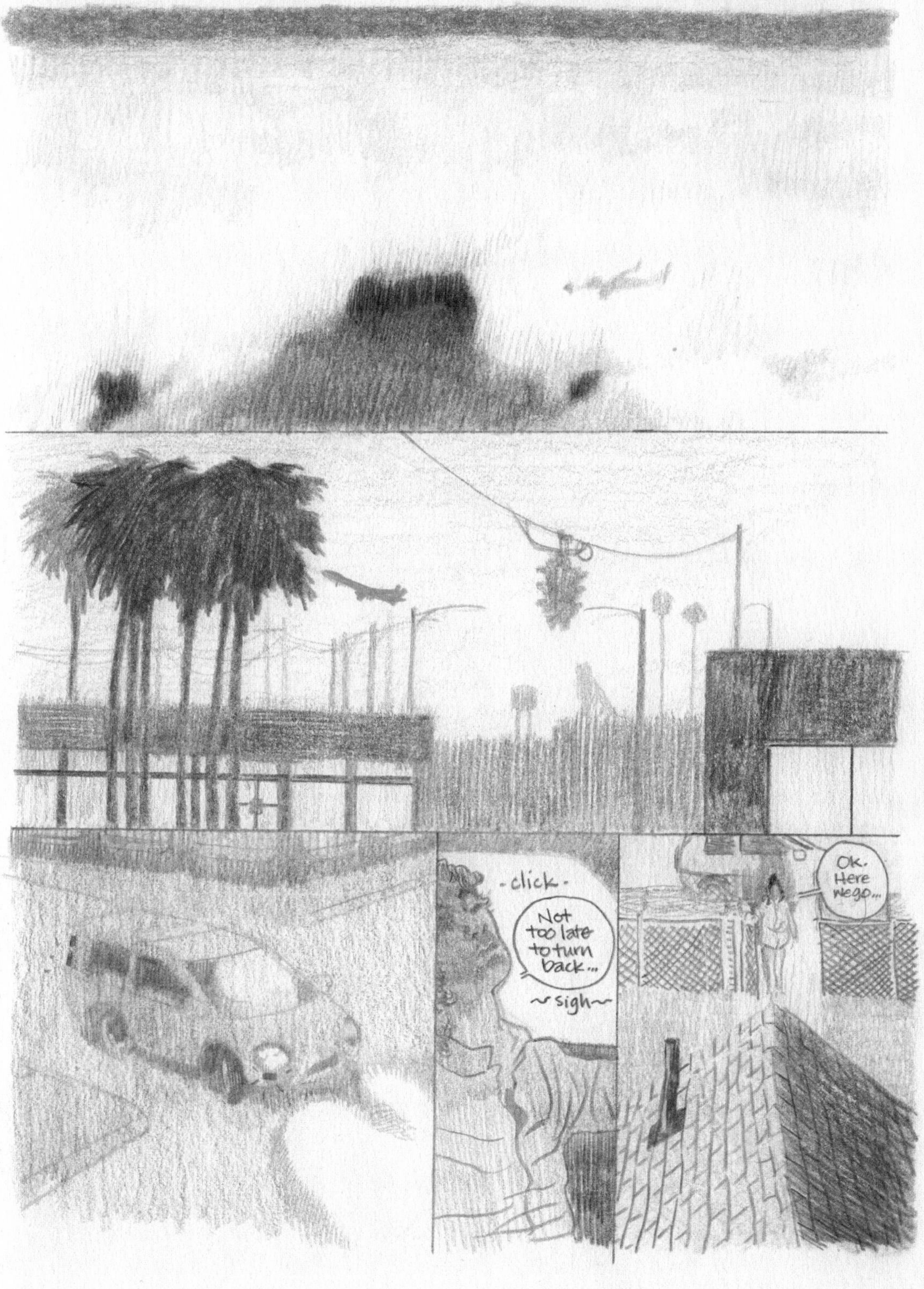
-click-
Not too late to turn back...
~sigh~
Ok. Here we go...

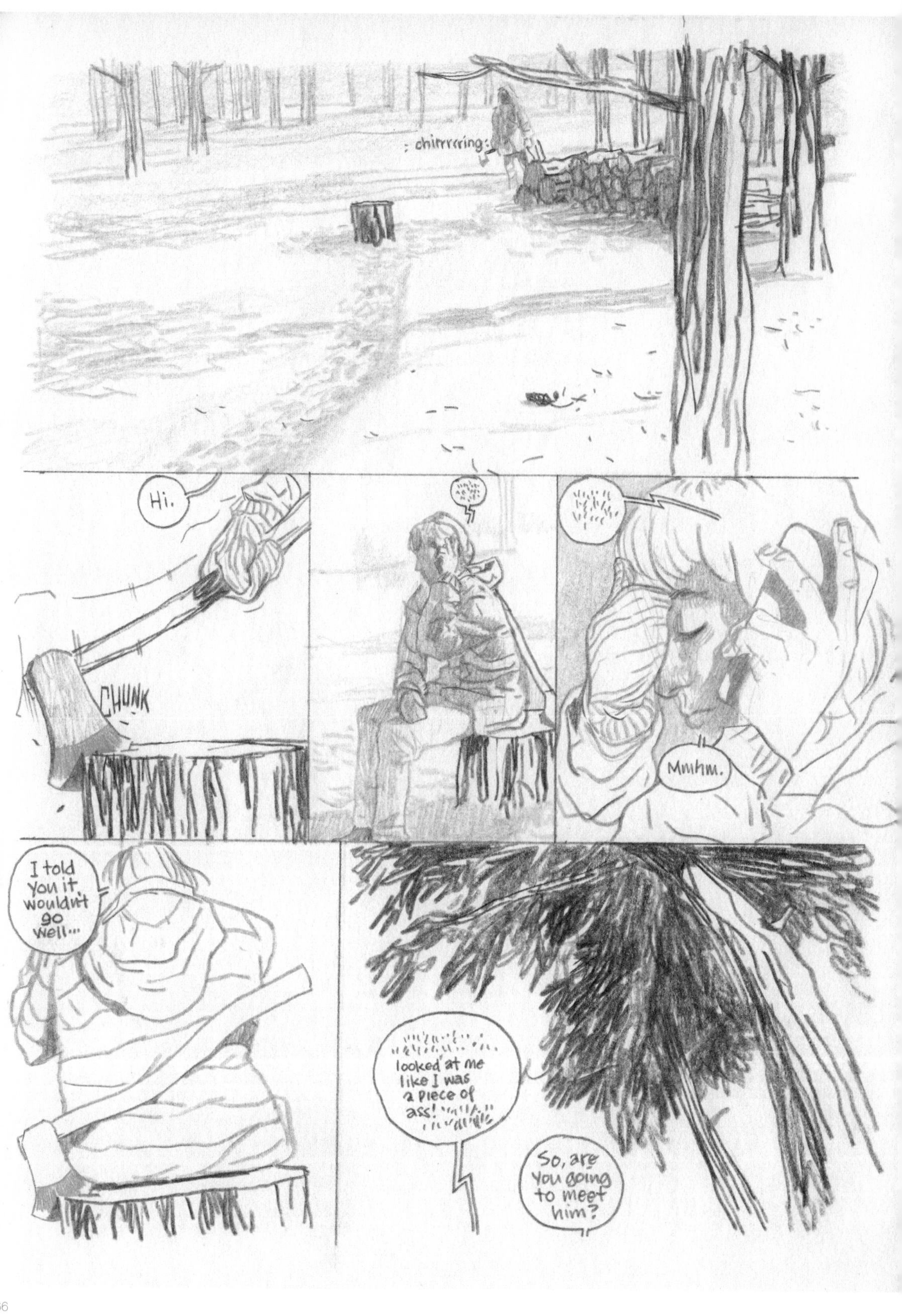

: chirrrrring :
Hi.
CHUNK
Mmhm.
I told you it wouldn't go well...
looked at me like I was a piece of ass!
So, are you going to meet him?

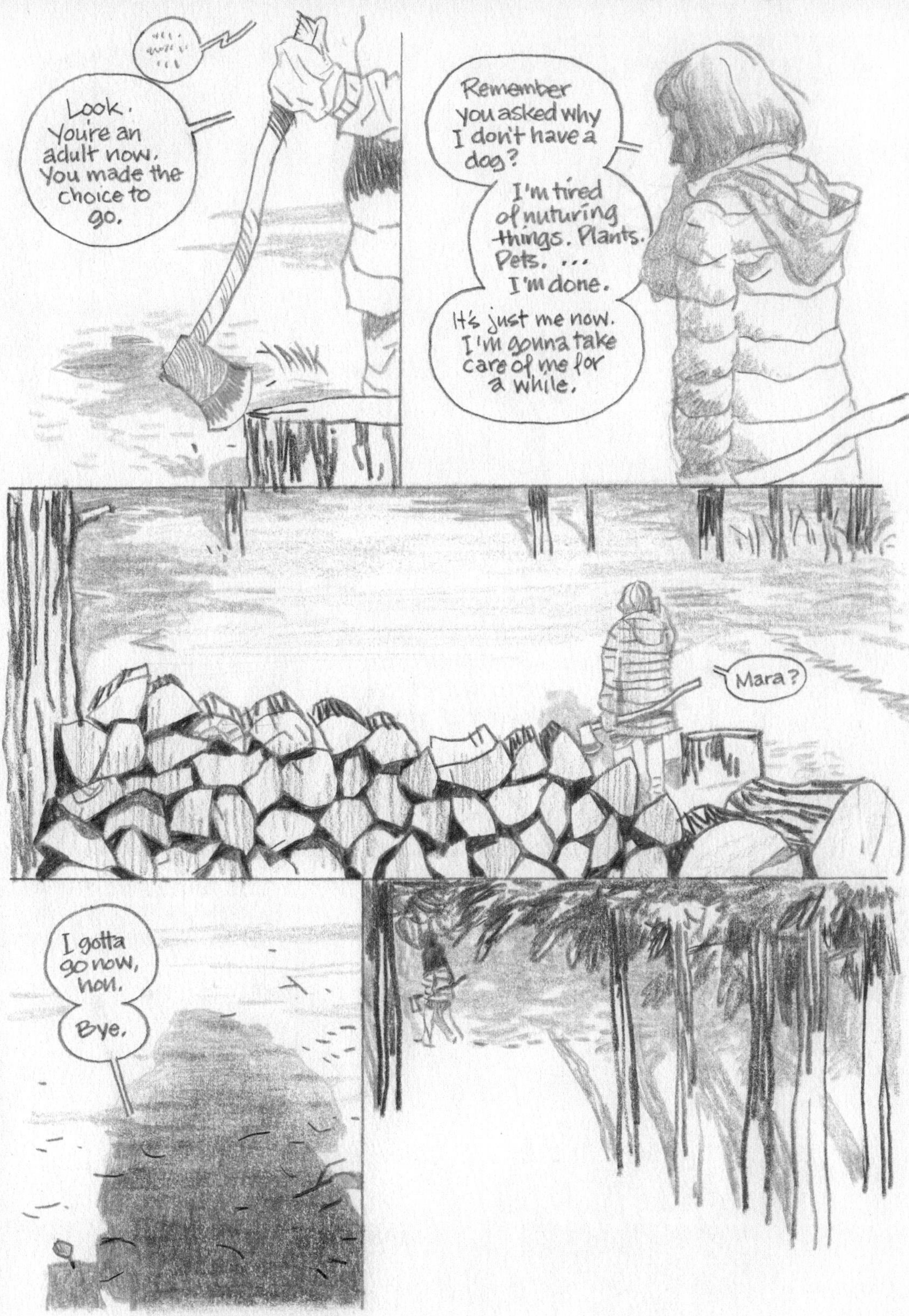
Look. You're an adult now. You made the choice to go.
Remember you asked why I don't have a dog?
I'm tired of nuturing things. Plants. Pets. ... I'm done.
It's just me now. I'm gonna take care of me for a while.
Mara?
I gotta go now, hon.
Bye.

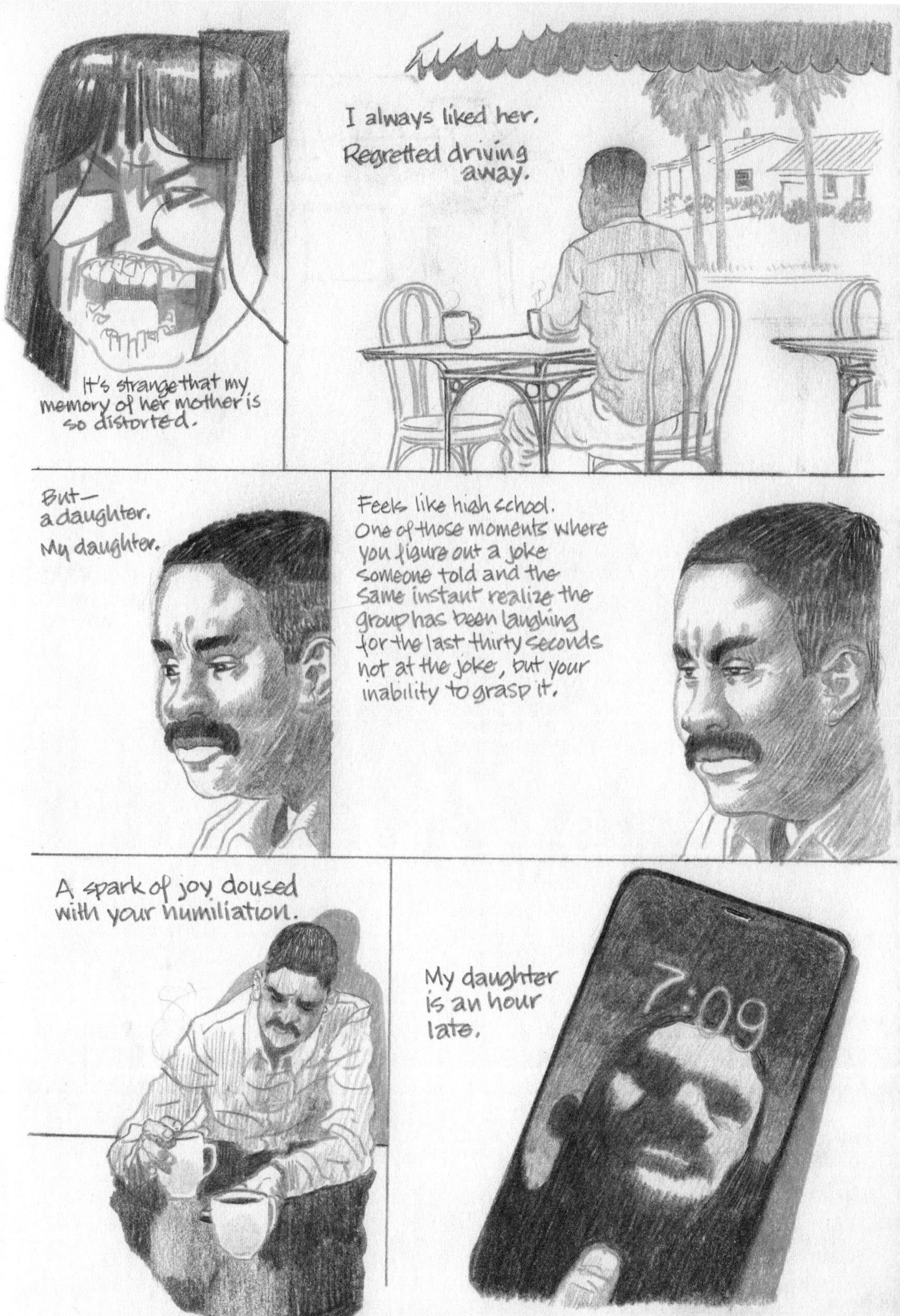
It's strange that my memory of her mother is so distorted.
I always liked her.
Regretted driving away.
But—
a daughter.
My daughter.
Feels like high school.
One of those moments where you figure out a joke someone told and the same instant realize the group has been laughing for the last thirty seconds not at the joke, but your inability to grasp it.
A spark of joy doused with your humiliation.
My daughter is an hour late.
7:09

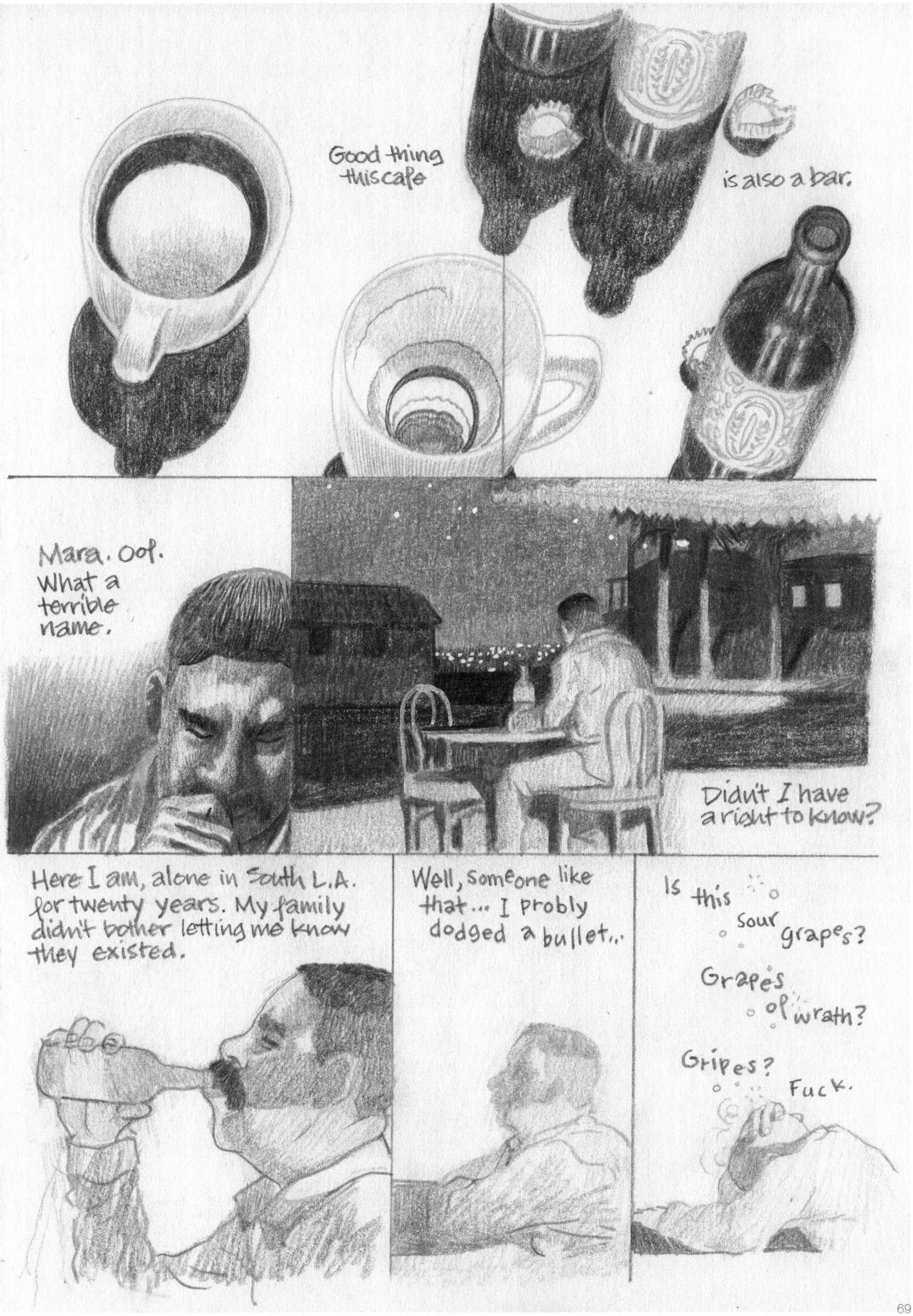
Good thing
this cafe
is also a bar.
Mara. Oof.
What a
terrible
name.
Didn't I have
a right to know?
Here I am, alone in South L.A.
for twenty years. My family
didn't bother letting me know
they existed.
Well, someone like
that... I probly
dodged a bullet...
Is this sour grapes?
Grapes of wrath?
Gripes?
Fuck.

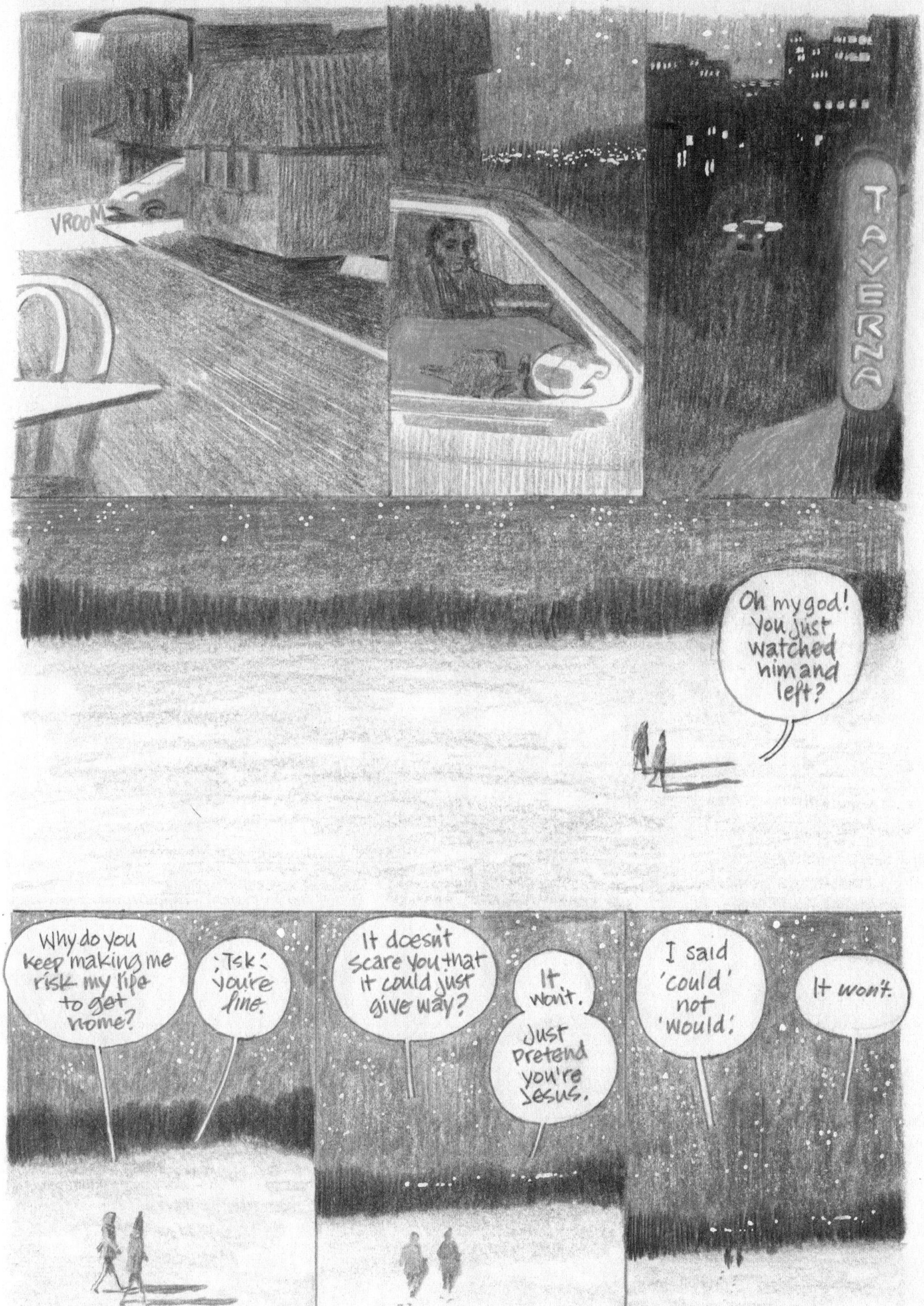
VROOM
TAVERNA
Oh my god! You just watched him and left?
Why do you keep making me risk my life to get home?
Tsk! You're fine.
It doesn't scare you that it could just give way?
It won't.
Just pretend you're Jesus.
I said 'could' not 'would'.
It won't.

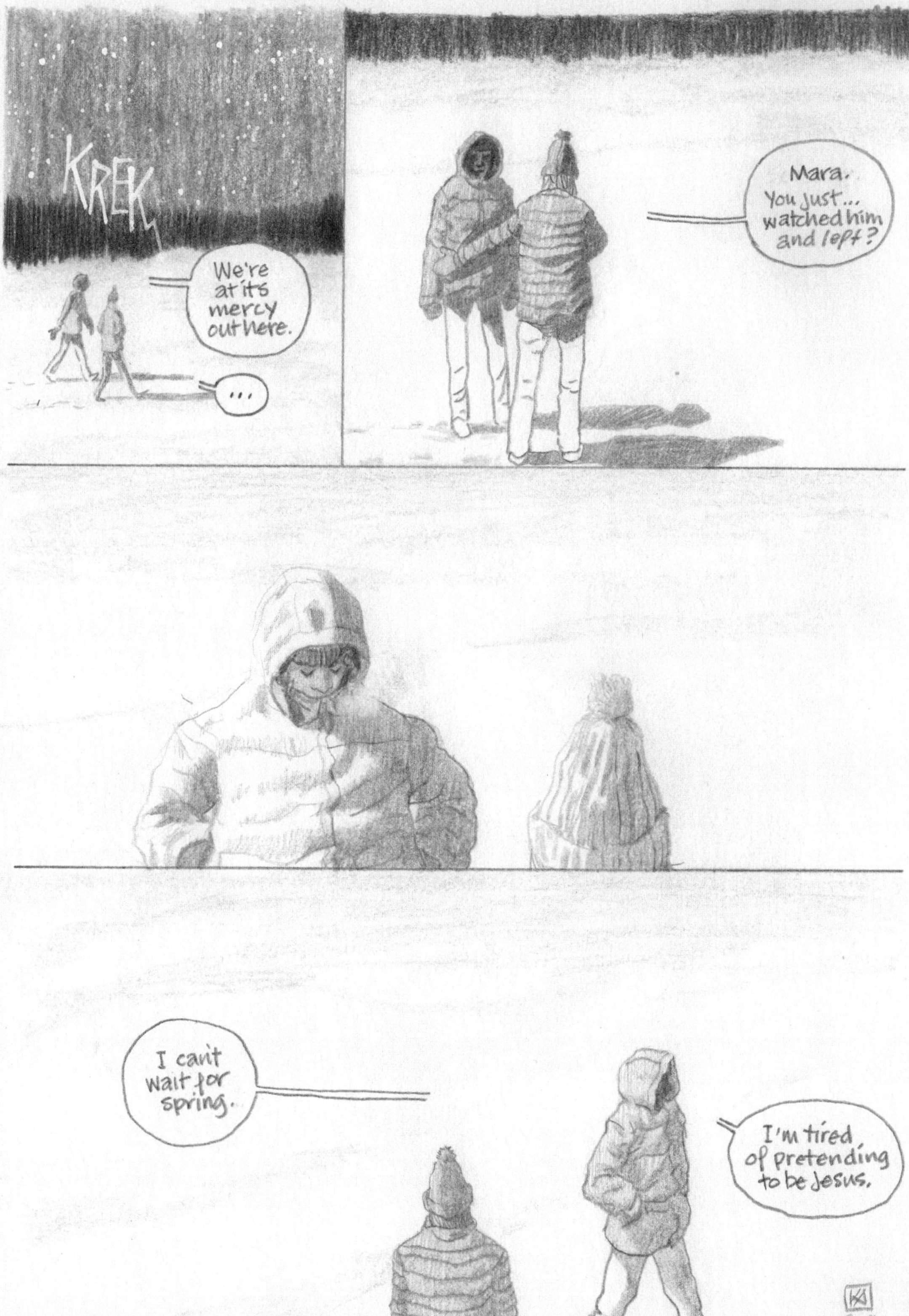
KREK
We're at it's mercy out here.
...
Mara. You just... watched him and left?
I can't wait for spring.
I'm tired of pretending to be Jesus.
2018

Mother Airplane

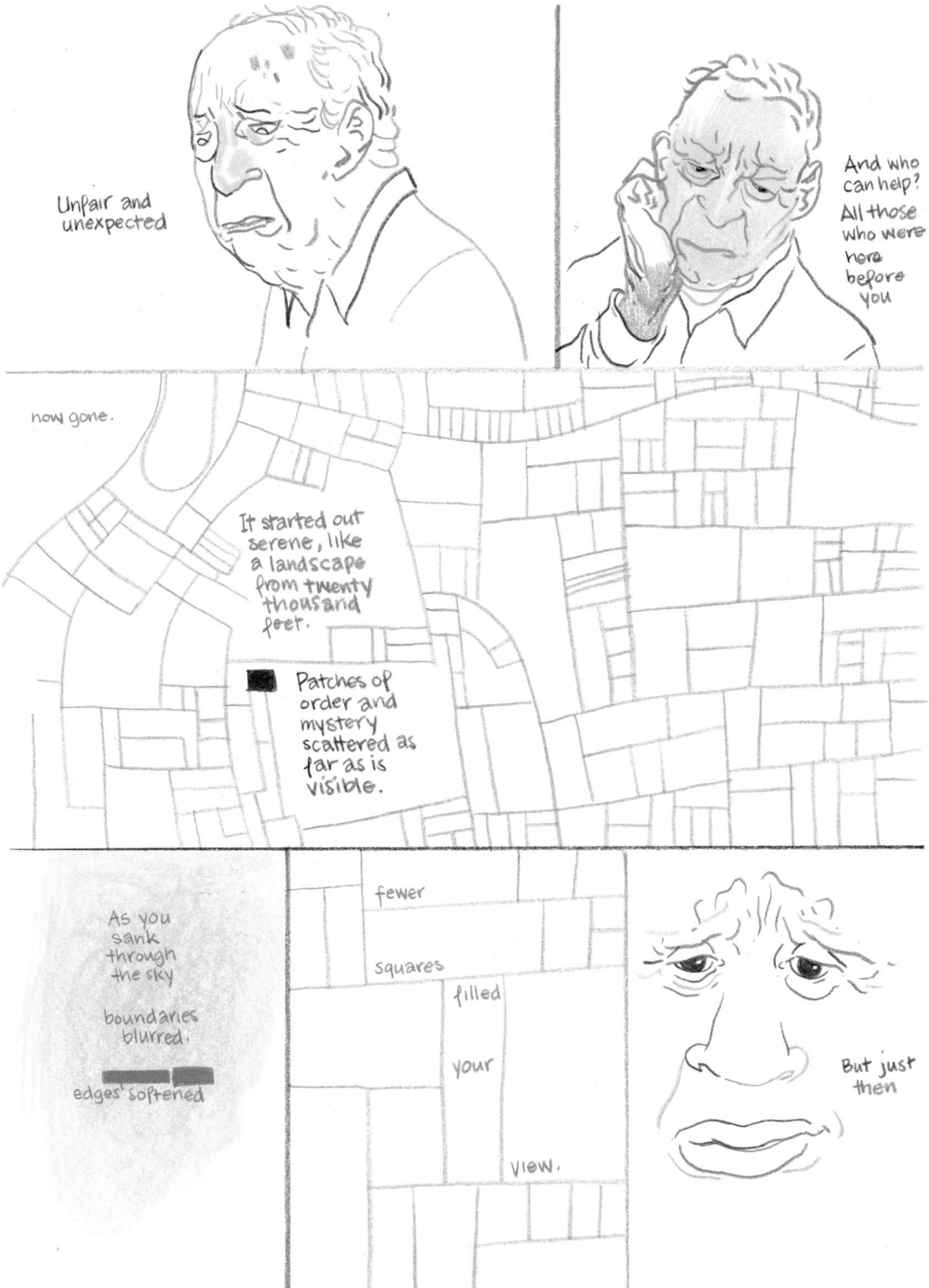
Unfair and unexpected
And who can help? All those who were here before you
now gone.
It started out serene, like a landscape from twenty thousand feet.
Patches of order and mystery scattered as far as is visible.
As you sank through the sky
boundaries blurred.
edges softened
fewer
squares
filled
your
view.
But just then

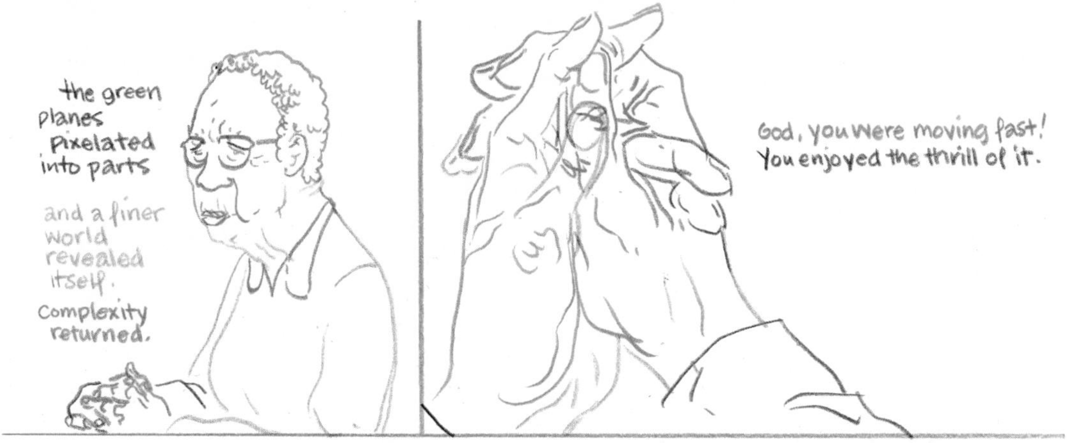
the green planes pixelated into parts
and a finer world revealed itself.
complexity returned.
God, you were moving fast! You enjoyed the thrill of it.

Forests became trees.

Blocks became house roofs

then shingles.

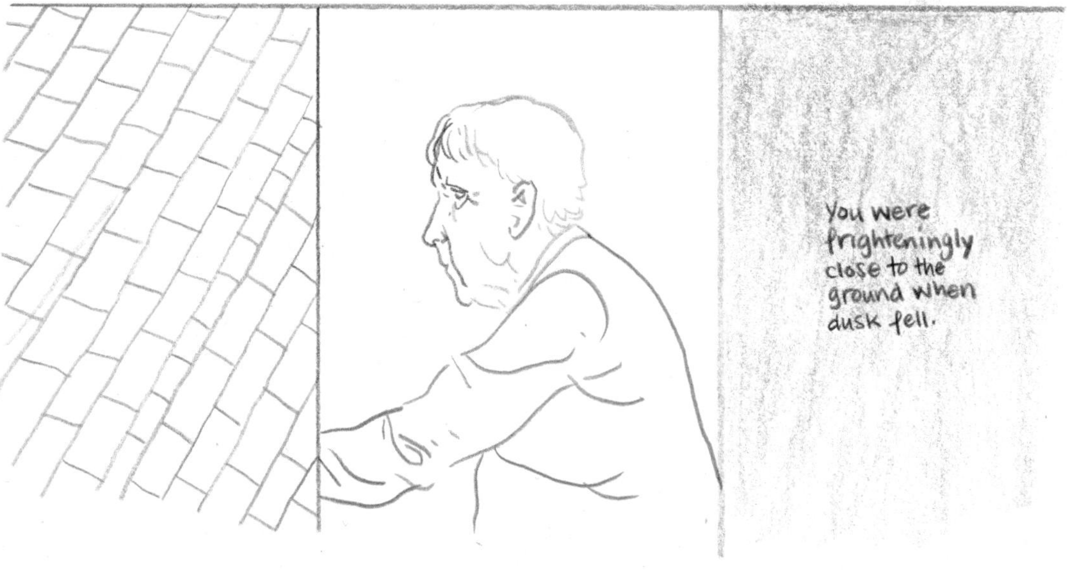
You were frighteningly close to the ground when dusk fell.

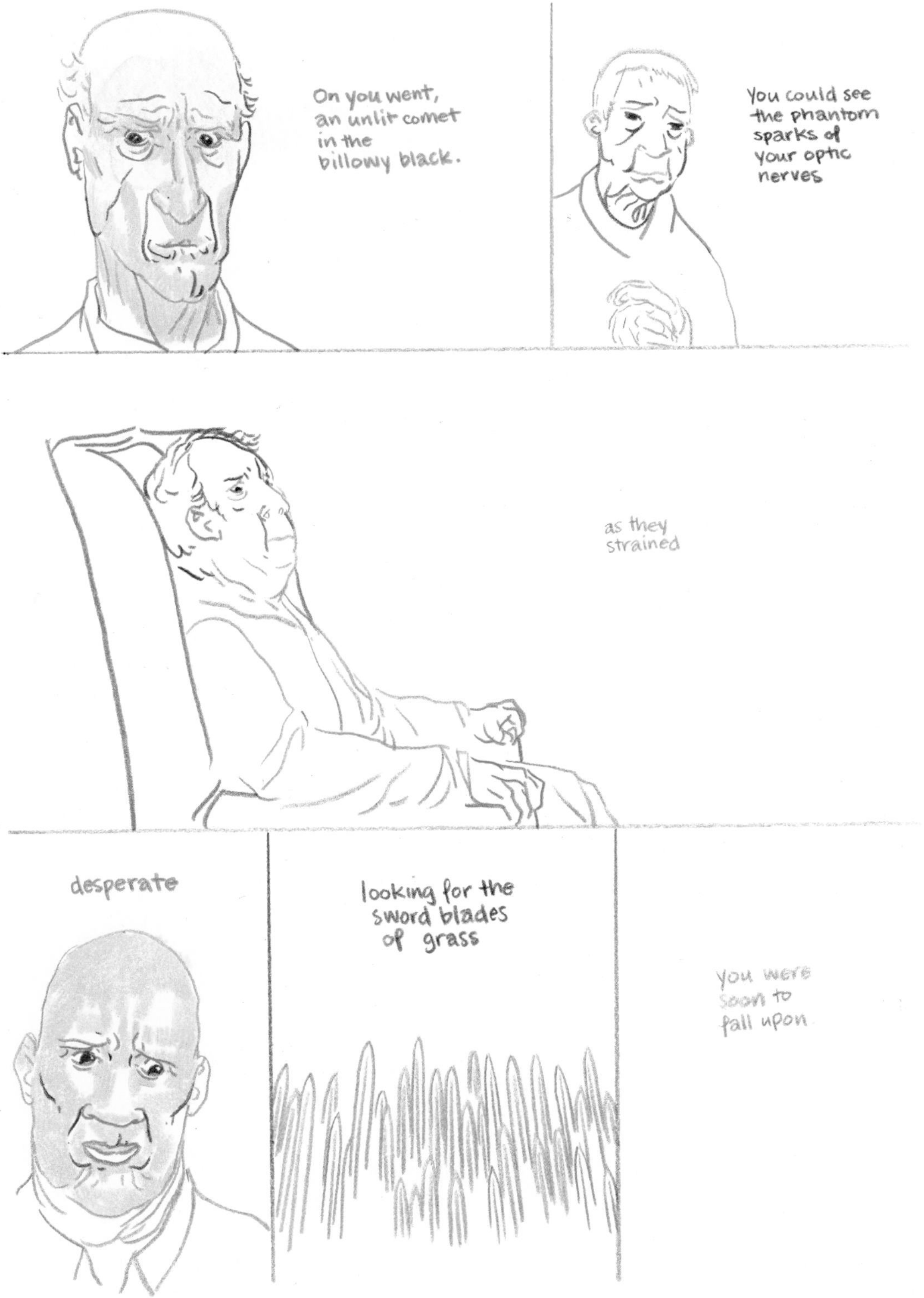
On you went, an unlit comet in the billowy black.
You could see the phantom sparks of your optic nerves
as they strained
desperate
looking for the sword blades of grass
you were soon to fall upon

Stolen Sketches

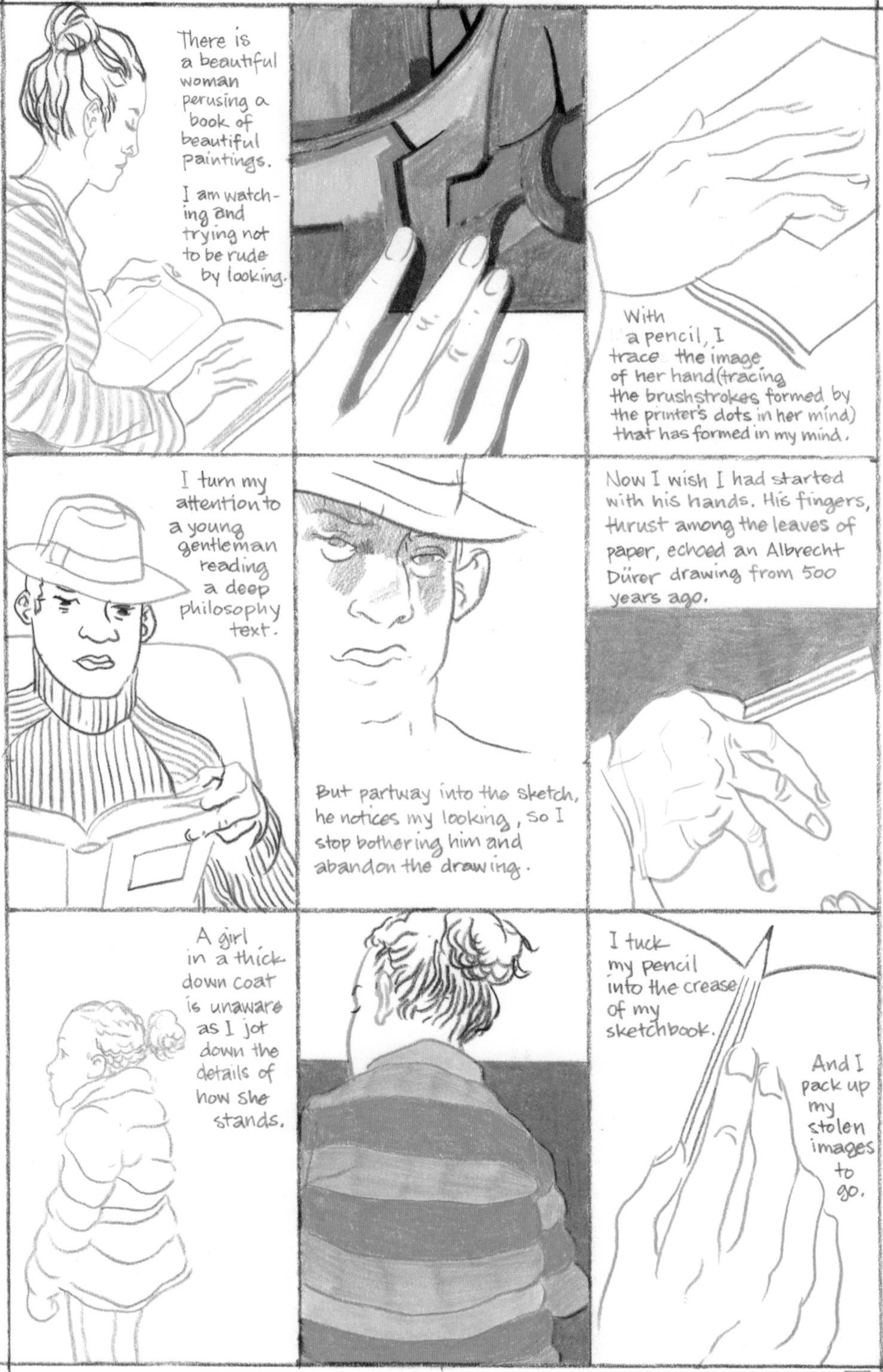

There is a beautiful woman perusing a book of beautiful paintings.
I am watching and trying not to be rude by looking.
With a pencil, I trace the image of her hand (tracing the brushstrokes formed by the printer's dots in her mind) that has formed in my mind.
I turn my attention to a young gentleman reading a deep philosophy text.
But partway into the sketch, he notices my looking, so I stop bothering him and abandon the drawing.
Now I wish I had started with his hands. His fingers, thrust among the leaves of paper, echoed an Albrecht Dürer drawing from 500 years ago.
A girl in a thick down coat is unaware as I jot down the details of how she stands.
I tuck my pencil into the crease of my sketchbook.
And I pack up my stolen images to go.

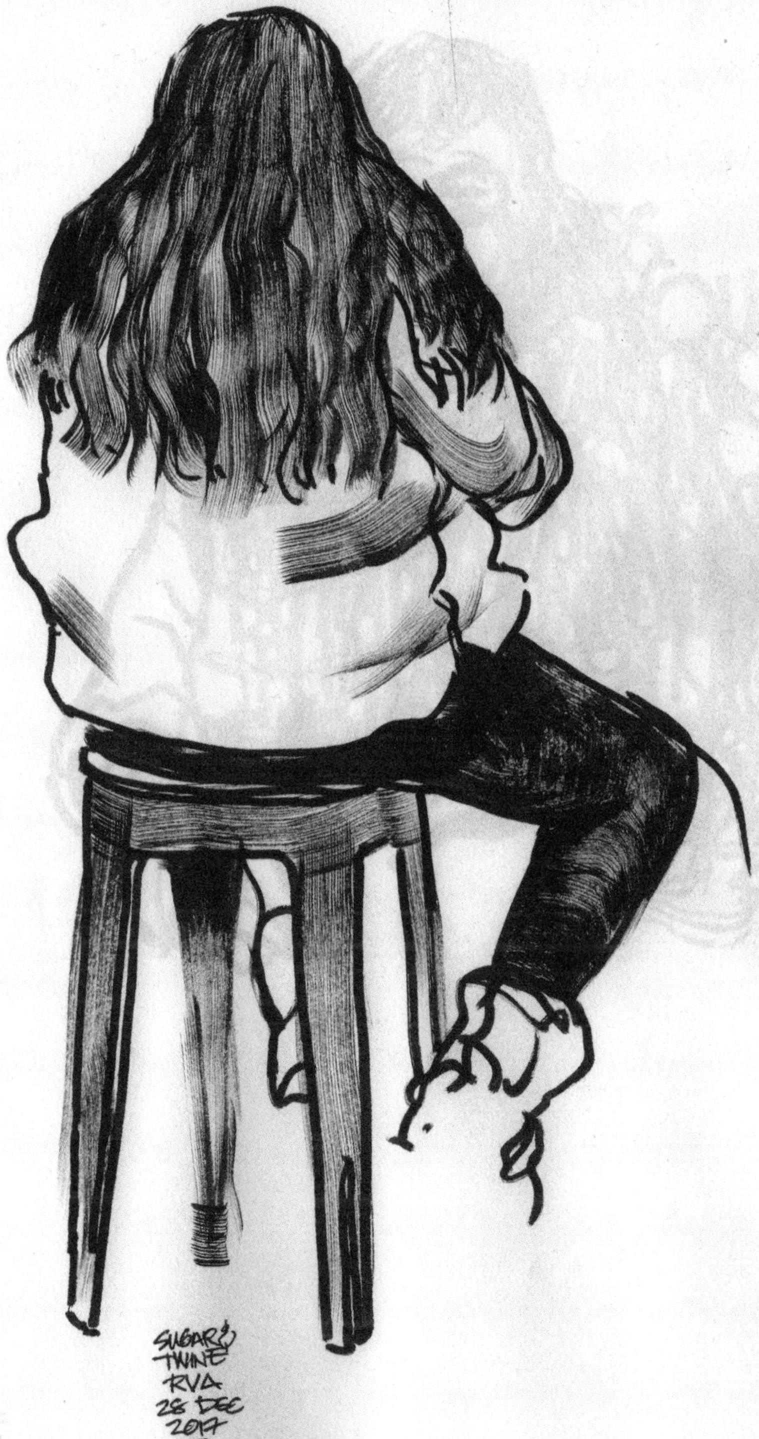
SUGAR & TWINE
RVA
28 DEC
2017

Dark Desert Dawn

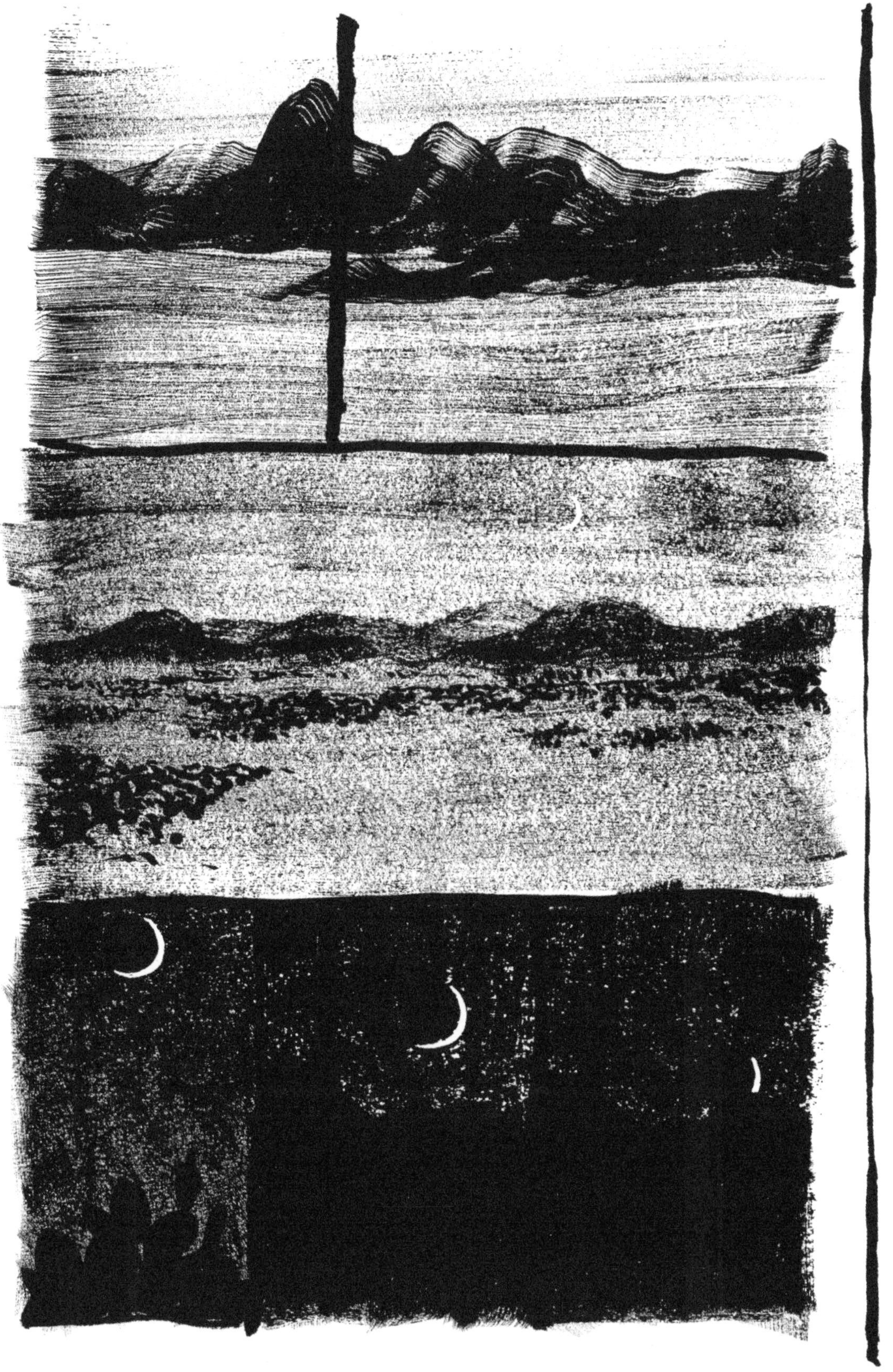

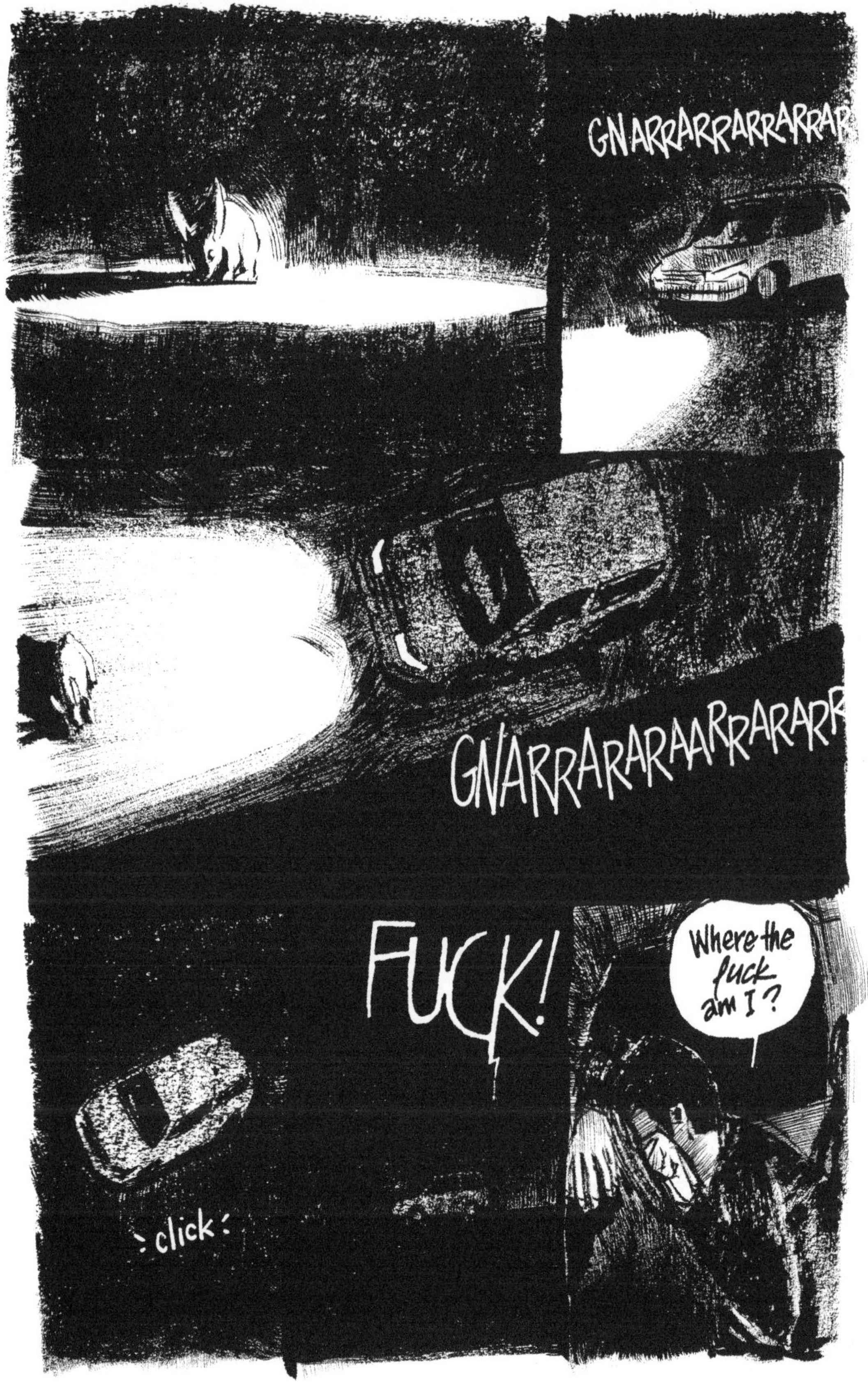
GNARRARRARRARRAR
GNARRARARAARRARARR
FUCK!
click
Where the fuck am I?

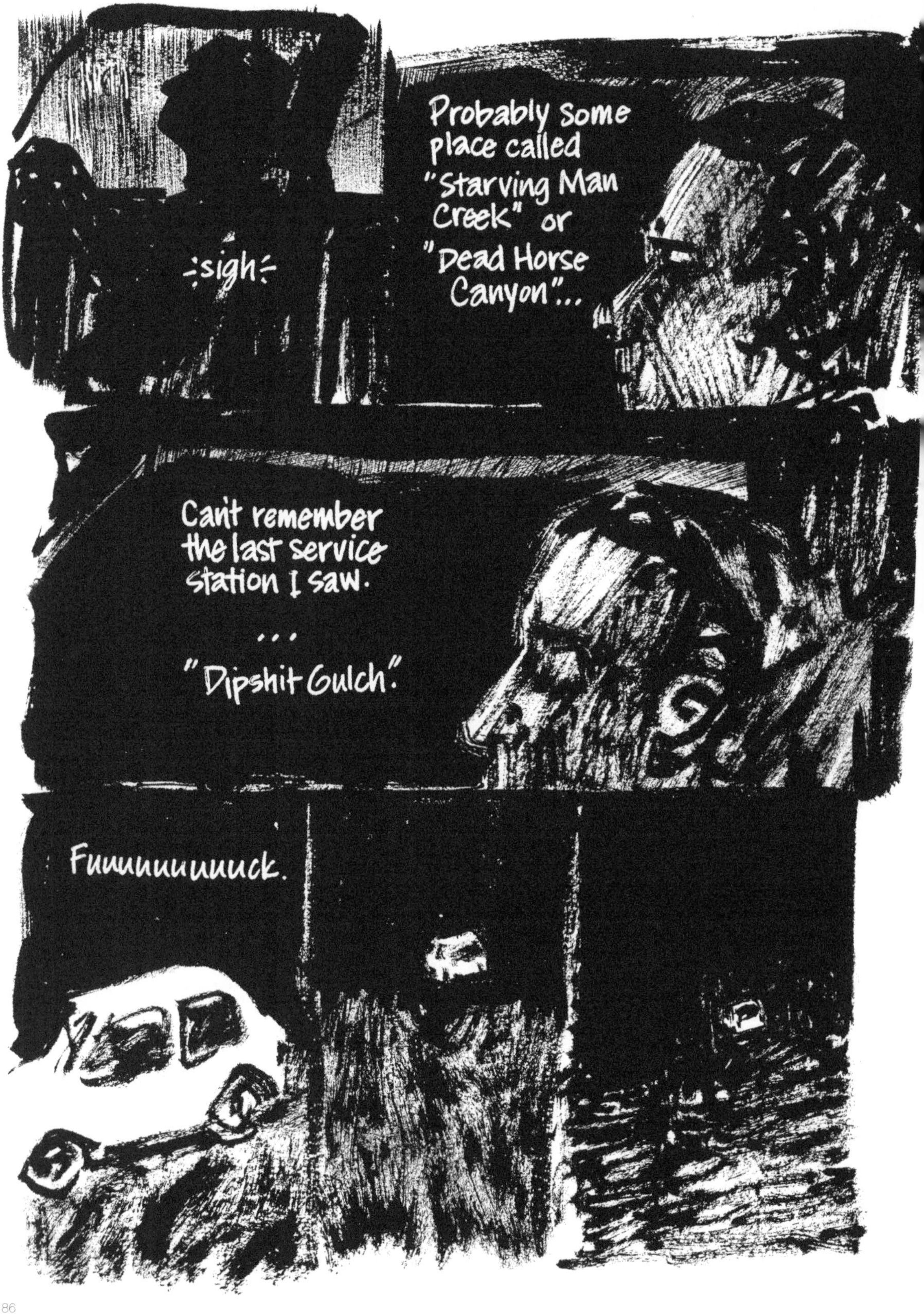
sigh
Probably some place called "Starving Man Creek" or "Dead Horse Canyon"...
Can't remember the last service station I saw.
...
"Dipshit Gulch."
Fuuuuuuuuuck.

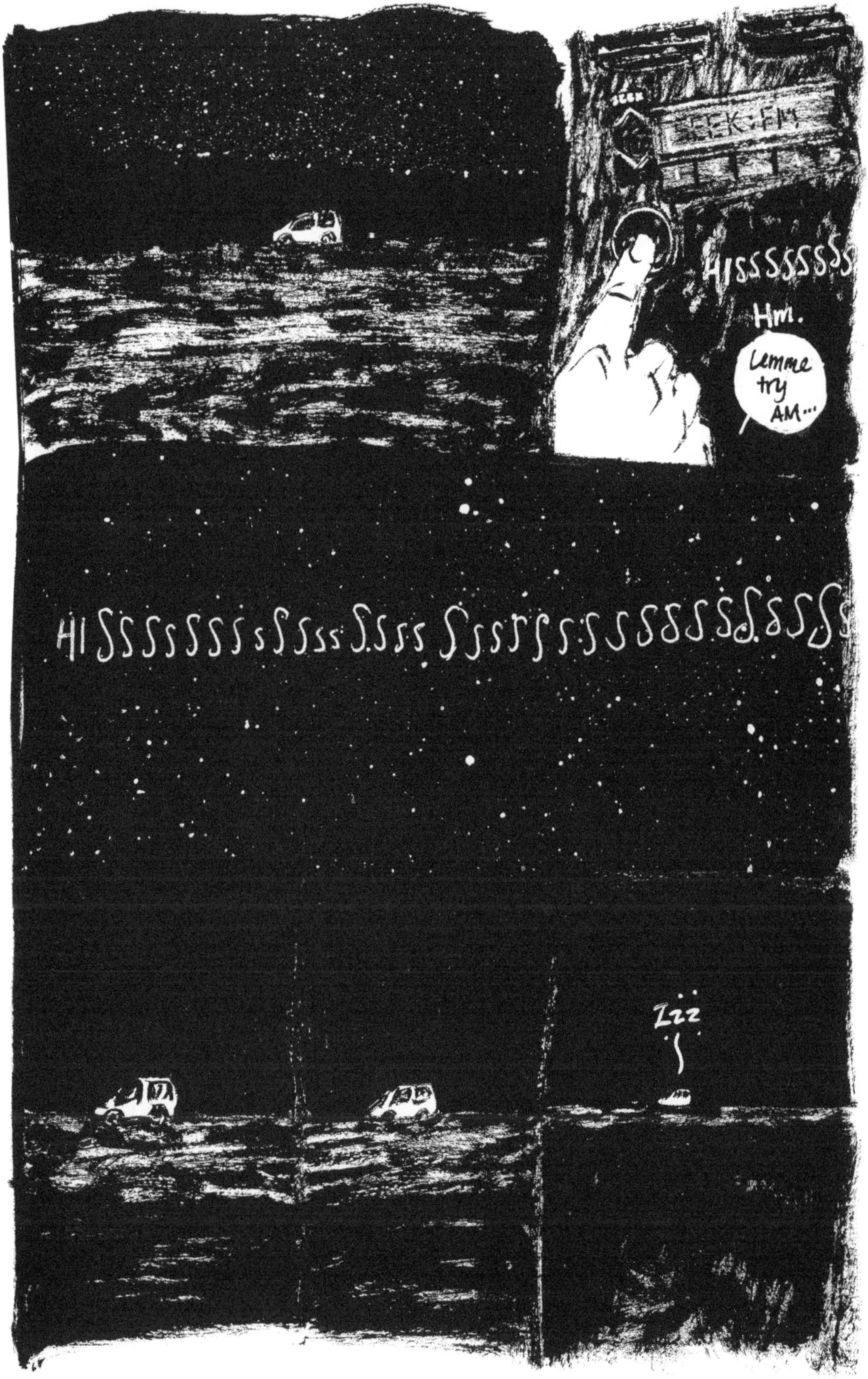
SEEK
SEEK:FM
HISSSSSSSS
Hm.
Lemme try AM...
HISSSSSSSSSSSSSSSSSSSSSSSSSSSSSSSSSSSS
Zzz

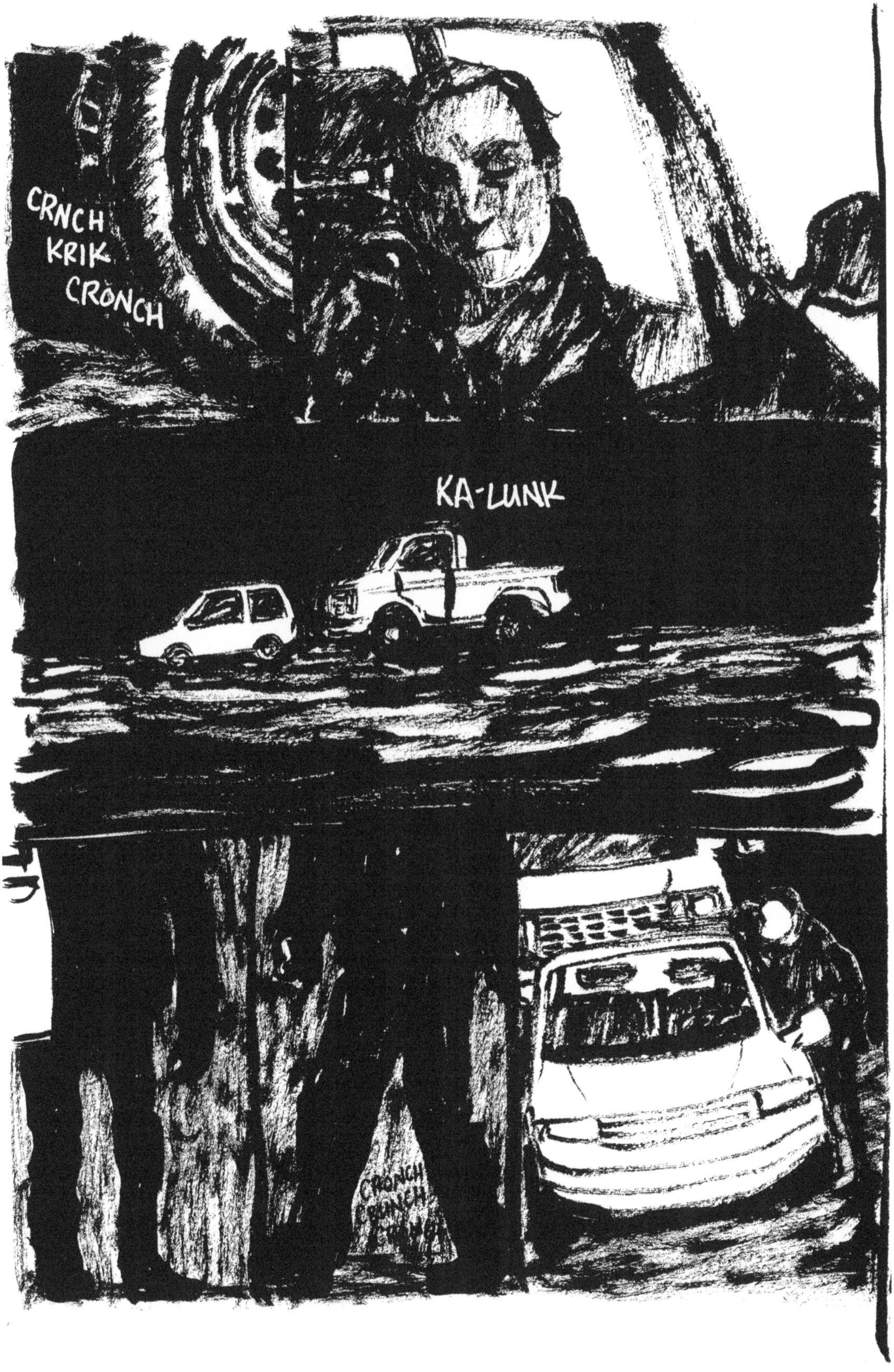
CRNCH
KRIK
CRǑNCH
KA-LUNK
CRONCH

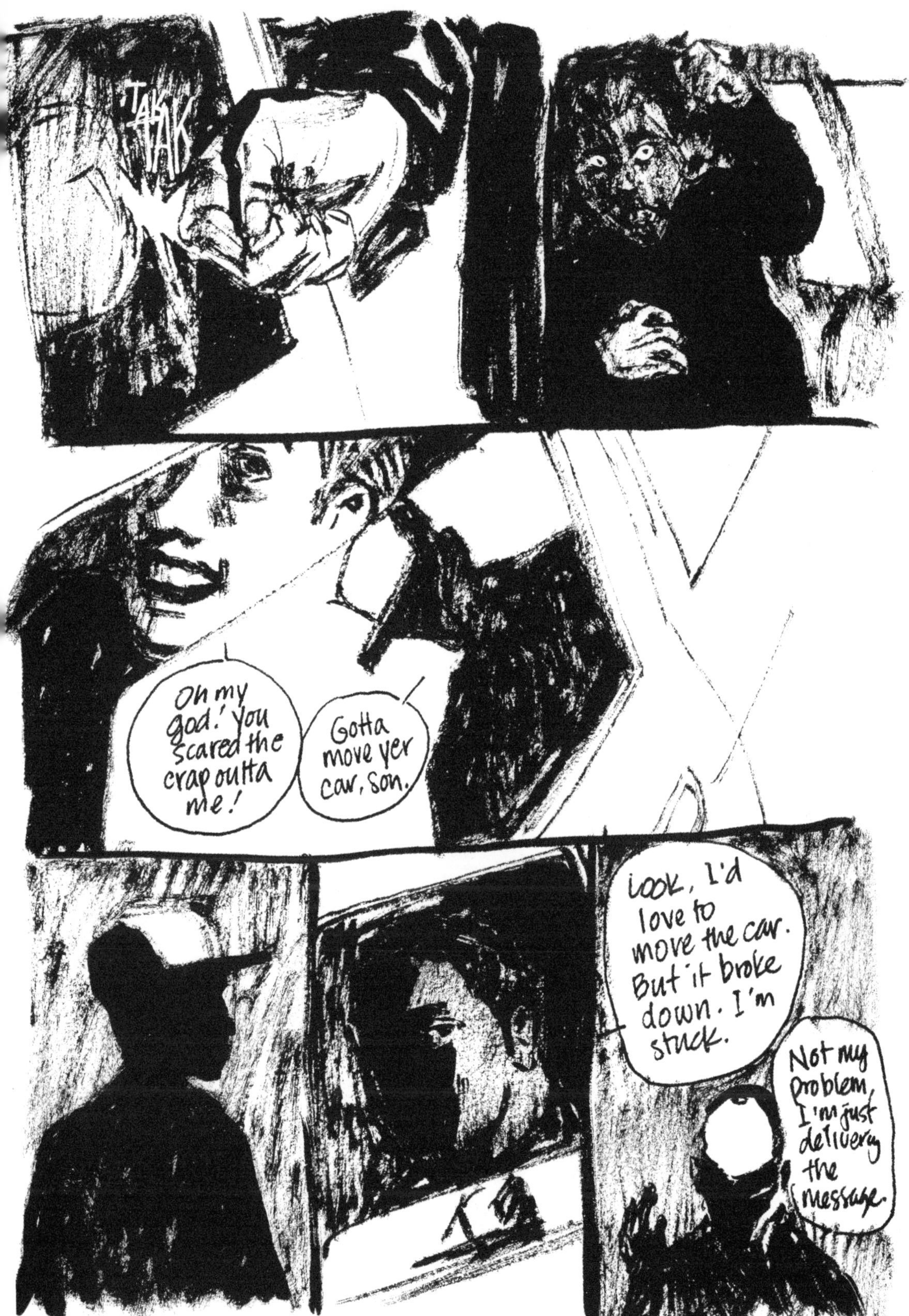
TAK TAK
Oh my god! You scared the crap outta me!
Gotta move yer car, son.
Look, I'd love to move the car. But it broke down. I'm stuck.
Not my problem, I'm just delivering the message.

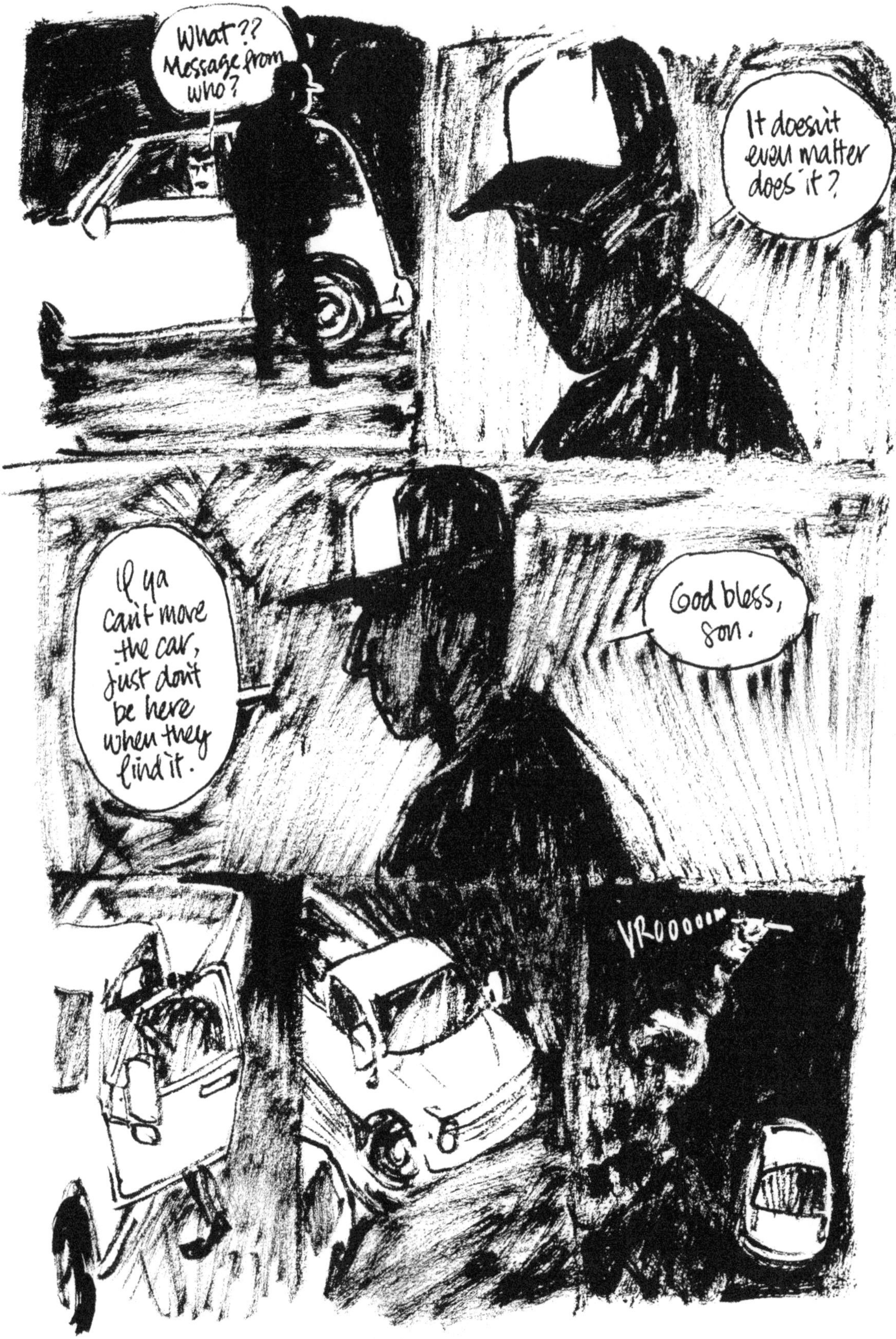
What?? Message from who?
It doesn't even matter does it?
If ya can't move the car, just don't be here when they find it.
God bless, son.
VROOOOM

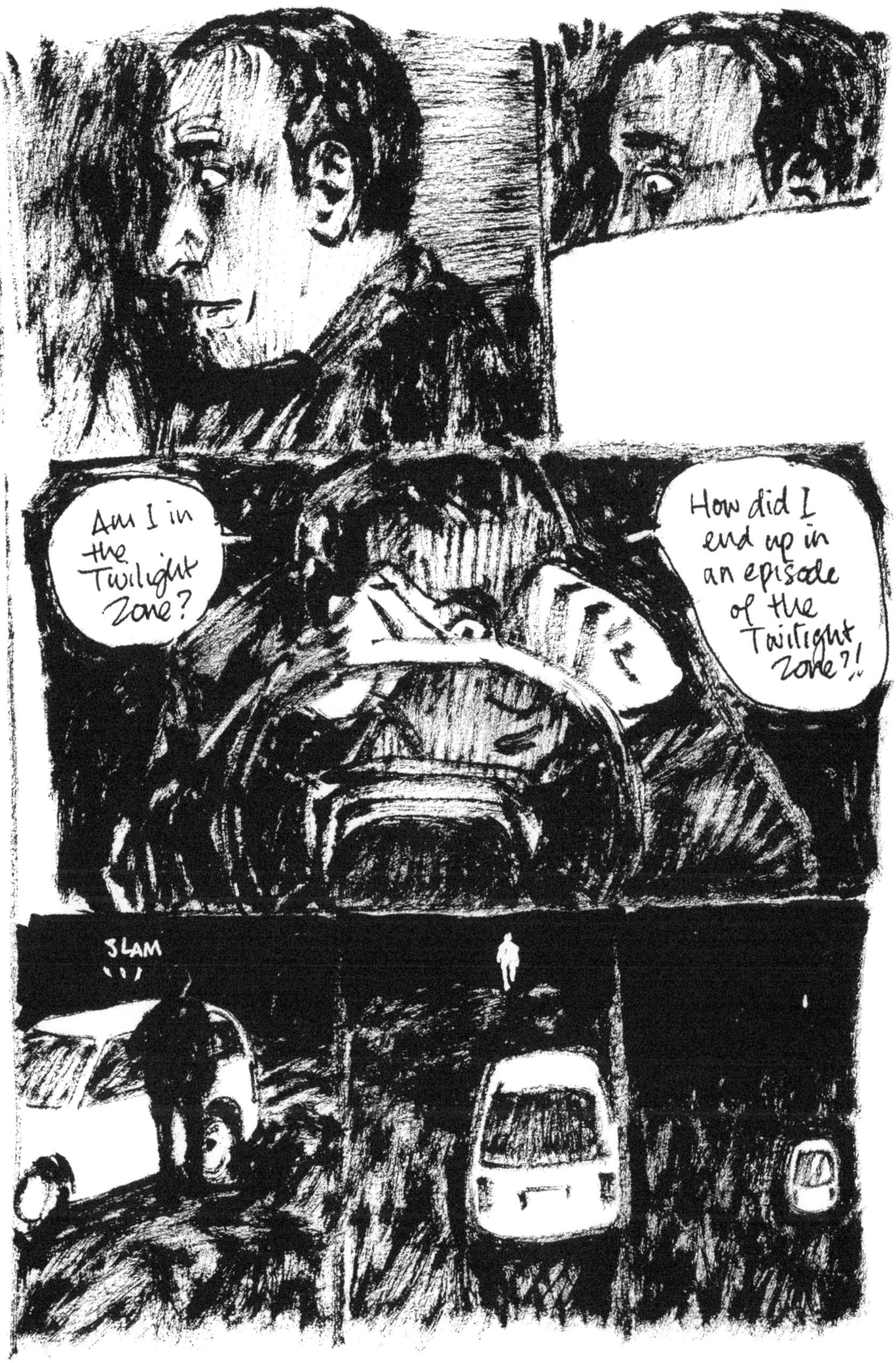
Am I in the Twilight Zone?
How did I end up in an episode of the Twilight Zone?!
SLAM

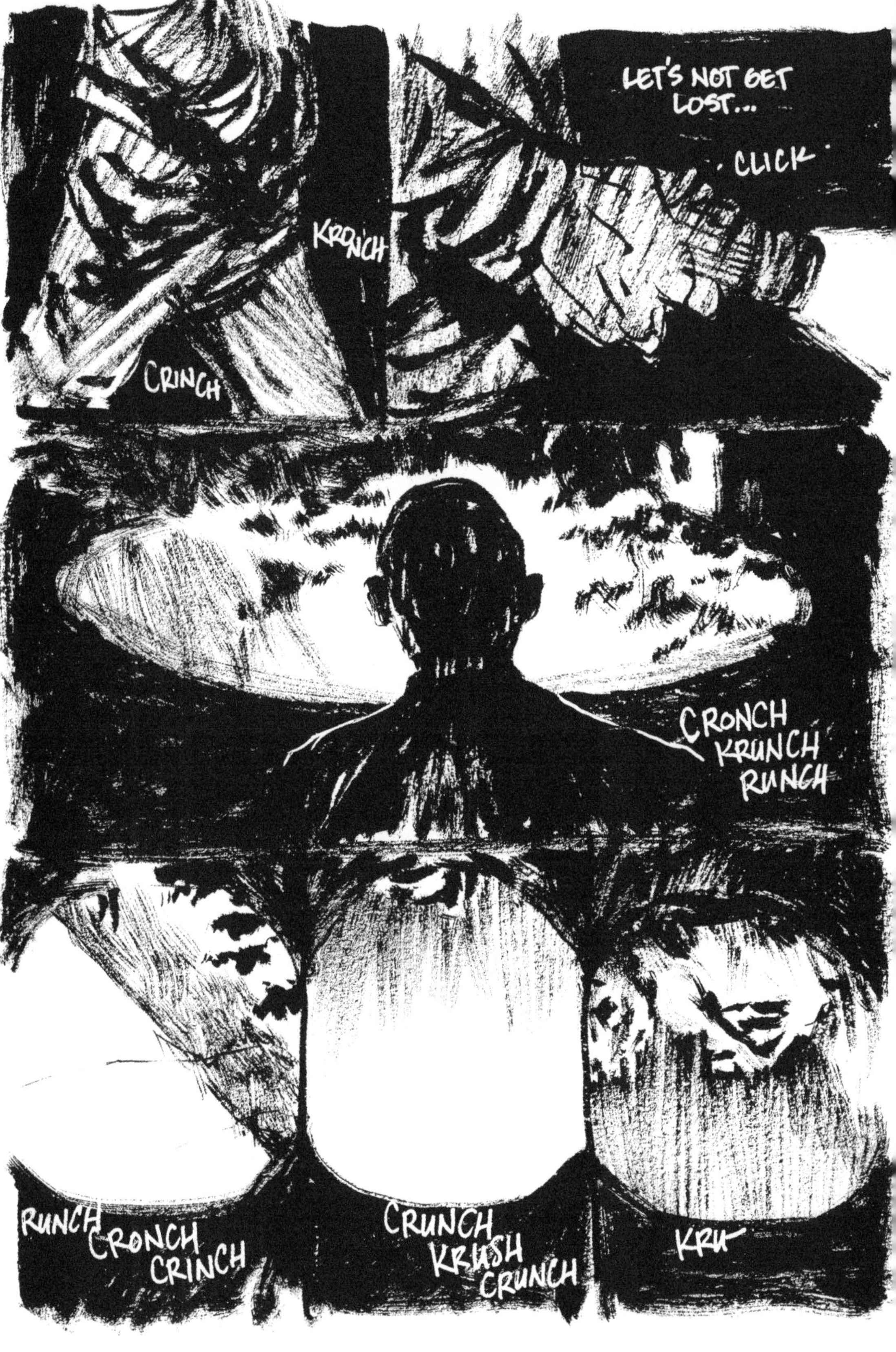
KRONCH
CRINCH
LET'S NOT GET LOST...
CLICK
CRONCH
KRUNCH
RUNCH
RUNCH
CRONCH
CRINCH
CRUNCH
KRUSH
CRUNCH
KRU

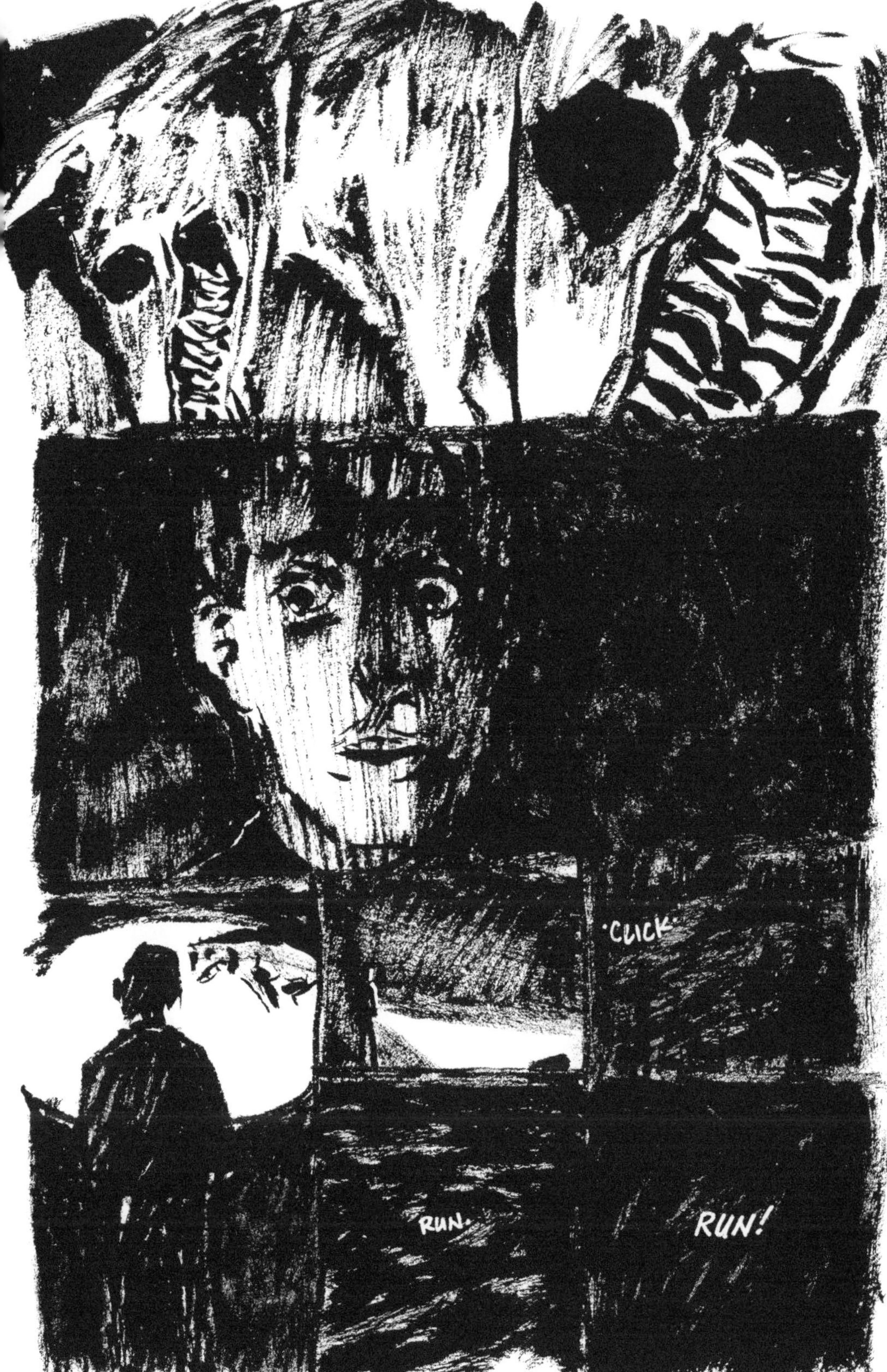
·CLICK·
RUN·
RUN!

KKKRINCH:
CRONCH:
KRUNCH KRUNCH CRONCH KRUNCH CRONCH KRUNCH
HEF HAF HUFF HUFF HEF HAF
NOISE...
WHAT'S THAT NOISE?

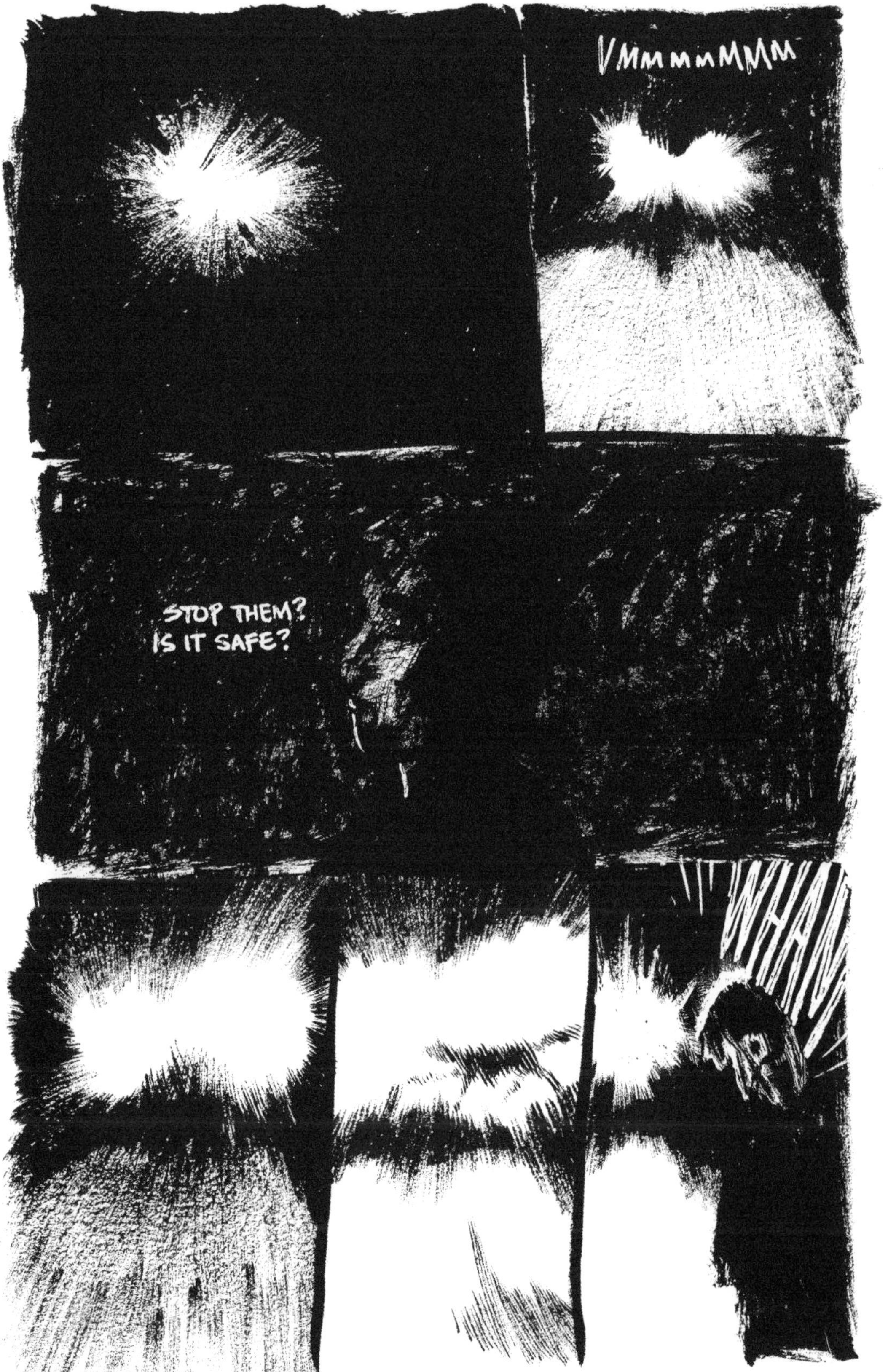
VMMMMMMM
STOP THEM?
IS IT SAFE?
WHA

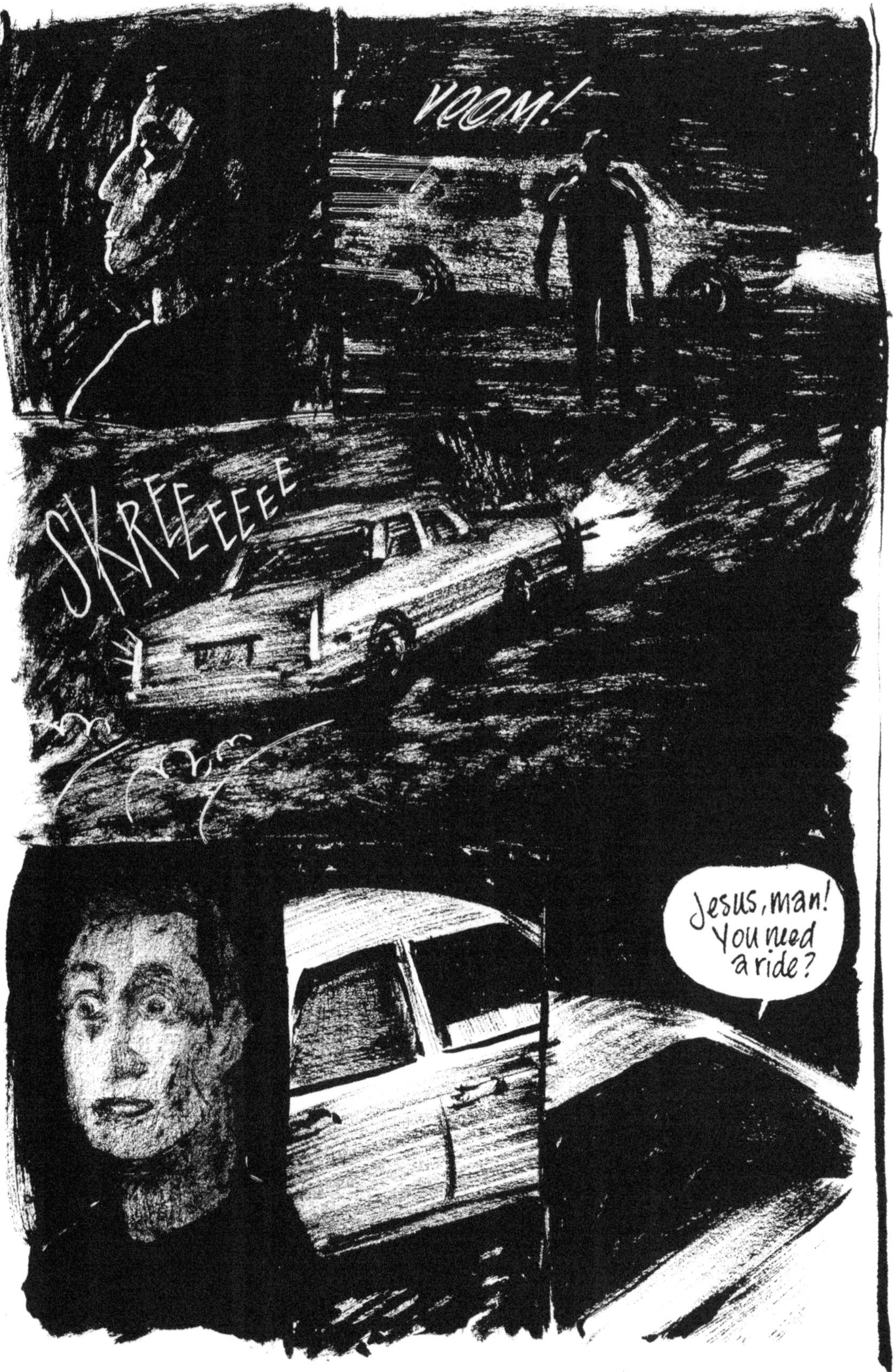
VROOM!
SKREEEEEEE
Jesus, man! You need a ride?

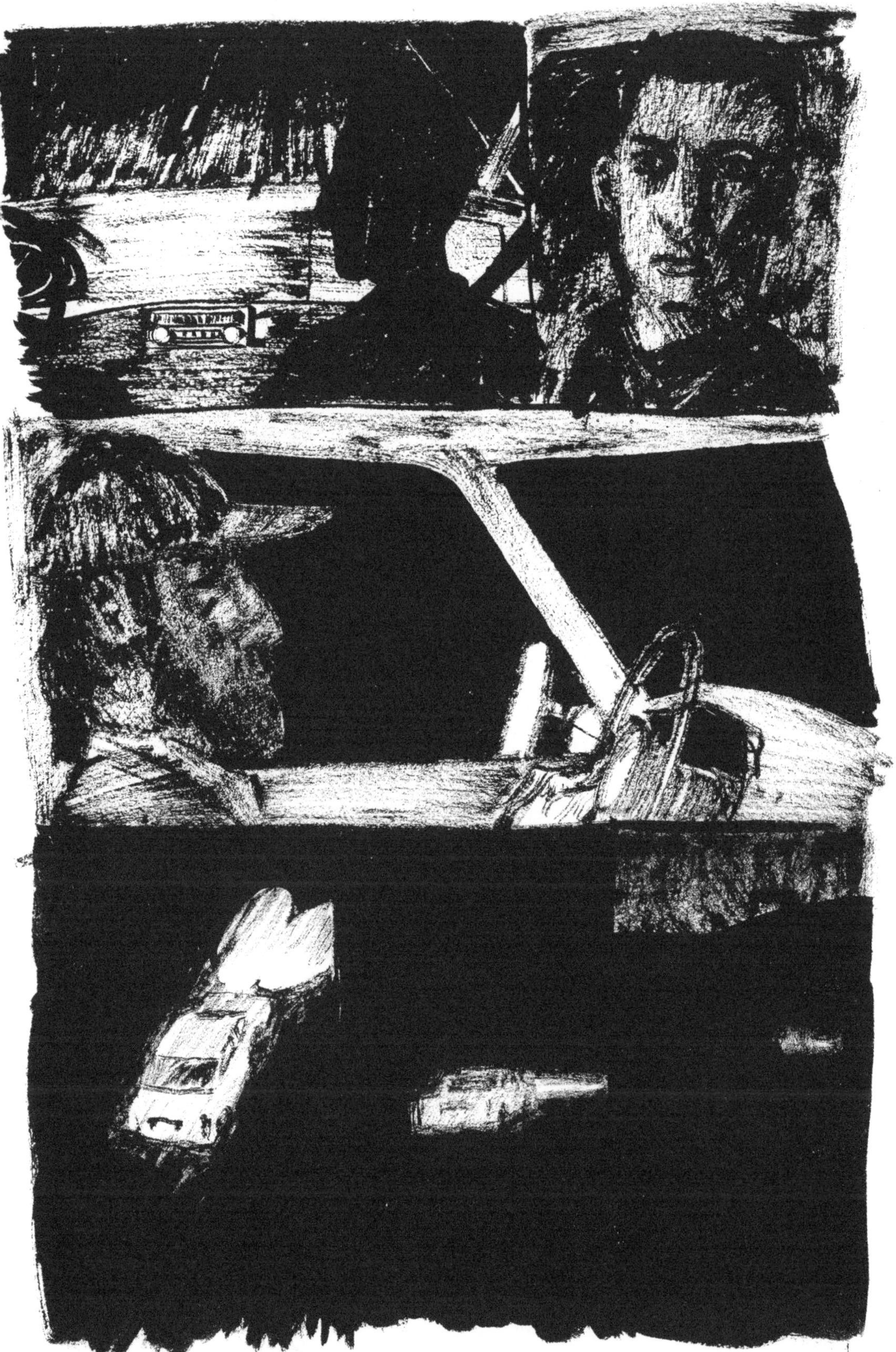

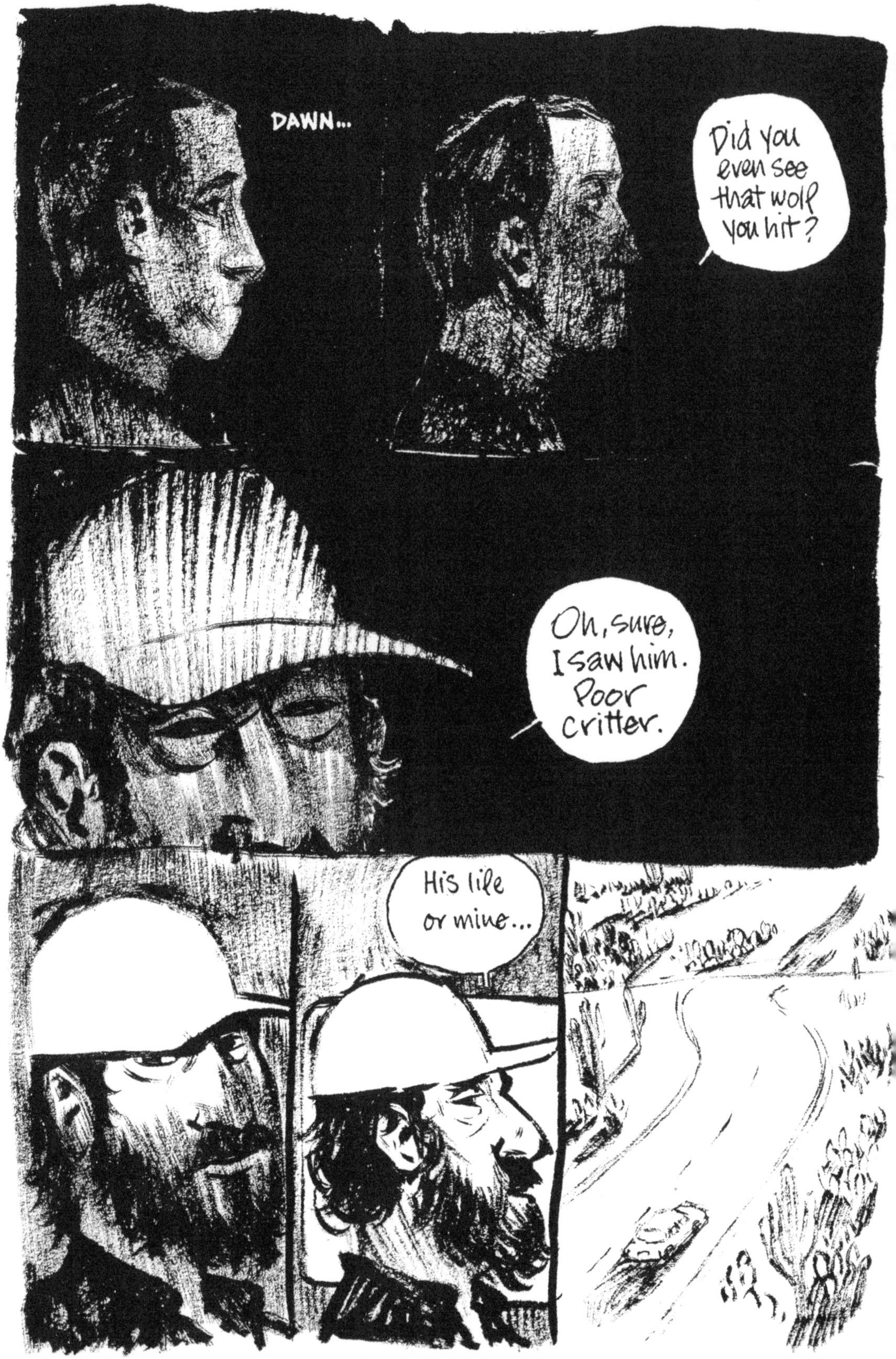
DAWN...
Did you even see that wolf you hit?
Oh, sure, I saw him. Poor critter.
His life or mine...

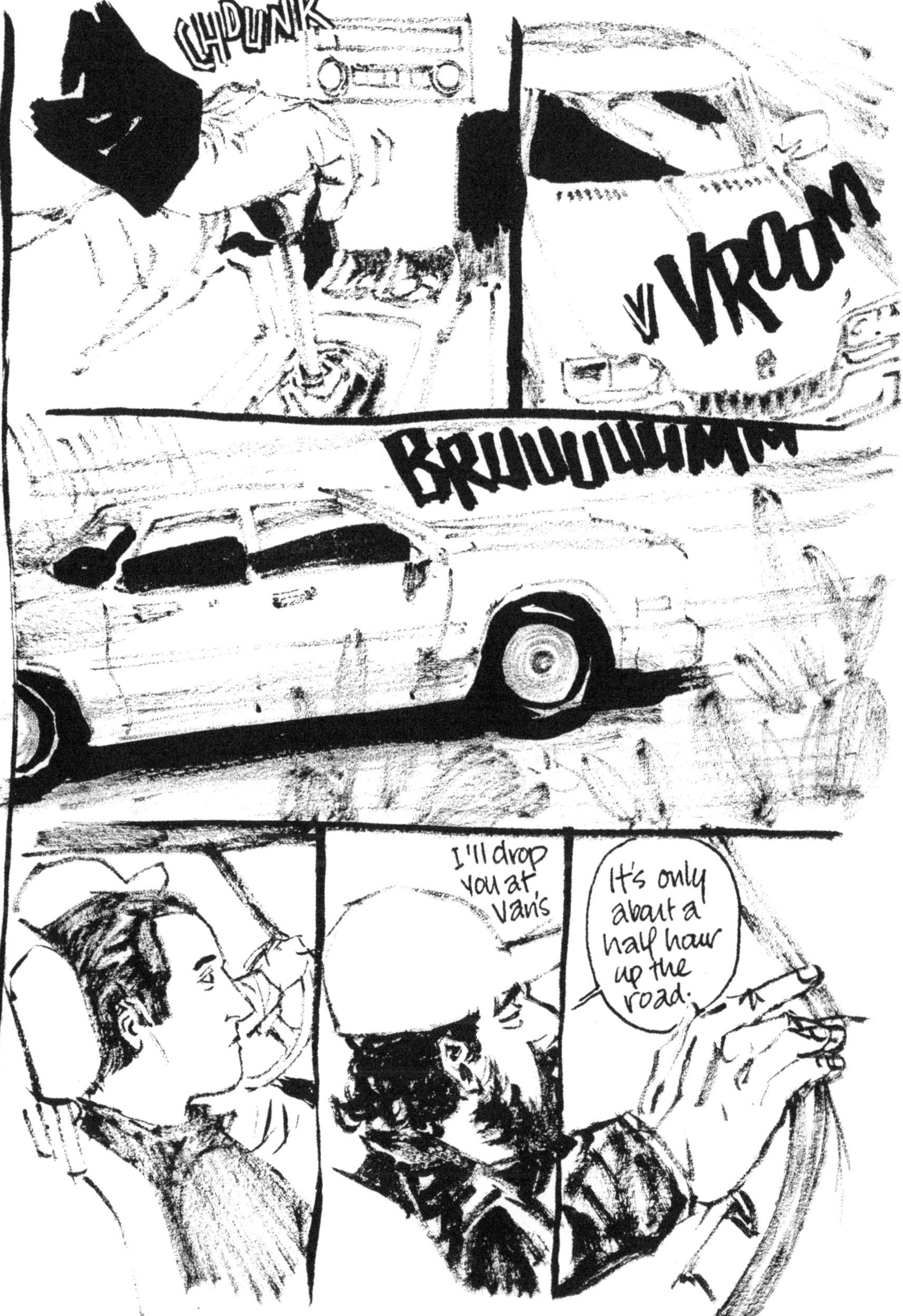
CHPUNK
VVROOM
BRUUUUUMM
I'll drop you at Van's
It's only about a half hour up the road.

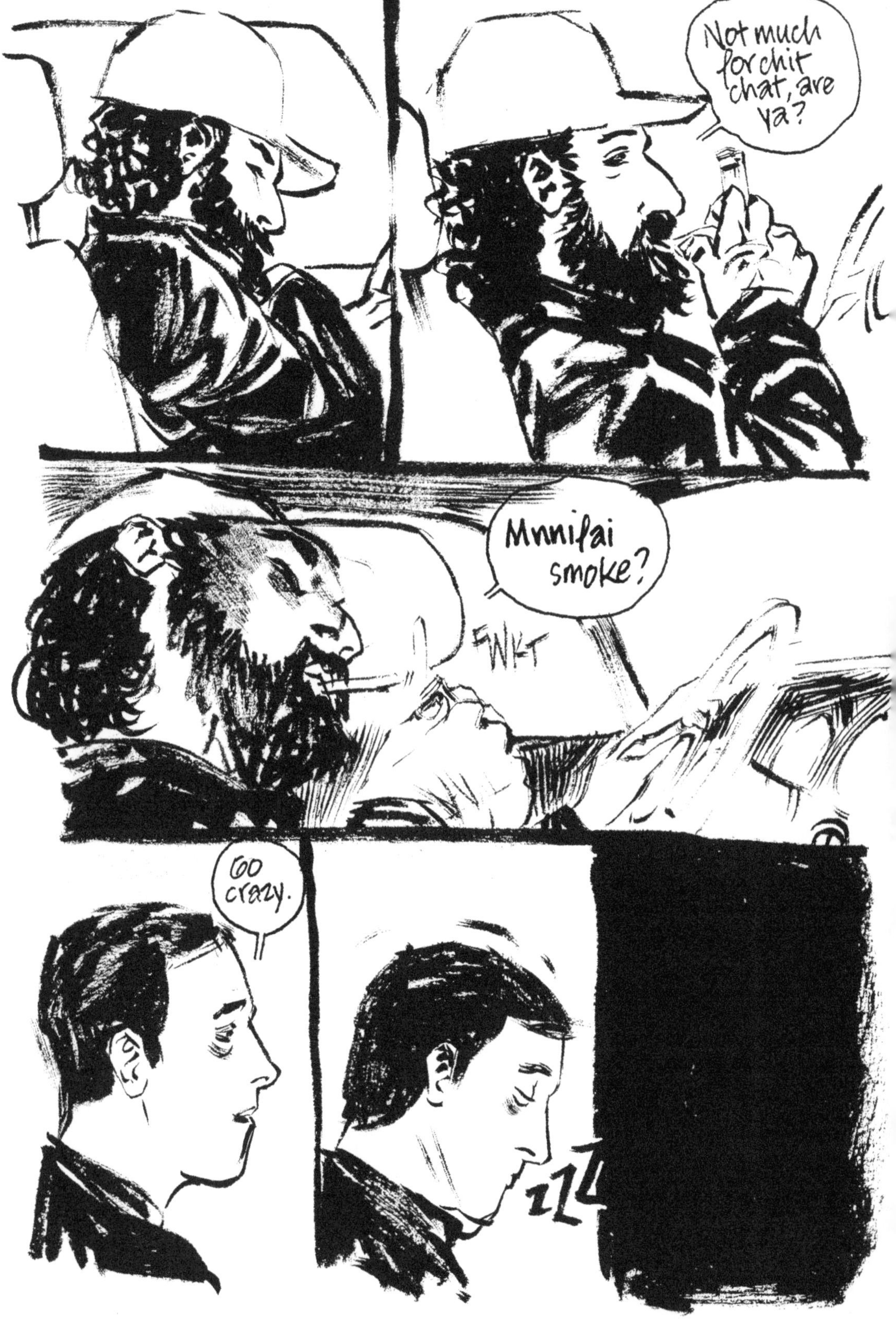
Not much for chit chat, are ya?
Mnnifai smoke?
FWKT
Go crazy.
ZZZ

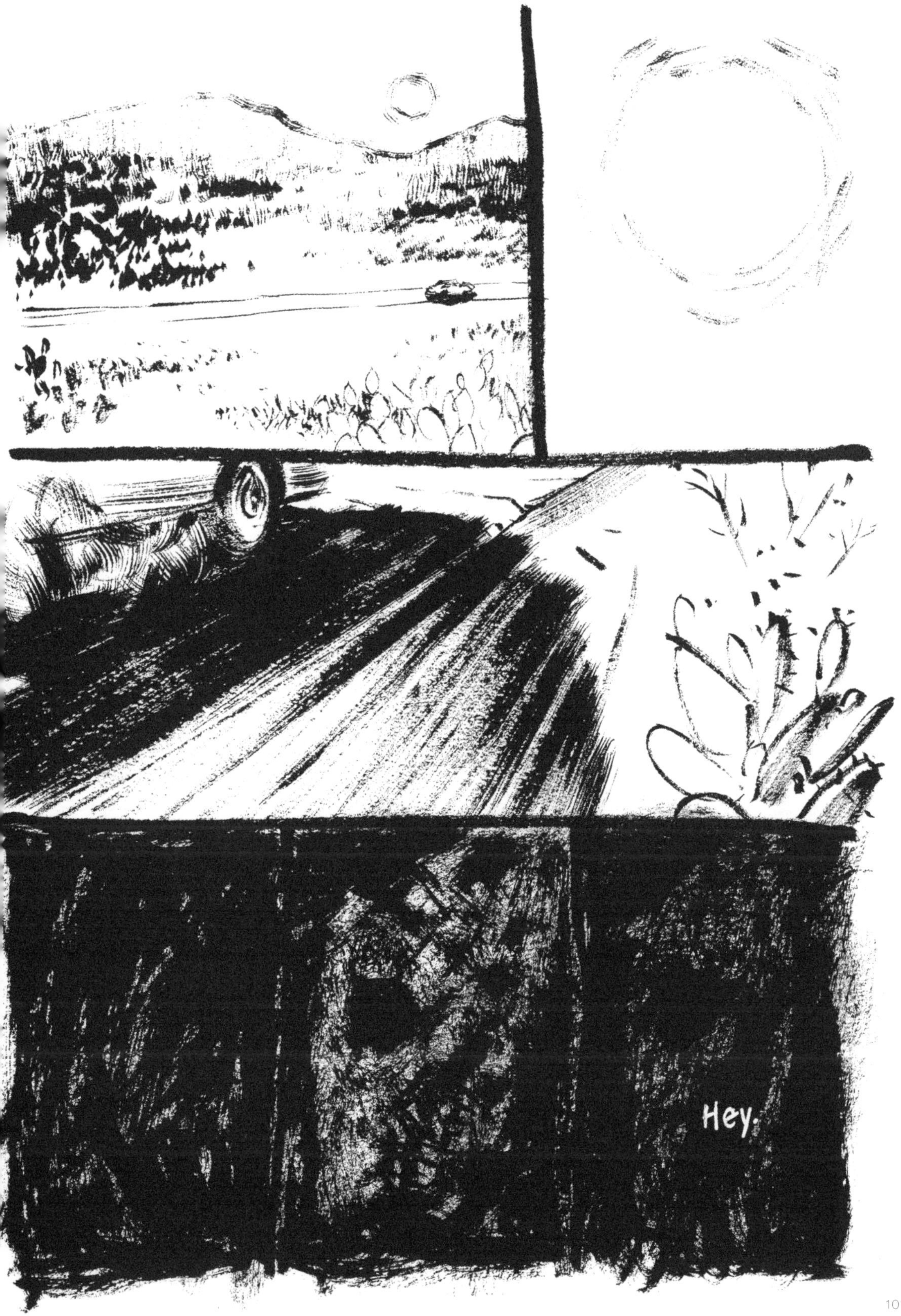
Hey.

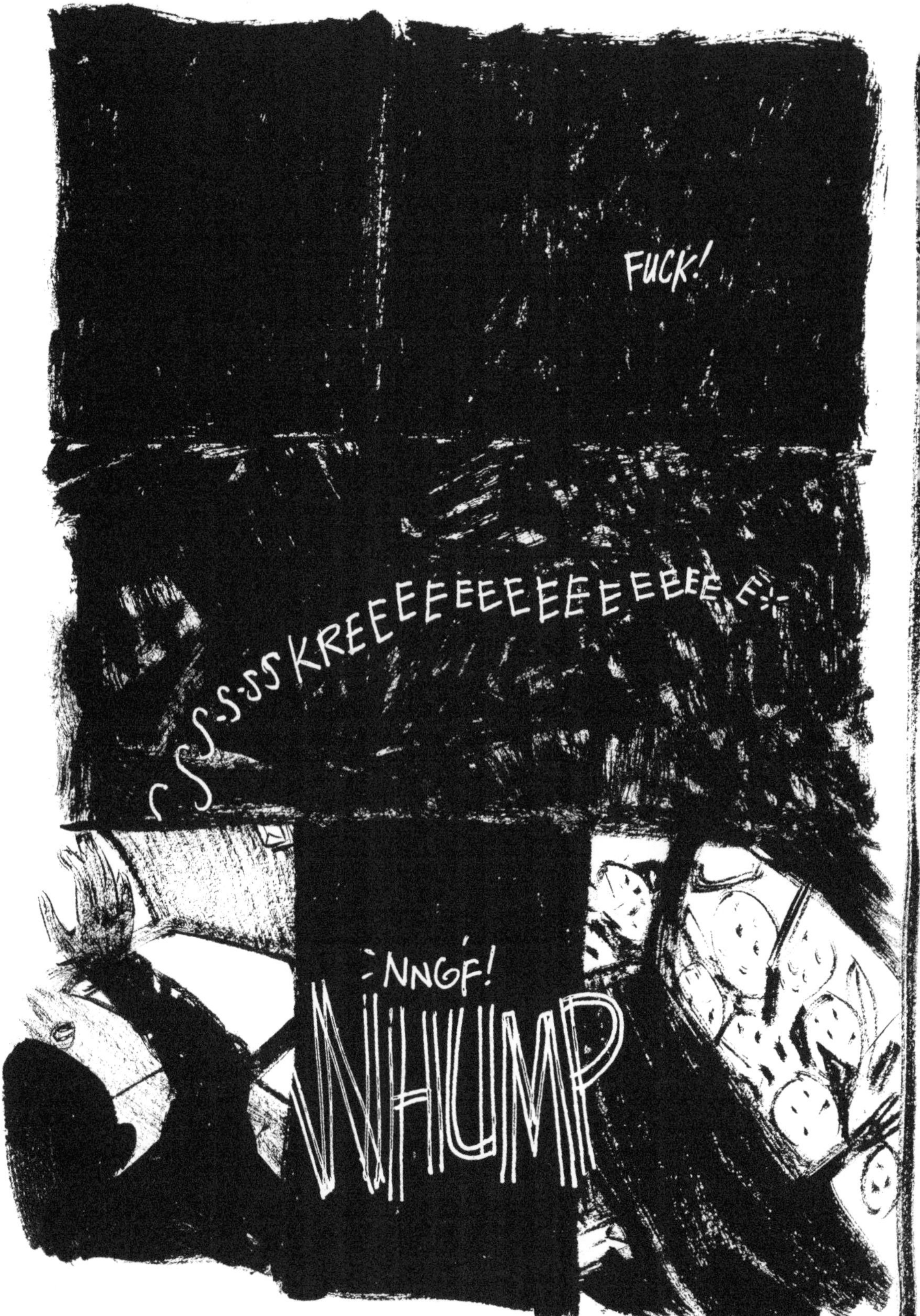
FUCK!
SSS-S-SS KREEEEEEEEEEEEEEEEE E
NNGF!
WHUMP

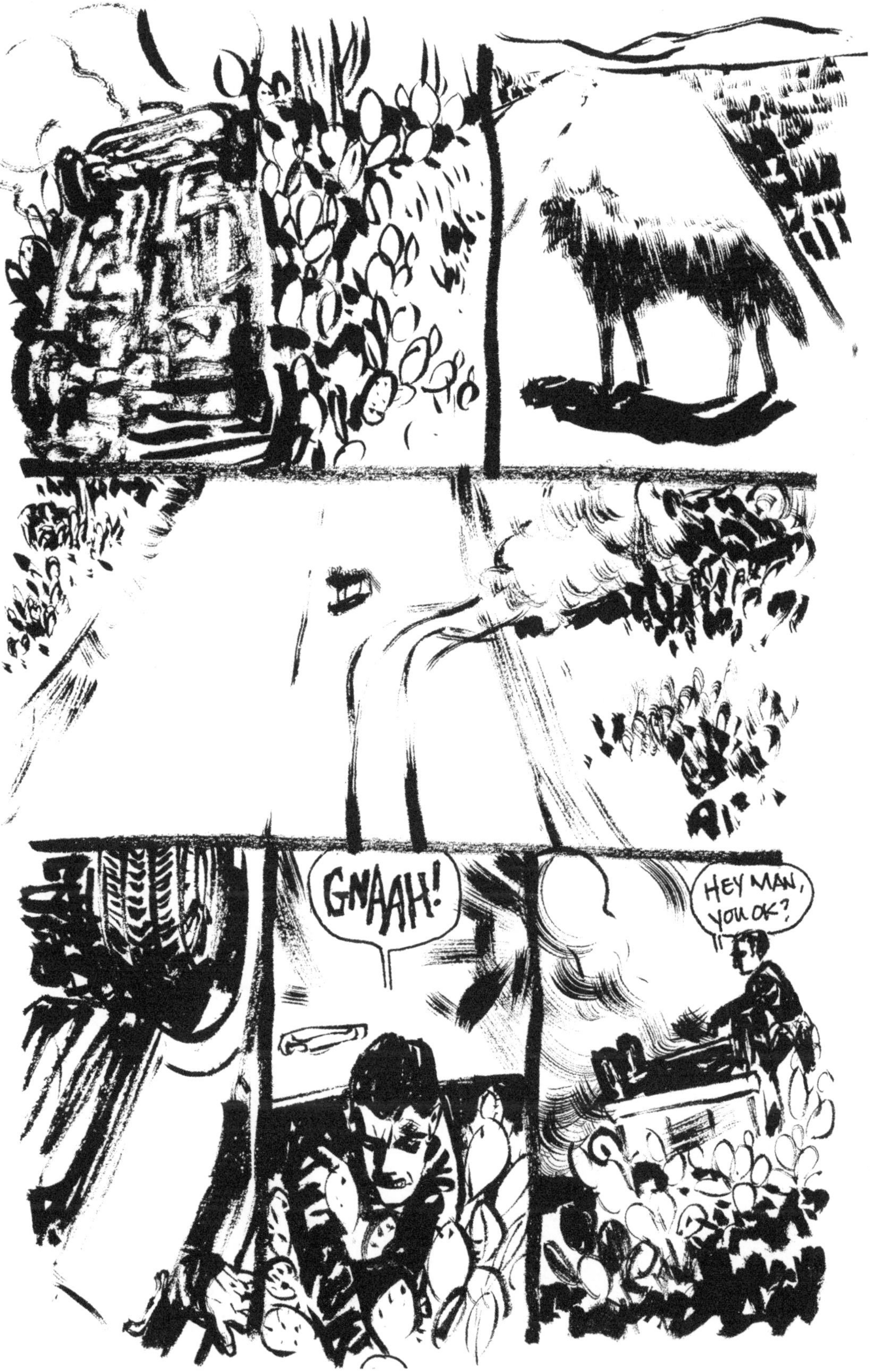
GNAAH!
HEY MAN, YOU OK?

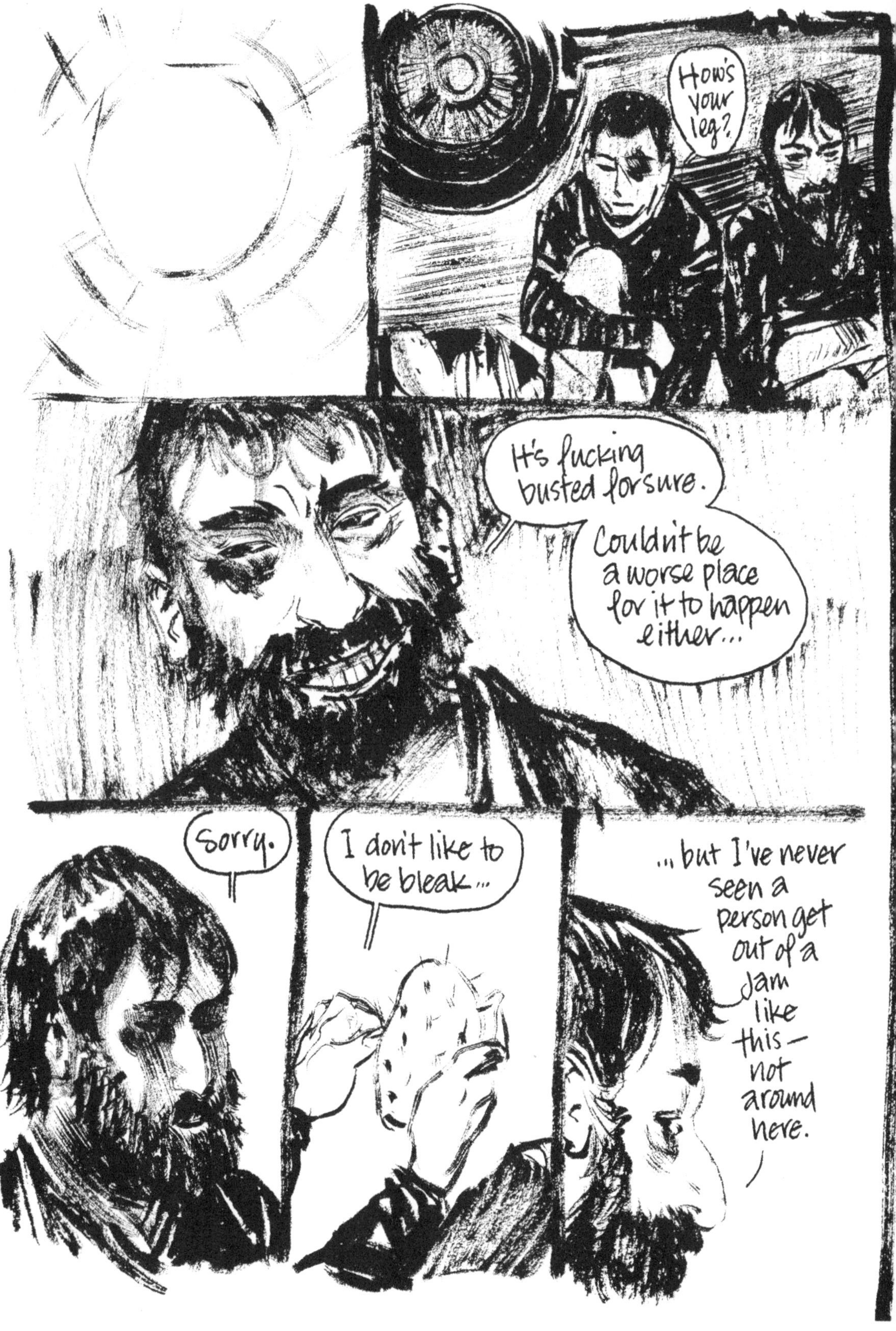
How's your leg?
It's fucking busted forsure.
Couldn't be a worse place for it to happen either...
Sorry.
I don't like to be bleak...
...but I've never seen a person get out of a jam like this— not around here.

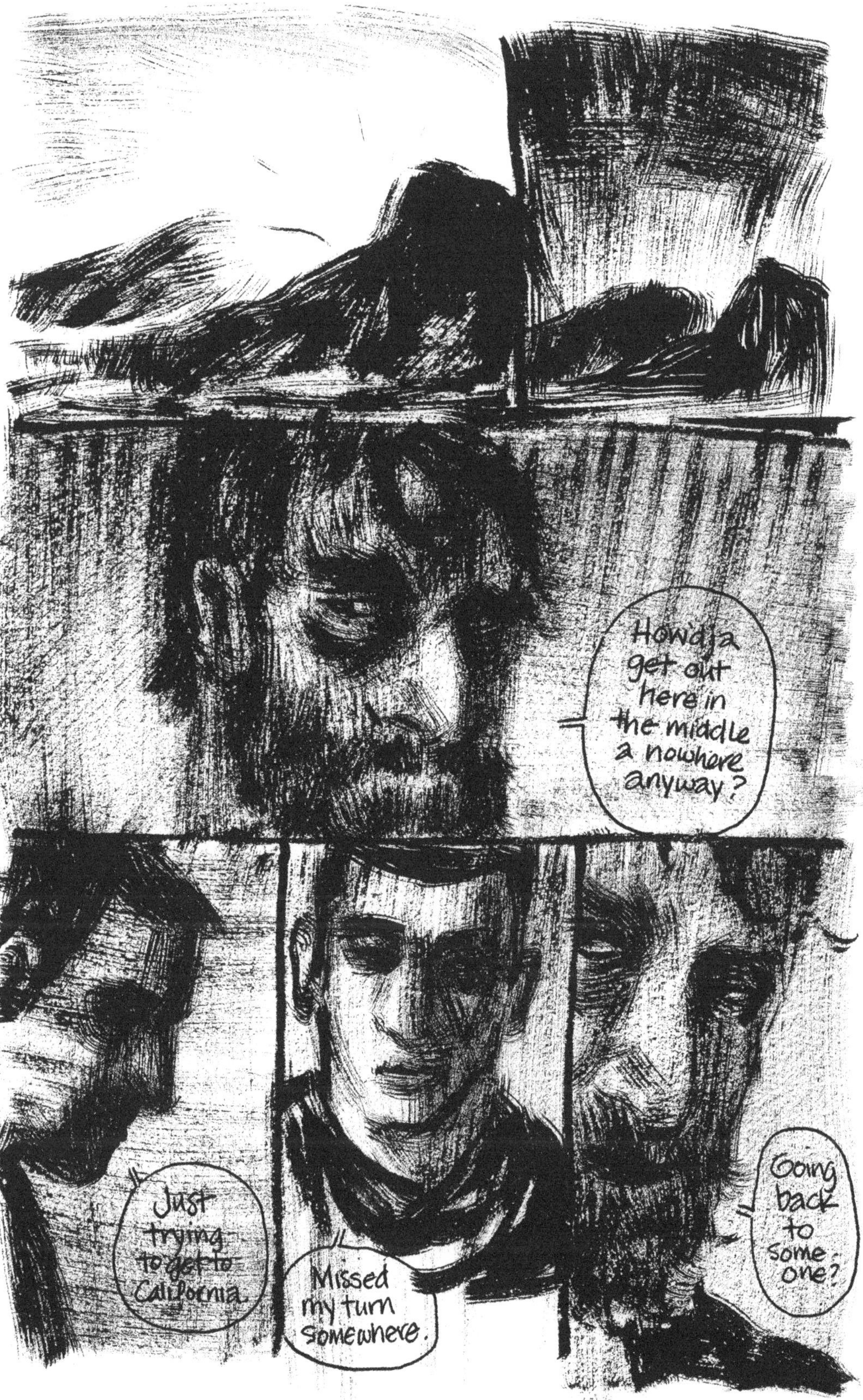
Howdja get out here in the middle a nowhere anyway?
Just trying to get to California.
Missed my turn somewhere.
Going back to someone?

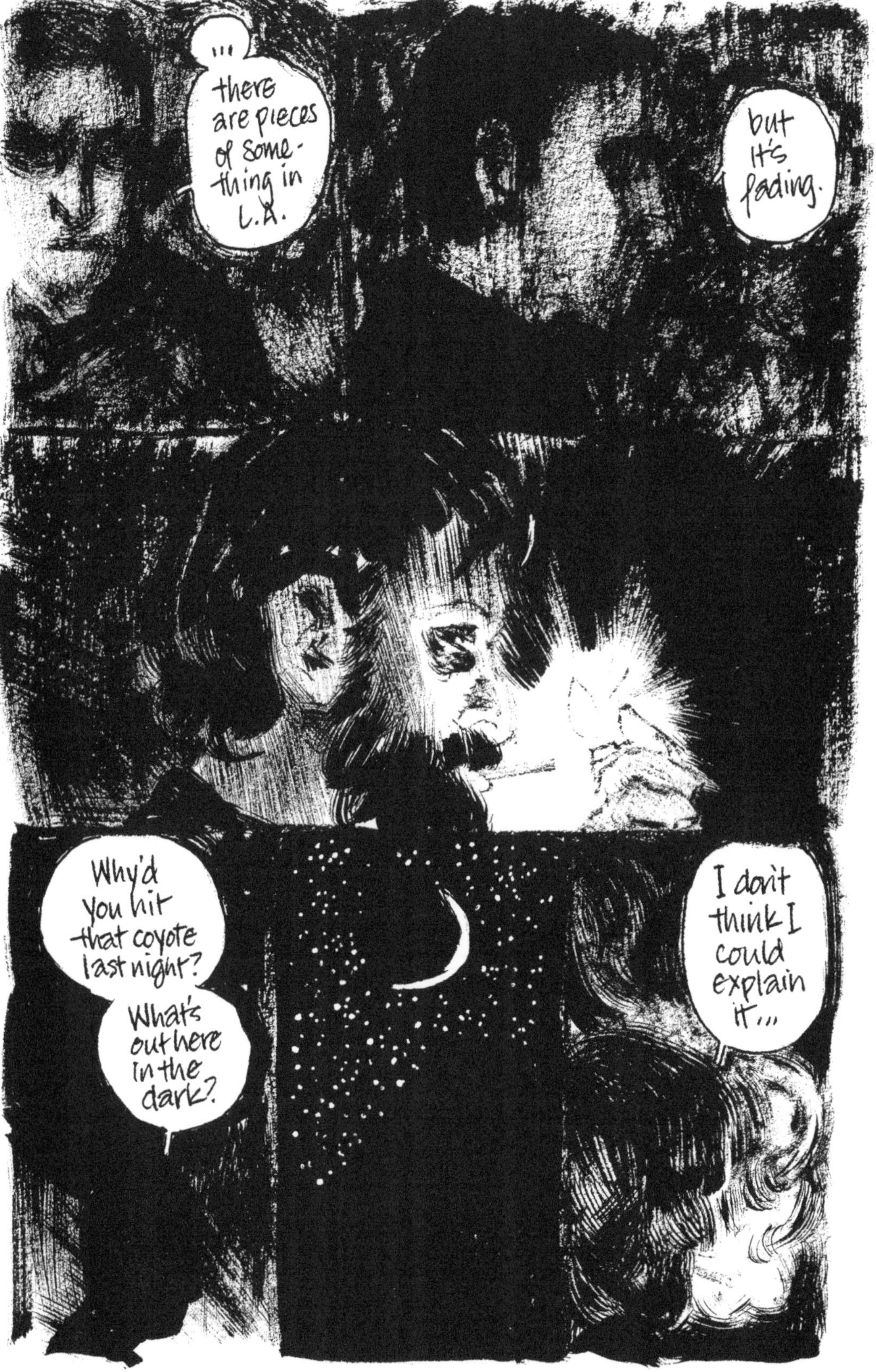
... there are pieces of some-thing in L.A.
but it's fading.
Why'd you hit that coyote last night?
What's out here in the dark?
I don't think I could explain it...

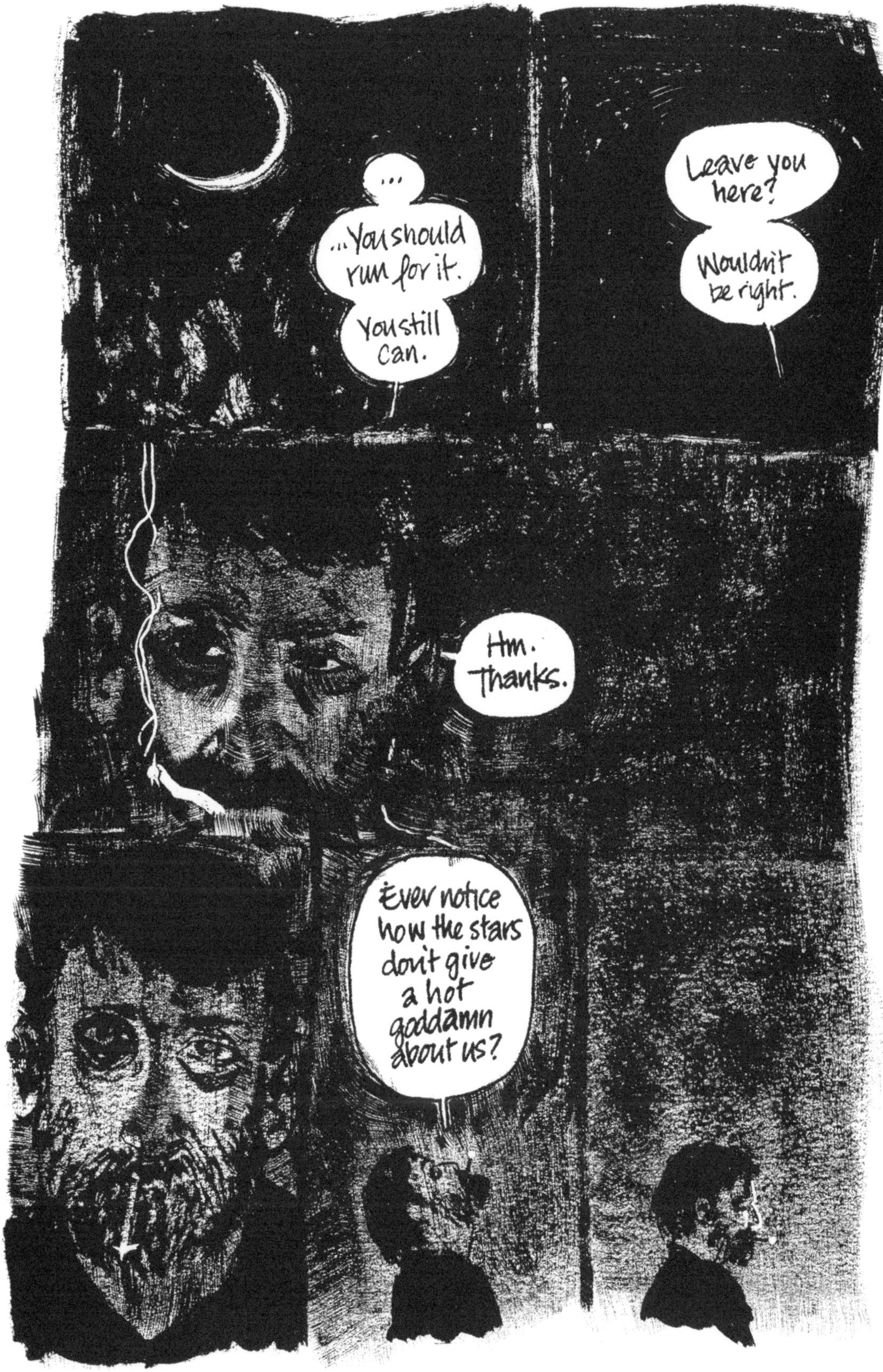
...
...You should run for it.
You still can.
Leave you here?
Wouldn't be right.
Hm. Thanks.
Ever notice how the stars don't give a hot goddamn about us?

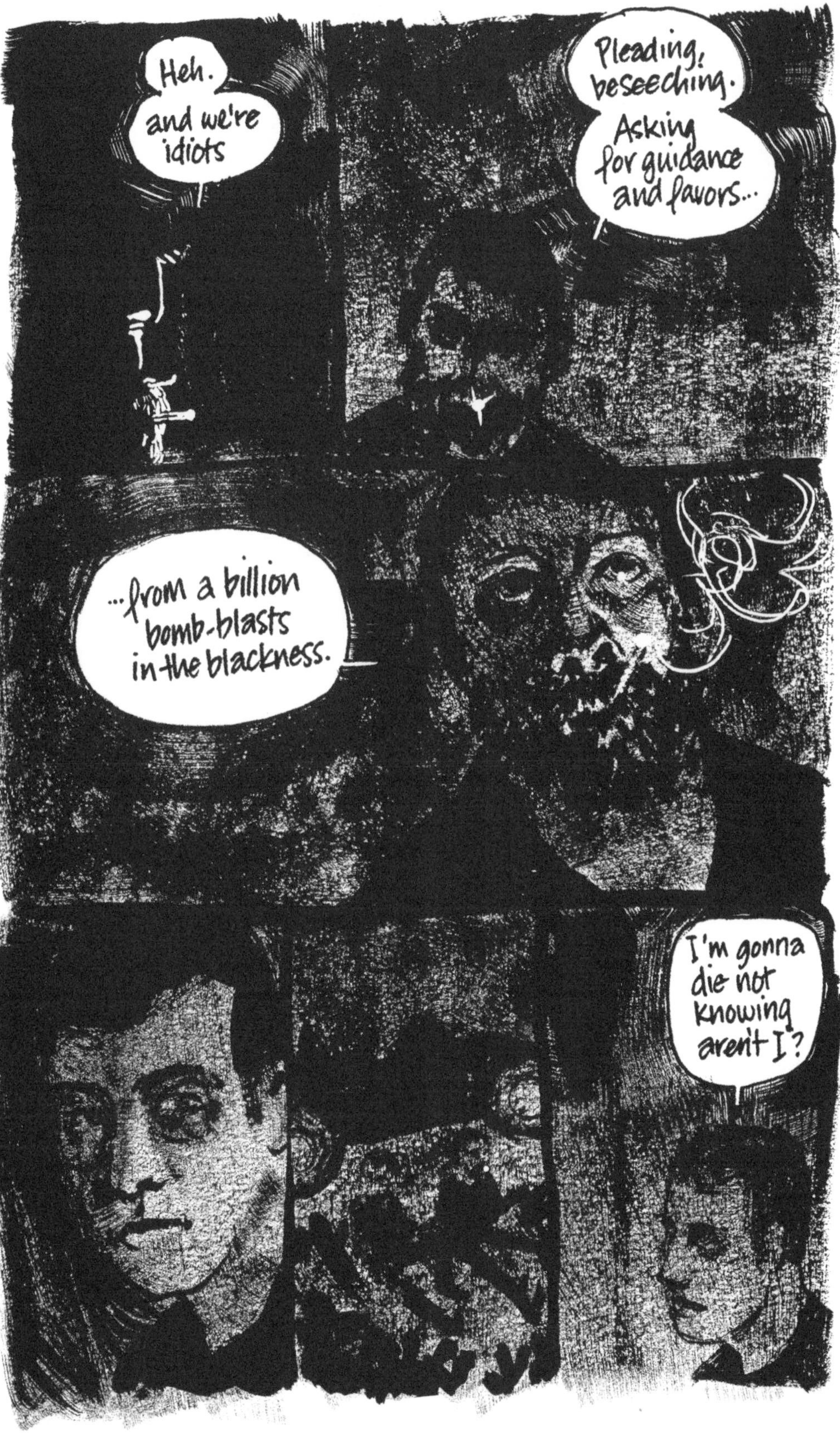
Heh.
and we're idiots
Pleading, beseeching.
Asking for guidance and favors...
...from a billion bomb-blasts in the blackness.
I'm gonna die not knowing aren't I?

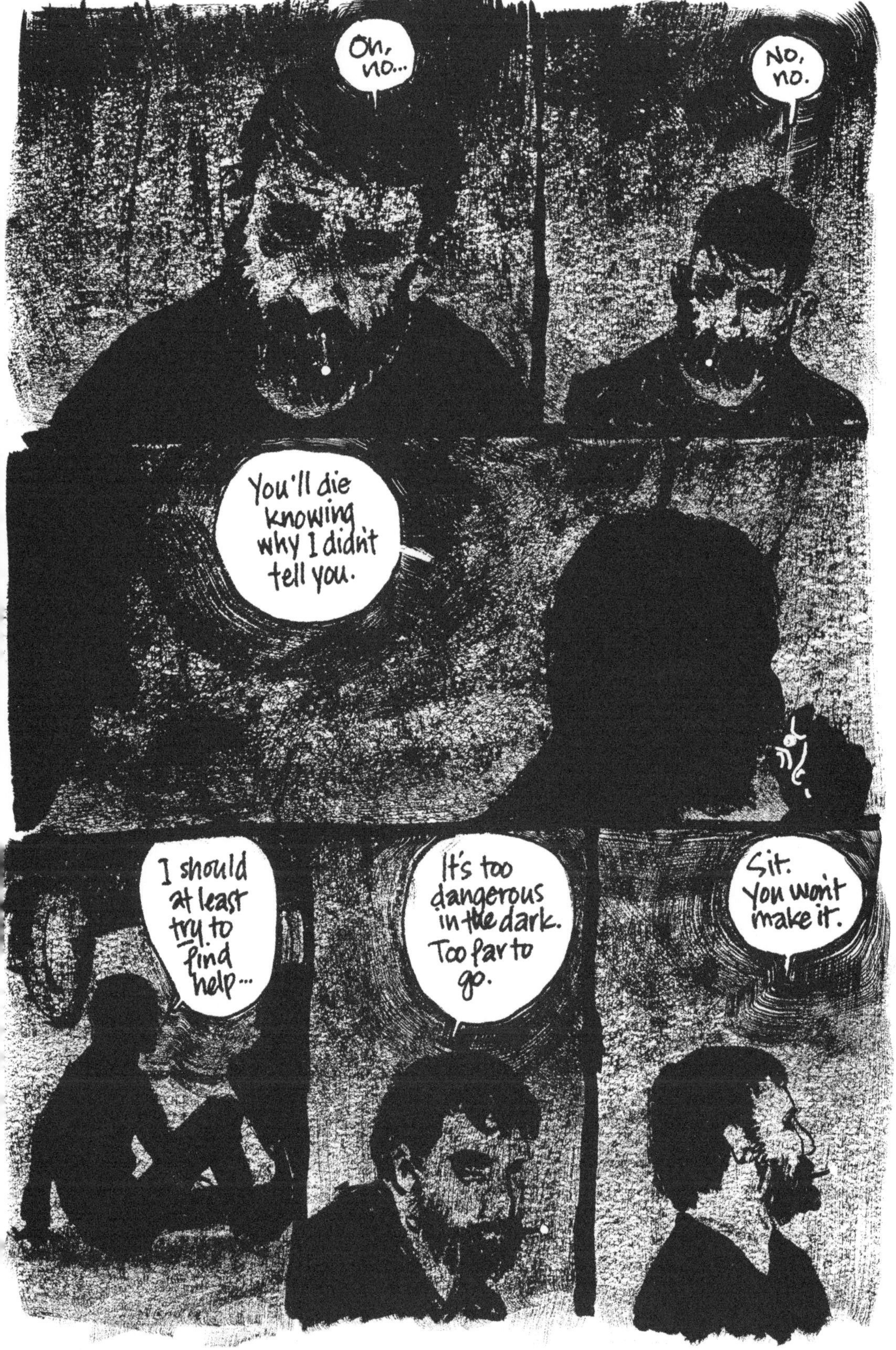
Oh, no...
No, no.
You'll die knowing why I didn't tell you.
I should at least try to find help...
It's too dangerous in the dark. Too far to go.
Sit. You won't make it.

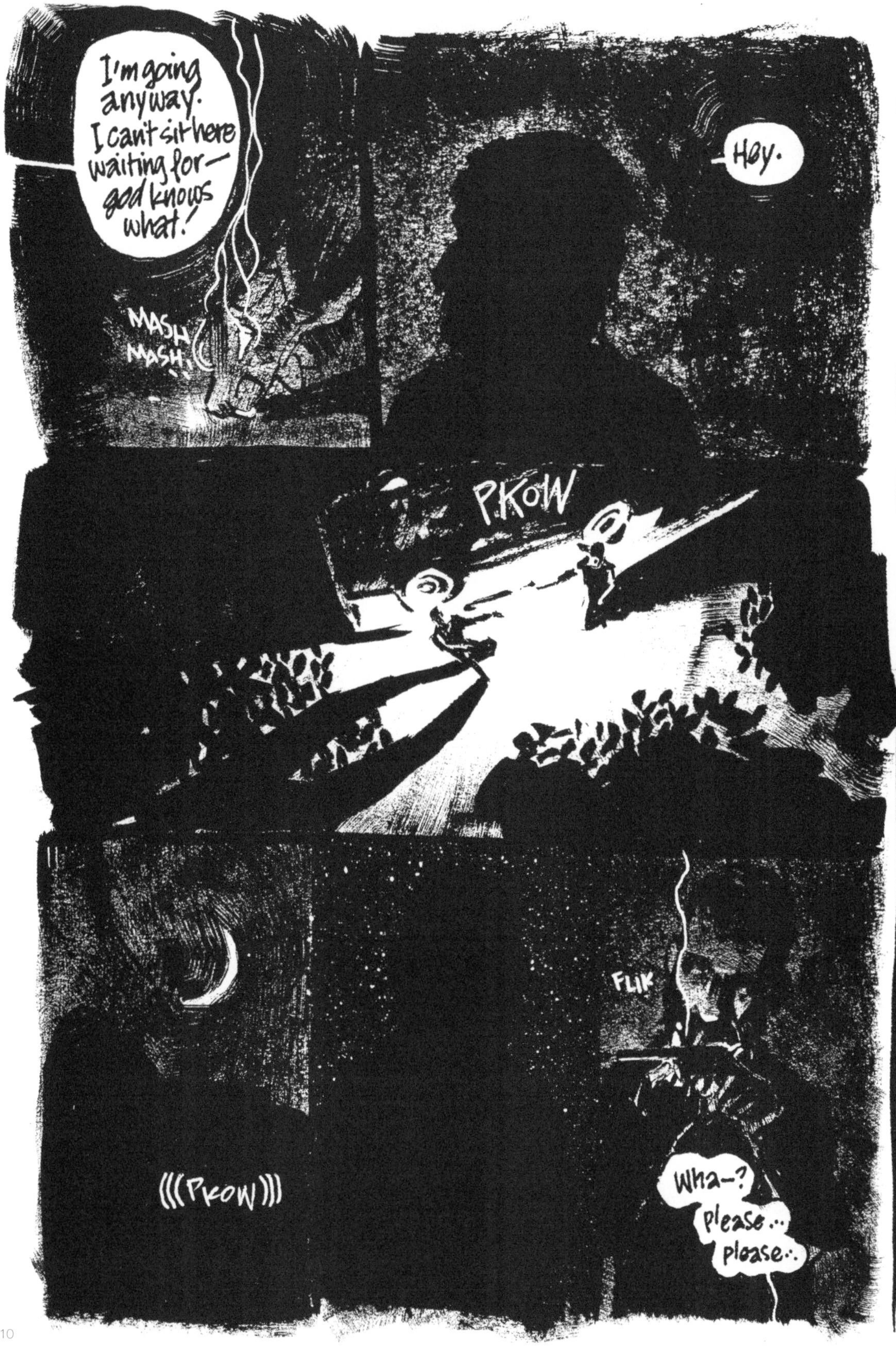
I'm going anyway. I can't sit here waiting for— god knows what!
MASH MASH
Hey.
P.KOW
FLIK
(((P.KOW)))
Wha–? Please... Please...

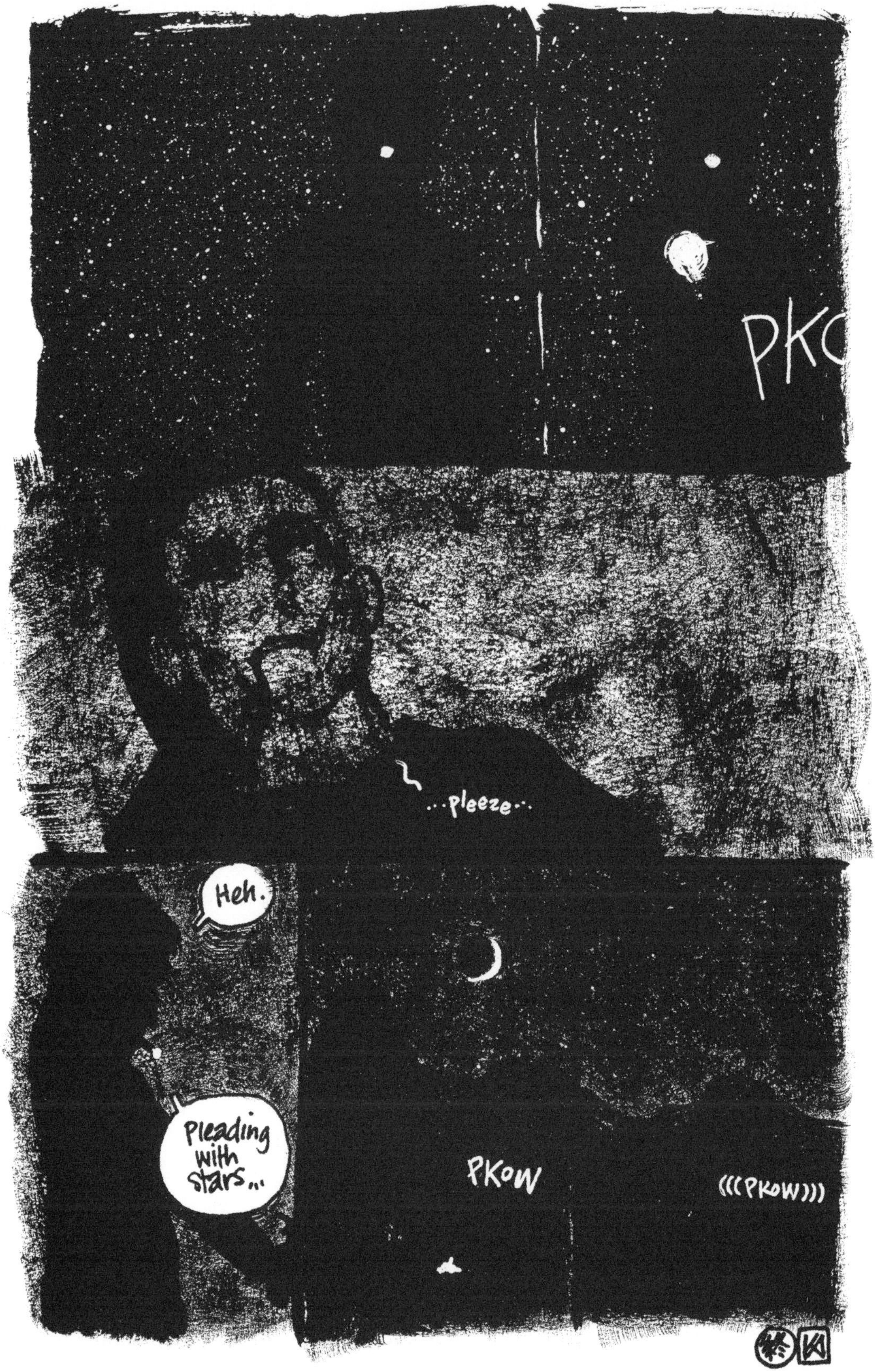
PKO
...pleeze...
Heh.
Pleading with stars...
PKOW
(((PKOW)))

A Bomb

YOU KNOW HOW A DEER STEPS FROM THE DARK INTO ONCOMING LIGHTS?

THAT'S WHAT IT WAS LIKE, DAD SAID.

THIS IS THE EARTH AND 'BLACK PLANET ONE', A NAME USED FOR: 17D 9H47:02:53

BUT THIS?

CATACLYSM!

THIS IS MY DAD AND ME WINNING A COSMIC LOTTERY.

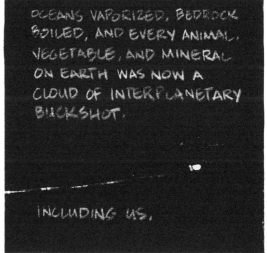

OCEANS VAPORIZED, BEDROCK BOILED, AND EVERY ANIMAL, VEGETABLE, AND MINERAL ON EARTH WAS NOW A CLOUD OF INTERPLANETARY BUCKSHOT.

INCLUDING US.

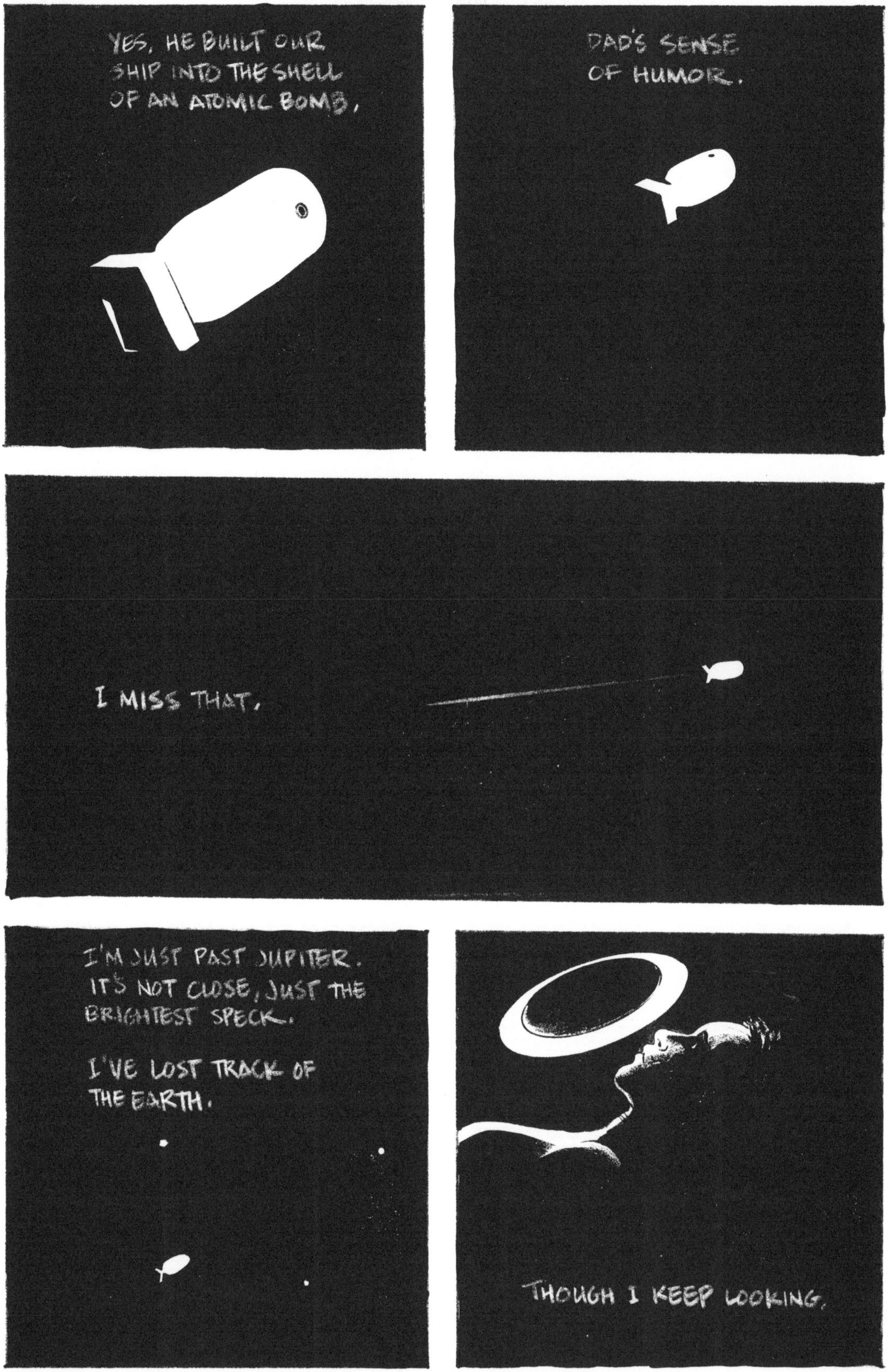

YES, HE BUILT OUR
SHIP INTO THE SHELL
OF AN ATOMIC BOMB,

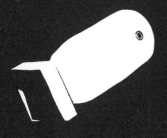

DAD'S SENSE
OF HUMOR.

I MISS THAT,

I'M JUST PAST JUPITER.
IT'S NOT CLOSE, JUST THE
BRIGHTEST SPECK.

I'VE LOST TRACK OF
THE EARTH.

THOUGH I KEEP LOOKING.

FOR A FEW DAYS AFTER WE
STILL CAUGHT SIGHT OF EARTH.

OR WHAT WAS
LEFT OF IT.

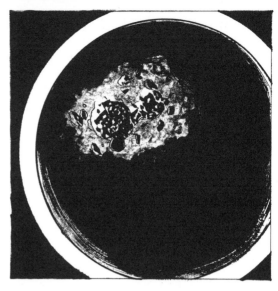

IT WAS STRANGE, TRYING TO
MENTALLY ADJUST THE IMAGE
OF THE PALE BLUE DOT

TO THIS CLUSTER OF GLOWING ORANGE
COALS GETTING SMALLER IN THE WINDOW.

IT WAS THE LOSS OF EVERYTHING.

THE CACOPHONY OF CROWDS, CRASHING SURF,
SUMMER CLOUDBURSTS. CLIFFS OF CHALK,
CRASS CUSSING OF MEN AND WOMEN. THUNDER
FROM LIGHTNING, STAMPEDING CATTLE, WILD
COURSING RIVERS. SMILES OF STRANGERS.
THE SCENT OF SPICY STEWS. HONEYBEES,
VERMILLION, WILDFLOWERS, SYCAMORES.
SIDEWALKS AND SAND. CRUSHED CANS, TAN
BODIES, THE SCENT OF SOIL IN THE HEAT AND
THE RAIN. FIRST SNOWS. WEATHERED WALLS,
THE WIND IN ALL ITS VELOCITIES. WREN SONG.
WEEDS. SALT AIR. SALT WATER. FRESH WATER.
WHISPERS OF LEAVES. WISPS OF FOG. WHALES,
MINNOWS. ALL LANGUAGES BUT MINE —
AND MOST OF MINE NO LONGER APPLIES.

I CLUNG TO THAT GUTTERING ORANGE COAL.

NOW IT'S GONE TOO.

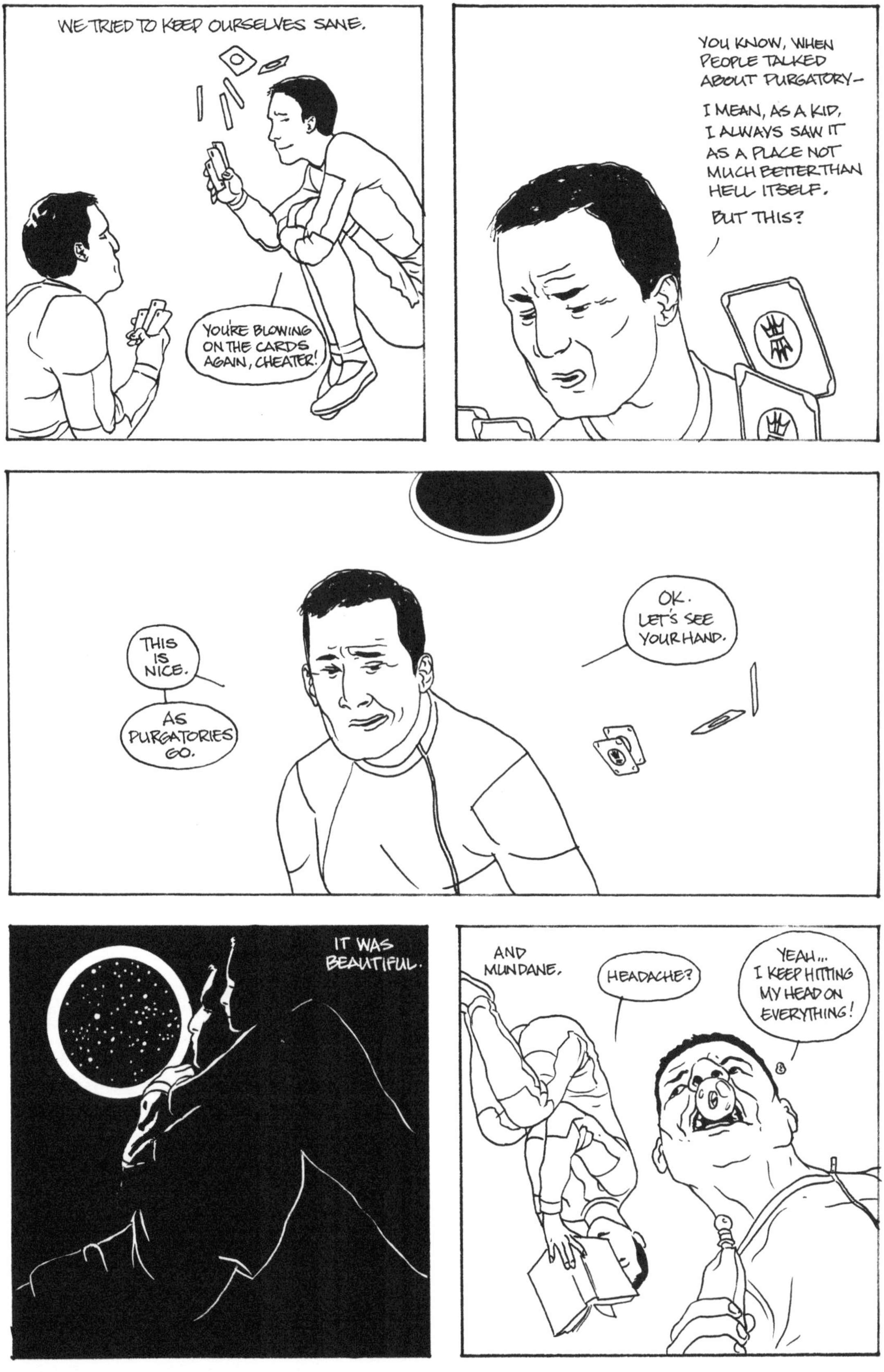
WE TRIED TO KEEP OURSELVES SANE.
YOU'RE BLOWING ON THE CARDS AGAIN, CHEATER!
YOU KNOW, WHEN PEOPLE TALKED ABOUT PURGATORY-
I MEAN, AS A KID, I ALWAYS SAW IT AS A PLACE NOT MUCH BETTER THAN HELL ITSELF.
BUT THIS?
THIS IS NICE.
AS PURGATORIES GO.
OK. LET'S SEE YOUR HAND.
IT WAS BEAUTIFUL.
AND MUNDANE.
HEADACHE?
YEAH... I KEEP HITTING MY HEAD ON EVERYTHING!

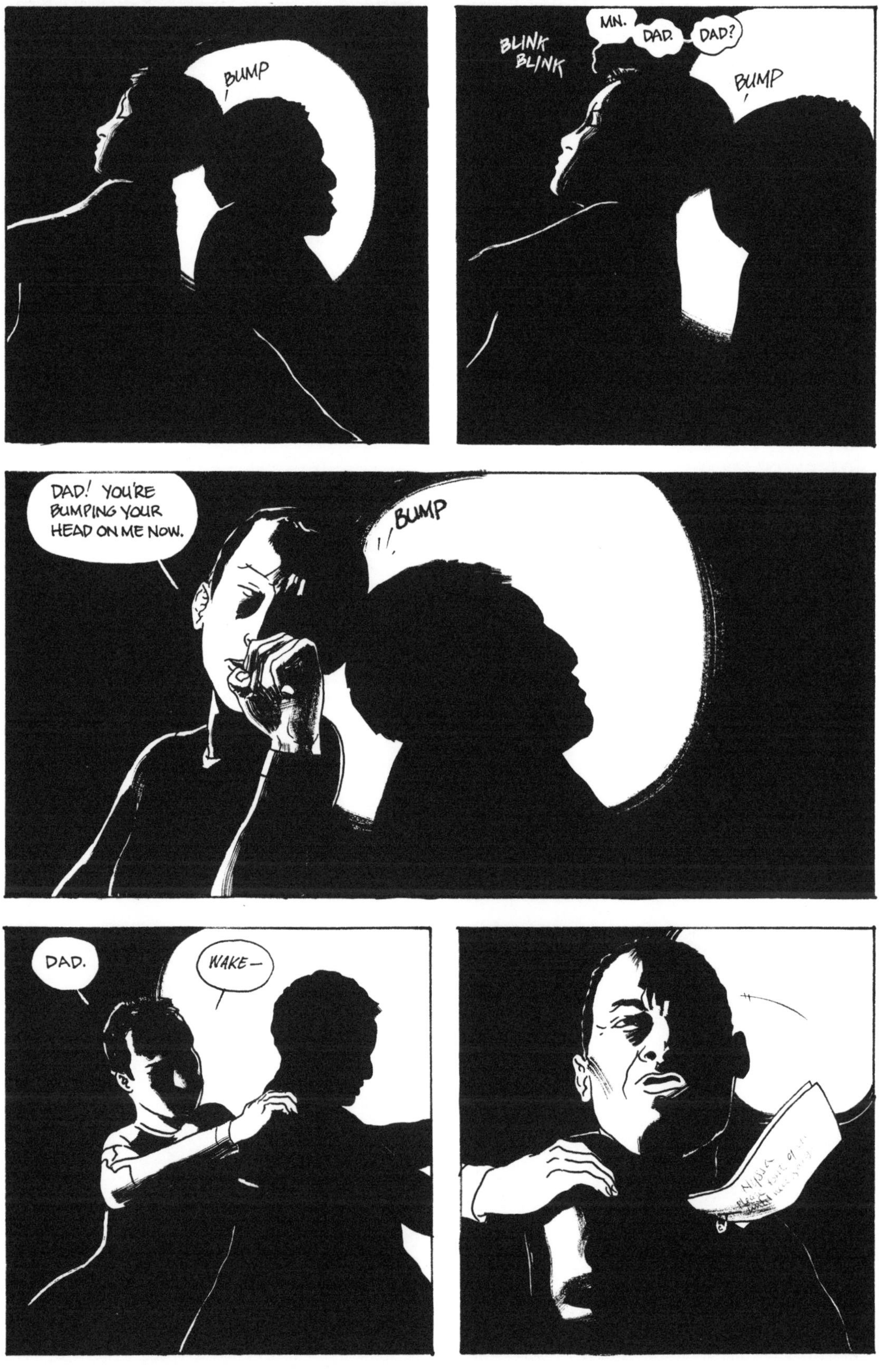
BUMP
BLINK BLINK
MN.
DAD.
DAD?
BUMP
DAD! YOU'RE BUMPING YOUR HEAD ON ME NOW.
BUMP
DAD.
WAKE—

NO ONE
Nyssa
please don't open
until necessary
HAS EVER KNOWN
LONELY LIKE I DO.

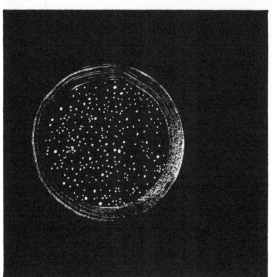

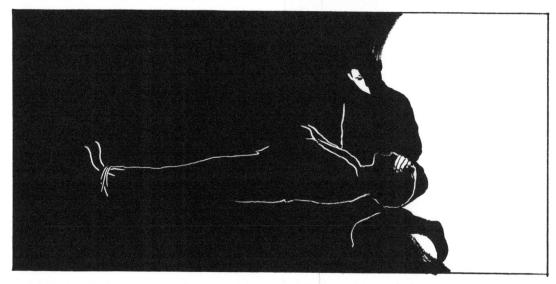

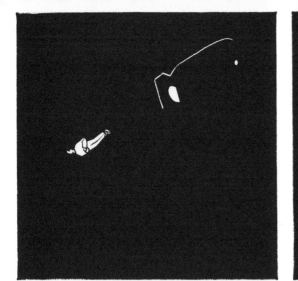

I COULDN'T EVEN WATCH HIS
BODY DRIFT AWAY.

SILENCE.

YOU THINK YOU
KNOW IT FROM
STILL SUMMER
DAYS IN PEACEFUL
GREEN FIELDS.

YOU DO NOT.

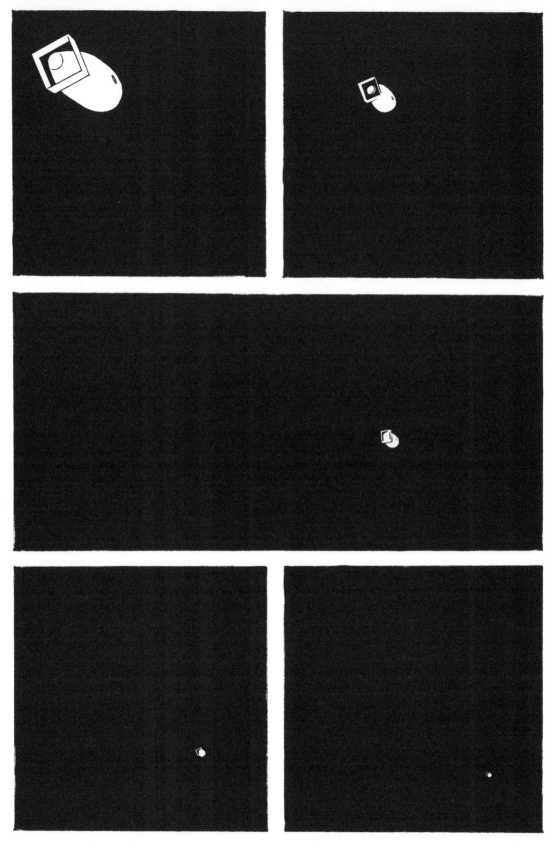

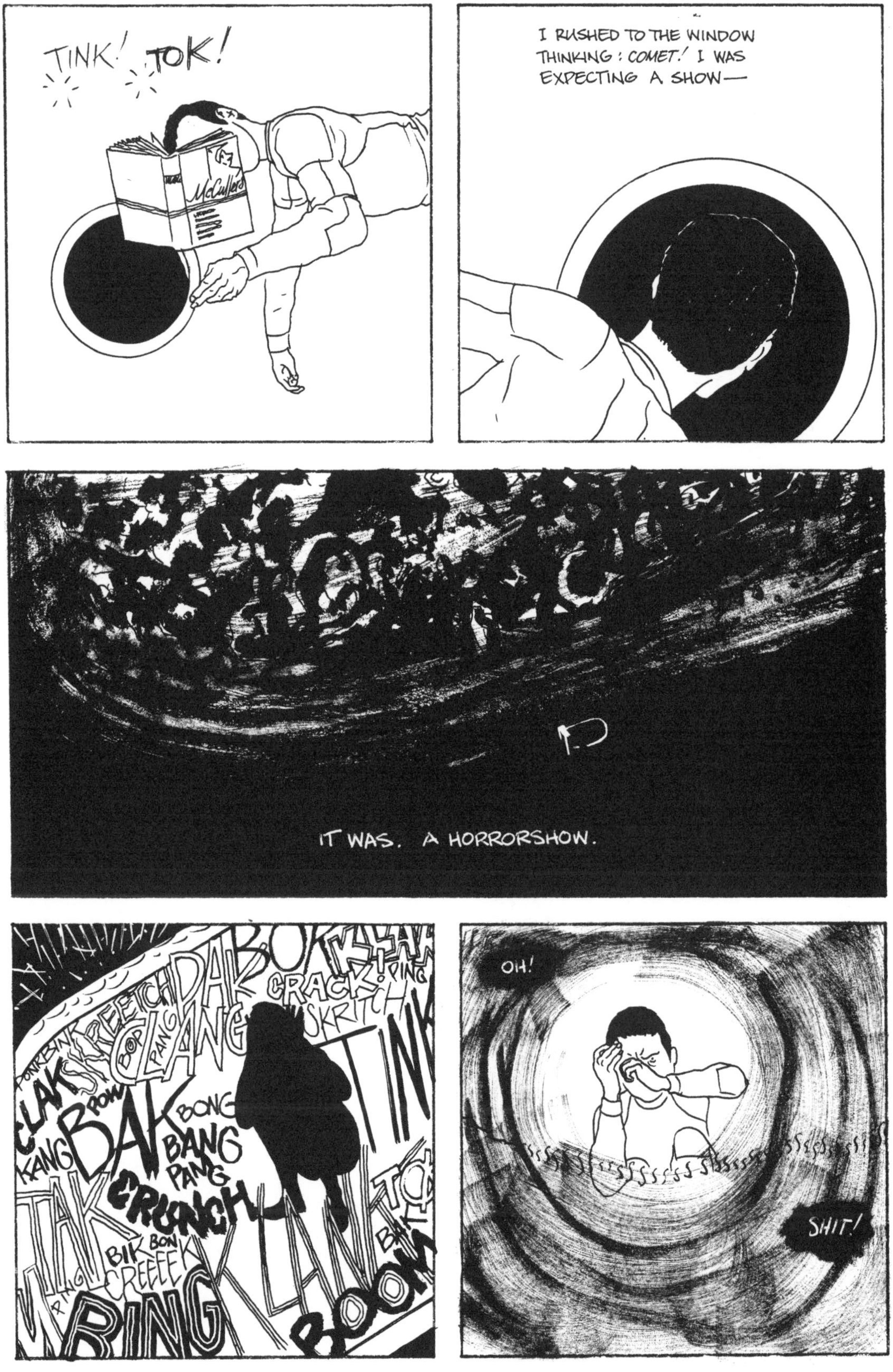
TINK! TOK!
I RUSHED TO THE WINDOW THINKING: COMET! I WAS EXPECTING A SHOW—
IT WAS. A HORRORSHOW.
CRACK!
PING
SKRITCH
CLANG
PANG
BOP
TINK
CLAK
BAK
BONG
BANG
PANG
KANG
TAK
CRUNCH
BIK
BON
CREEEEK
RING
BAK
BOOM
OH!
SHIT!

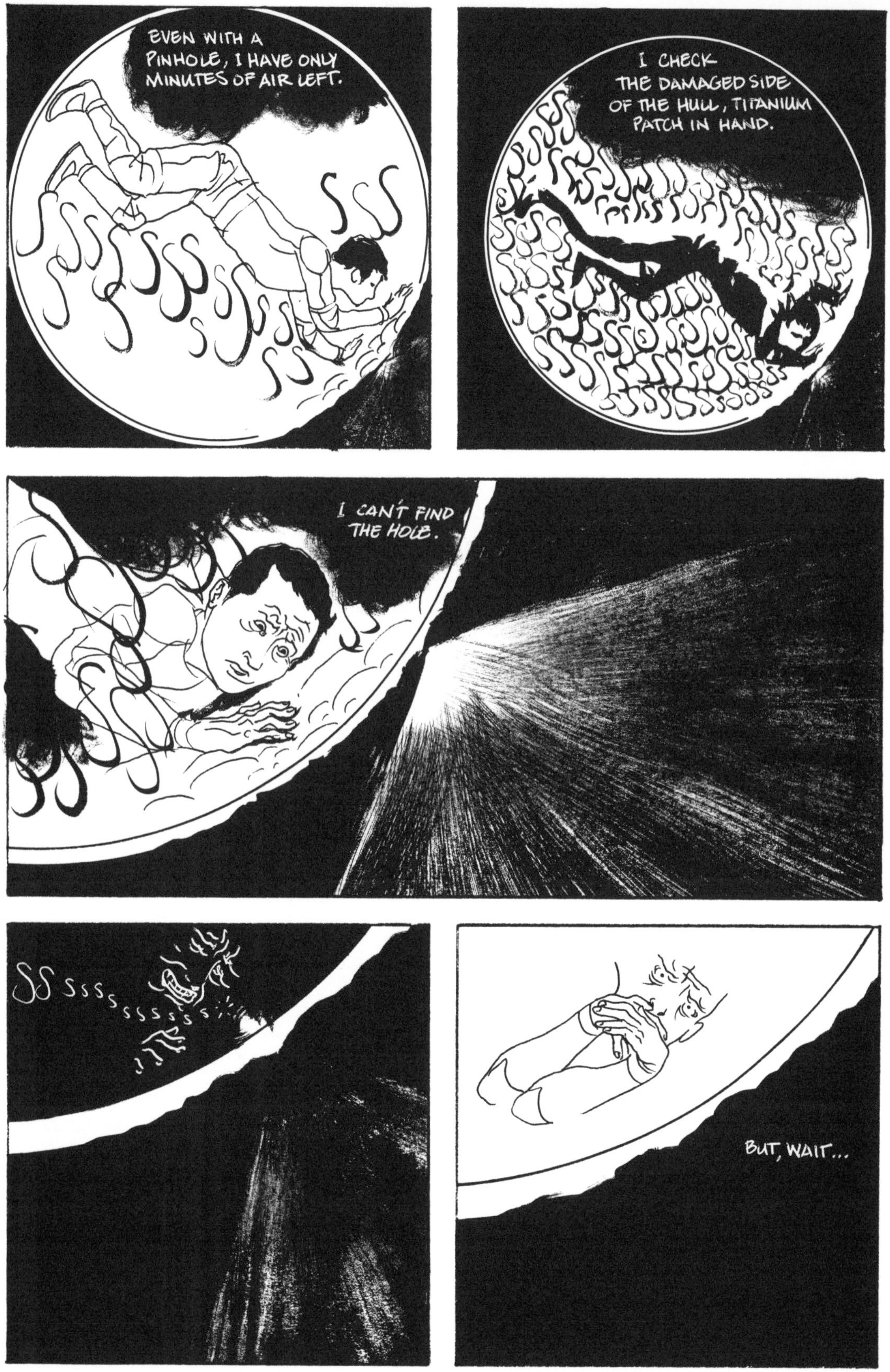
EVEN WITH A PINHOLE, I HAVE ONLY MINUTES OF AIR LEFT.
I CHECK THE DAMAGED SIDE OF THE HULL, TITANIUM PATCH IN HAND.
I CAN'T FIND THE HOLE.
BUT, WAIT...

I'M STILL BREATHING.

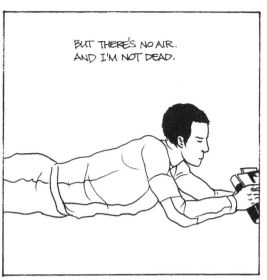

BUT THERE'S NO AIR.
AND I'M NOT DEAD.

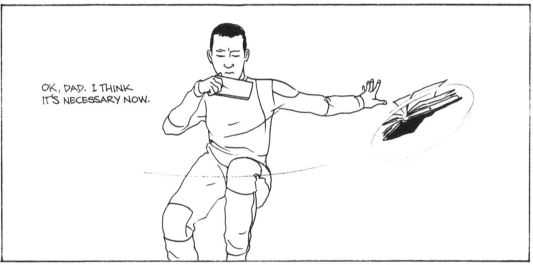

OK, DAD. I THINK
IT'S NECESSARY NOW.

I'M NOT EVEN HUMAN.

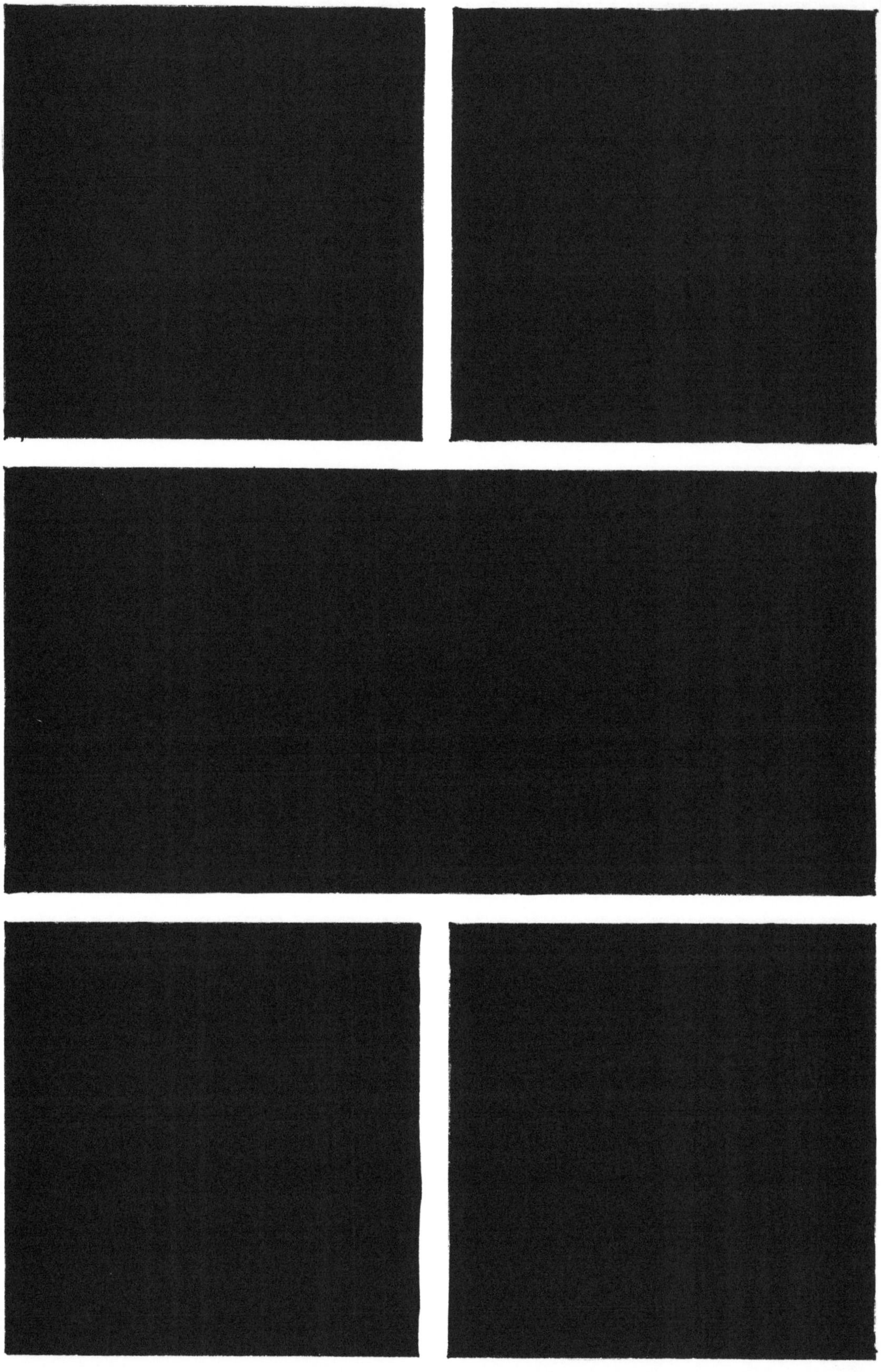

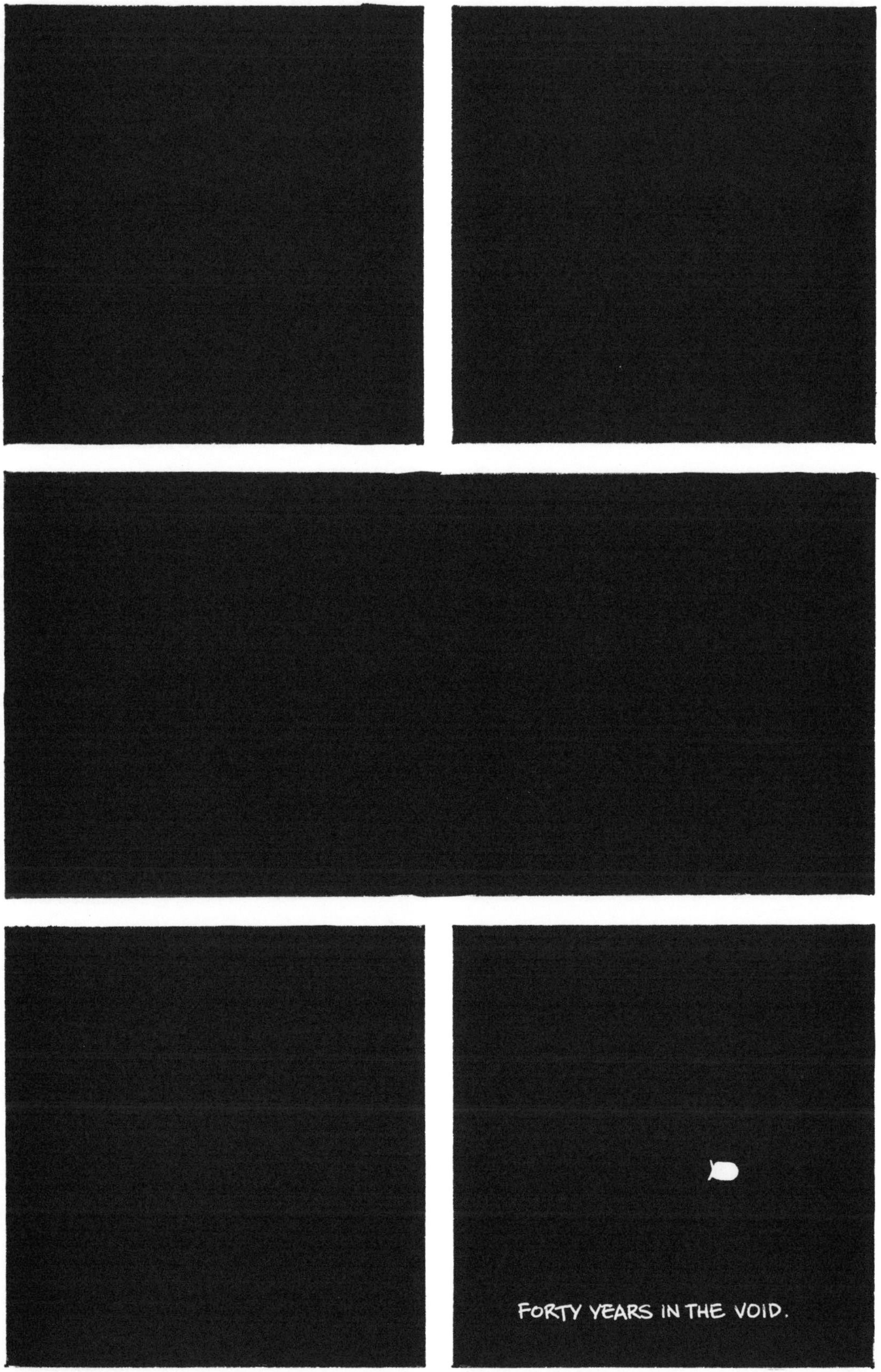

FORTY YEARS IN THE VOID.

I AM *THIRSTY* FOR LIGHT AND WARMTH.

BUT CRUISING AMONG COUNTLESS COLD CANDLES.

THE EARTH WILL ALWAYS BE A PHANTOM LIMB.

BUT OVER TIME, I'VE COME TO RECOGNIZE THE GENIUS OF WHAT MY FATHER ACHIEVED —

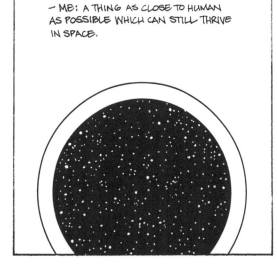

— ME: A THING AS CLOSE TO HUMAN AS POSSIBLE WHICH CAN STILL THRIVE IN SPACE.

AND IN A SLOW, CREEPING WAY,
I'VE COME TO REALIZE:

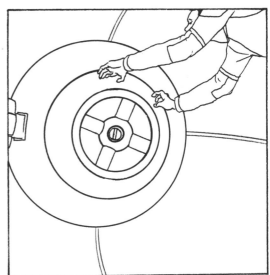

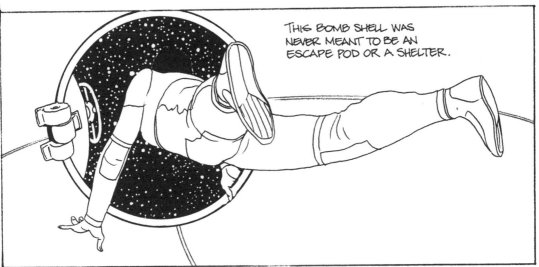

THIS BOMB SHELL WAS
NEVER MEANT TO BE AN
ESCAPE POD OR A SHELTER.

IT WAS A COCOON.

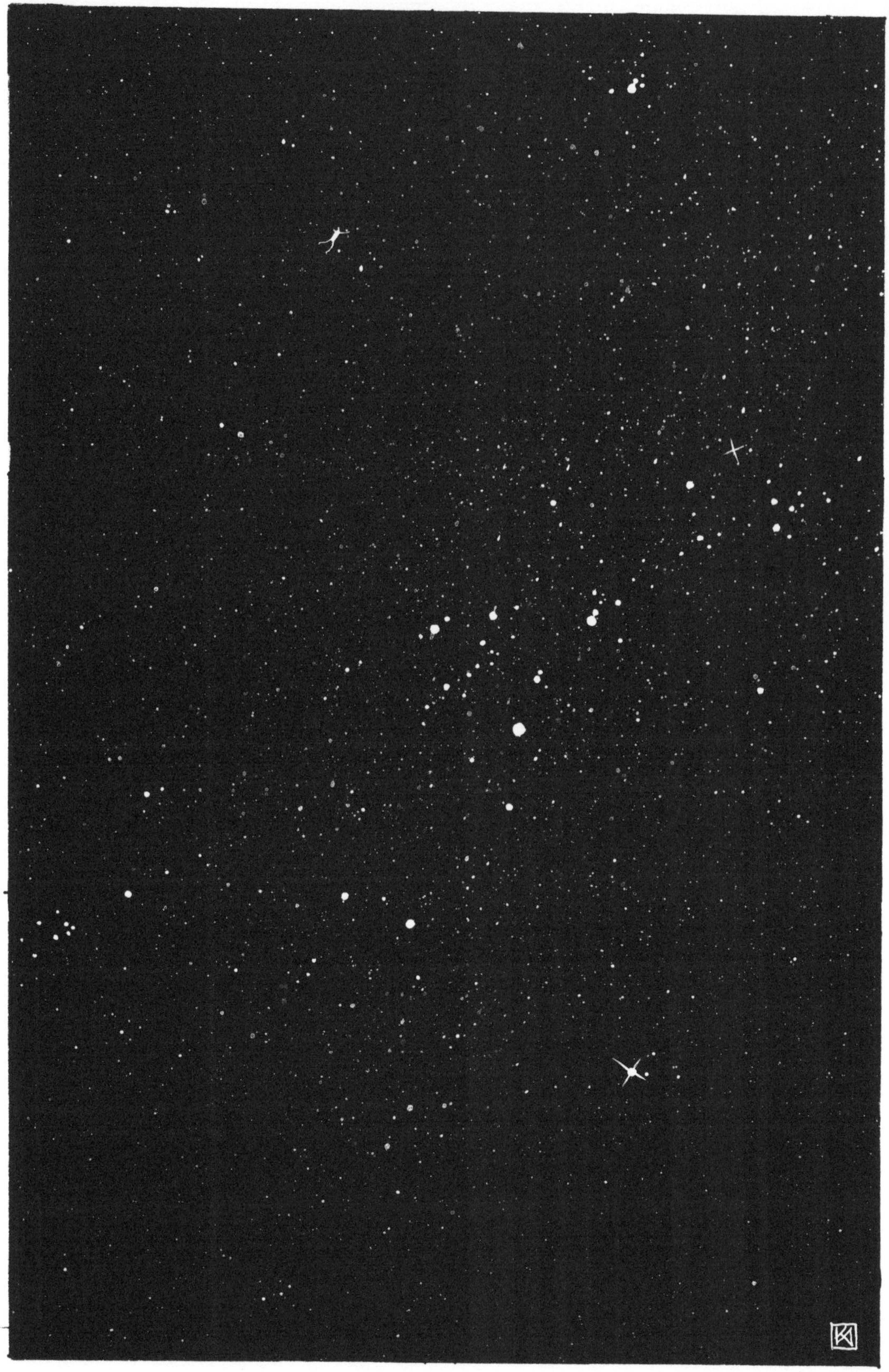

E

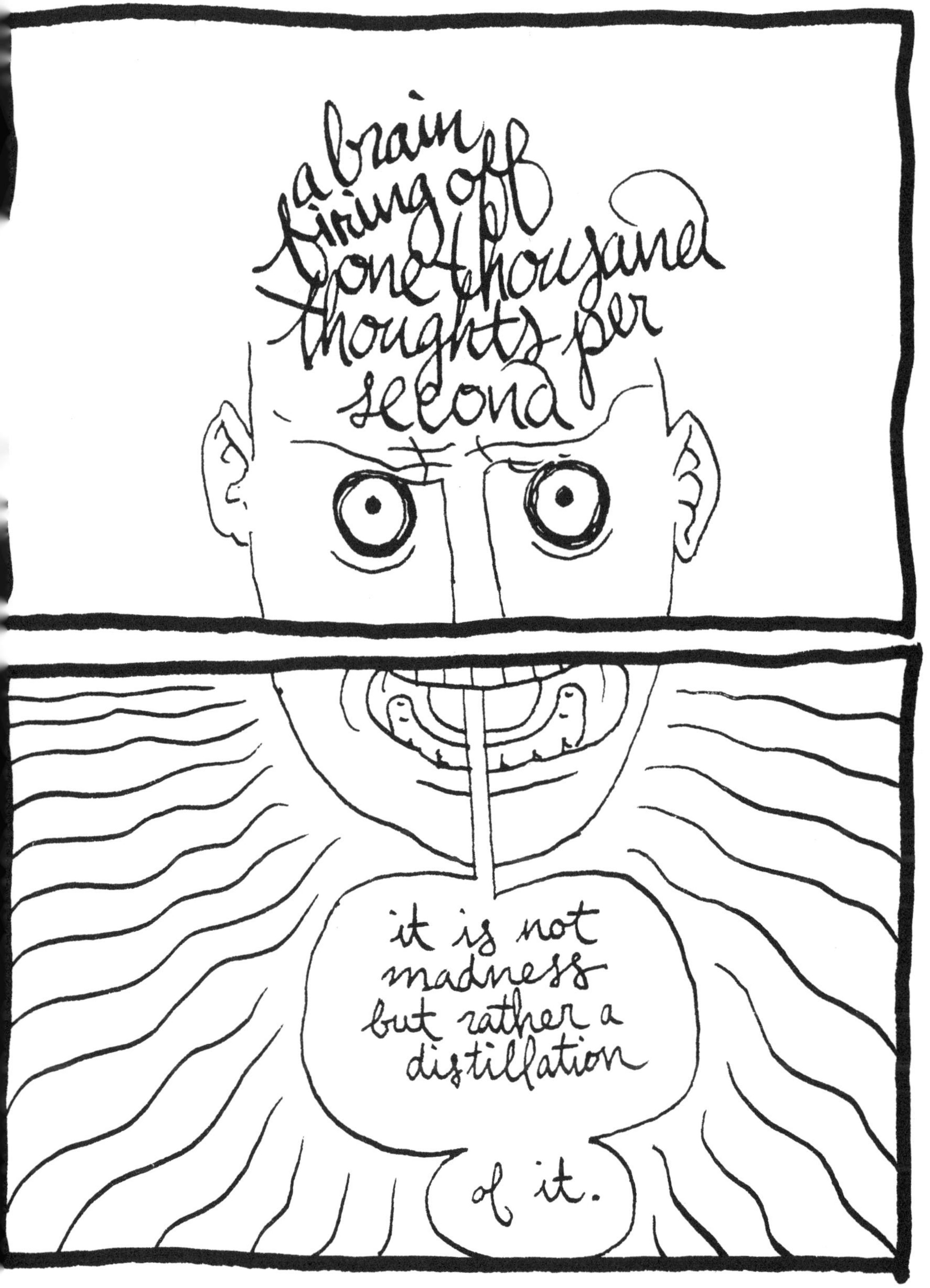
a brain firing off one thousand thoughts per second
it is not madness but rather a distillation
of it.

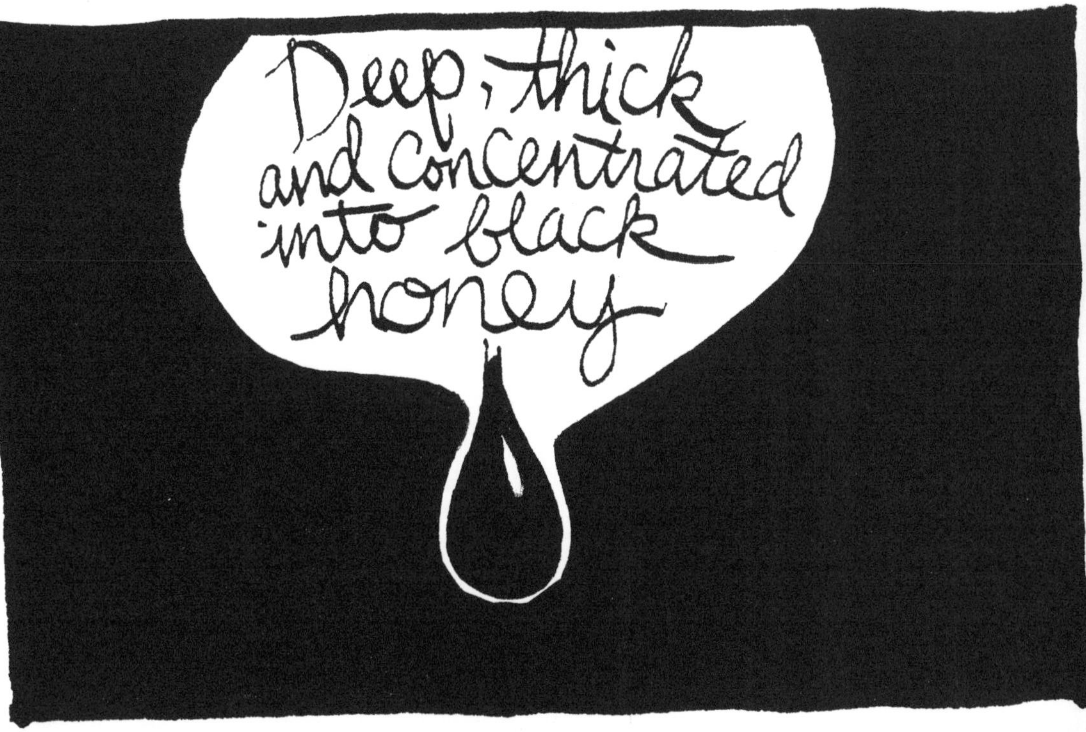
Deep, thick and concentrated into black honey

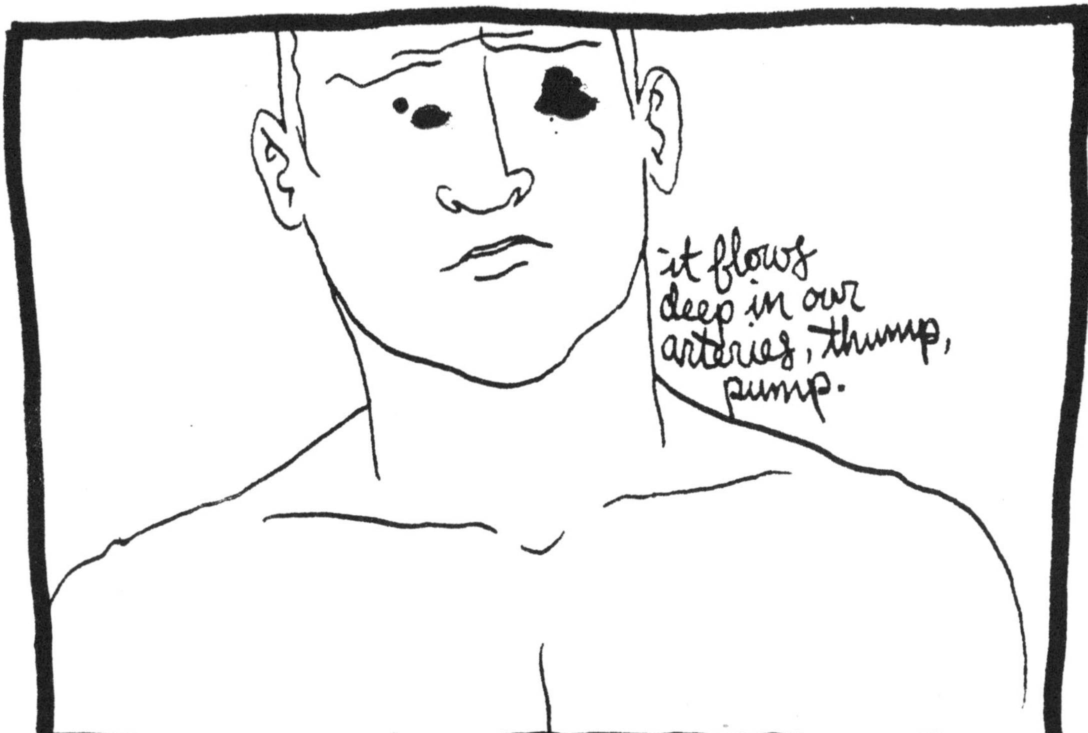
it flows deep in our arteries, thump, pump.

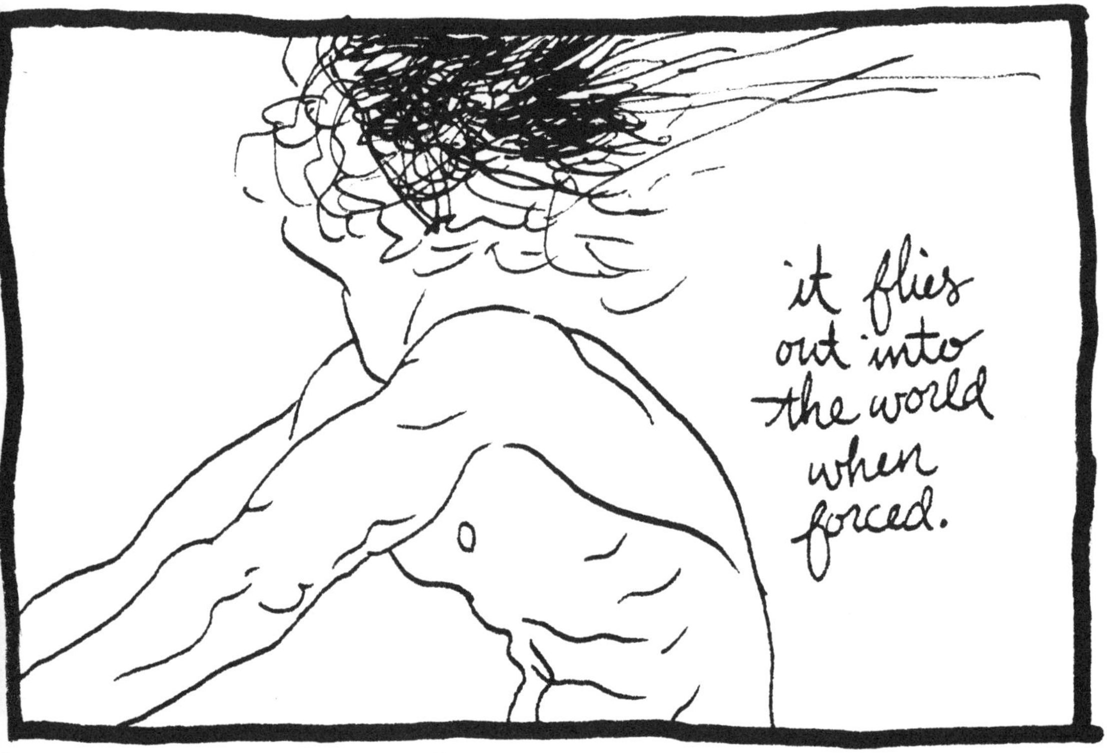
it flies out into the world when forced.

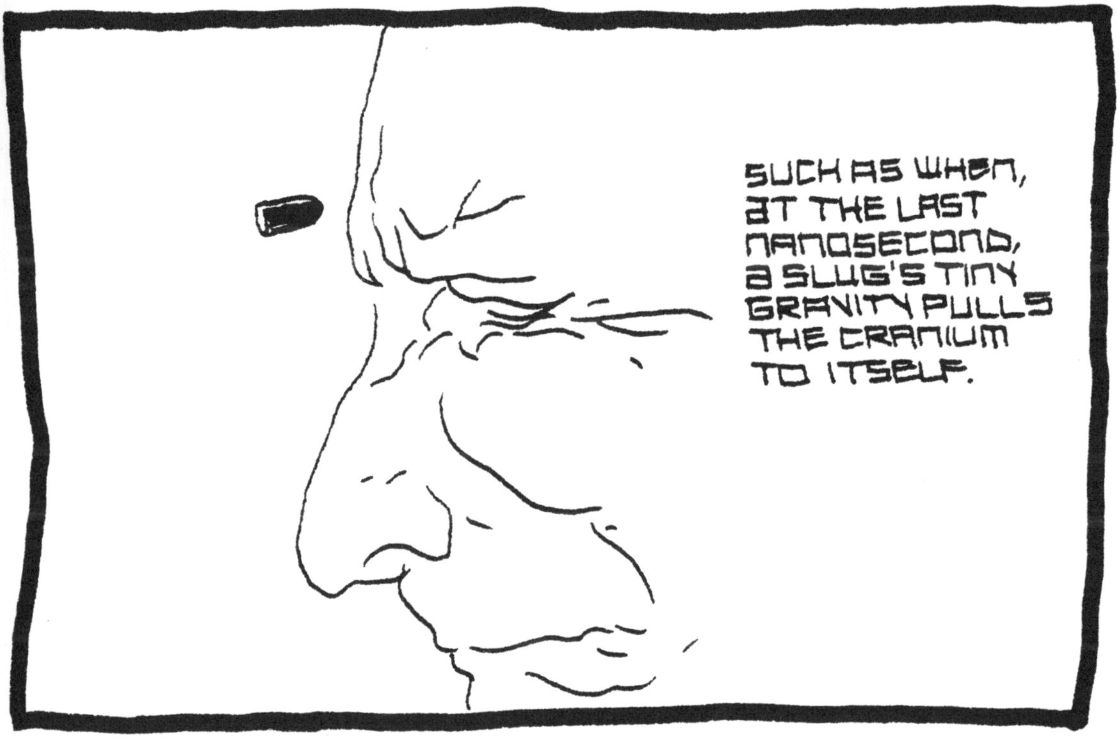
SUCH AS WHEN, AT THE LAST NANOSECOND, A SLUG'S TINY GRAVITY PULLS THE CRANIUM TO ITSELF.

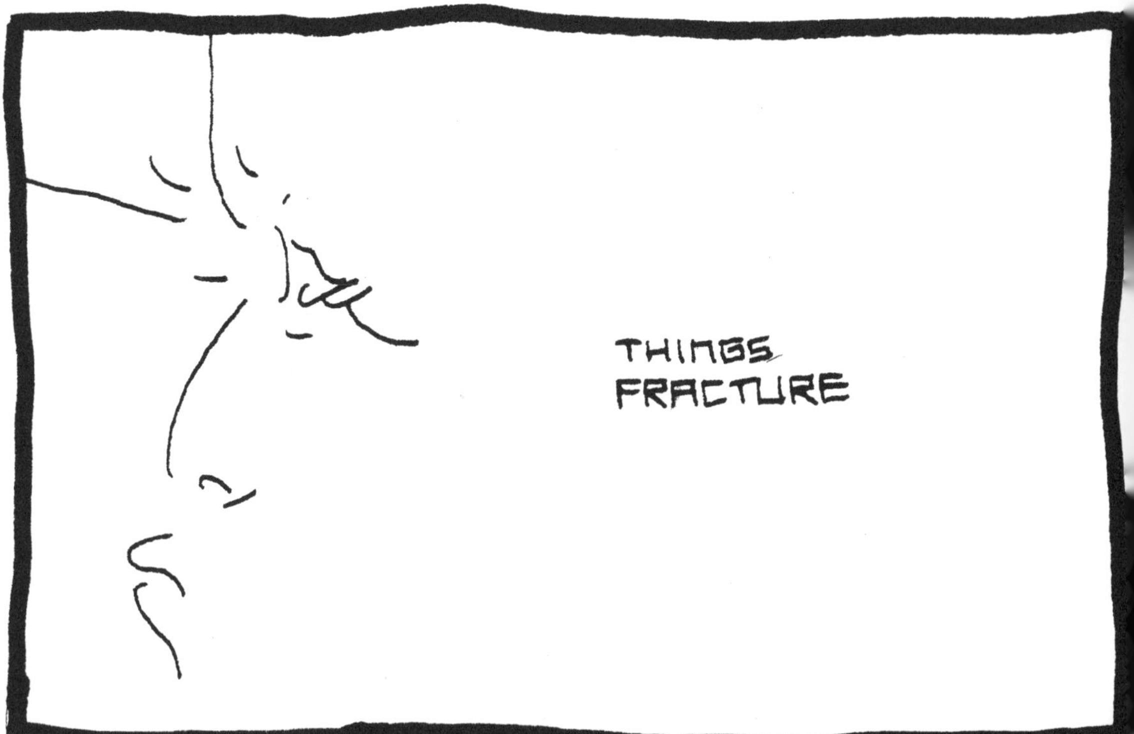
THINGS
FRACTURE

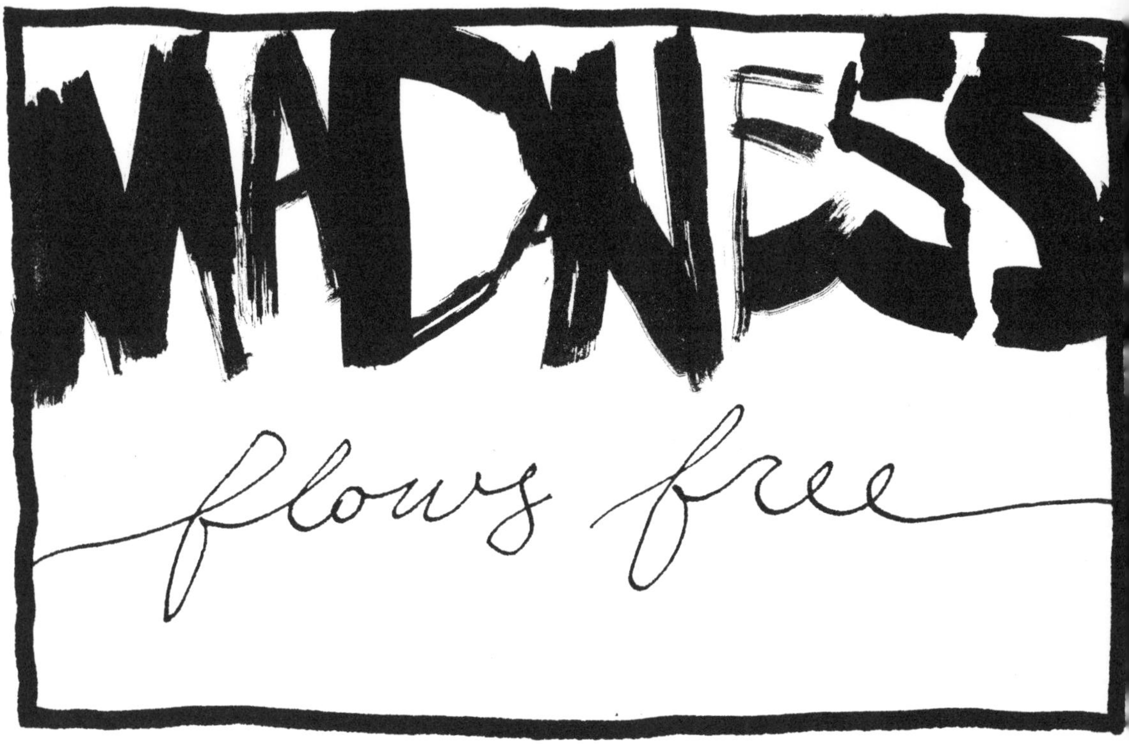
MADNESS
flows free

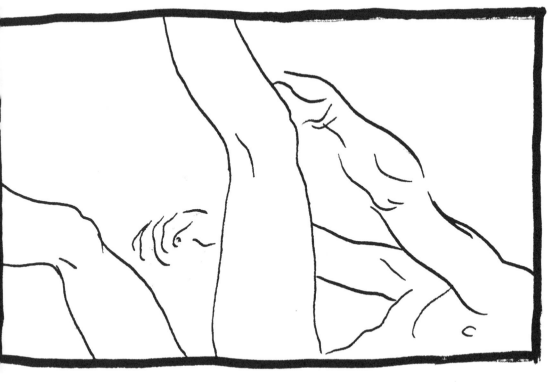

and a body, shorn of too much madness, falls.

lifeless.

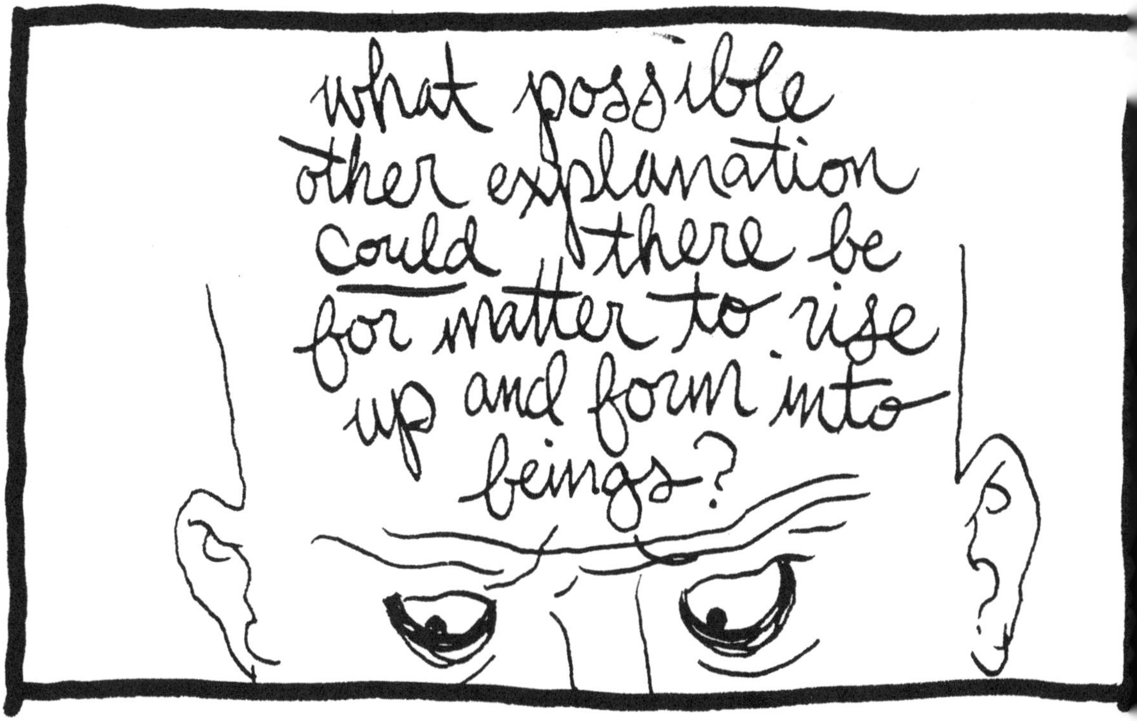
what possible other explanation could there be for matter to rise up and form into beings?

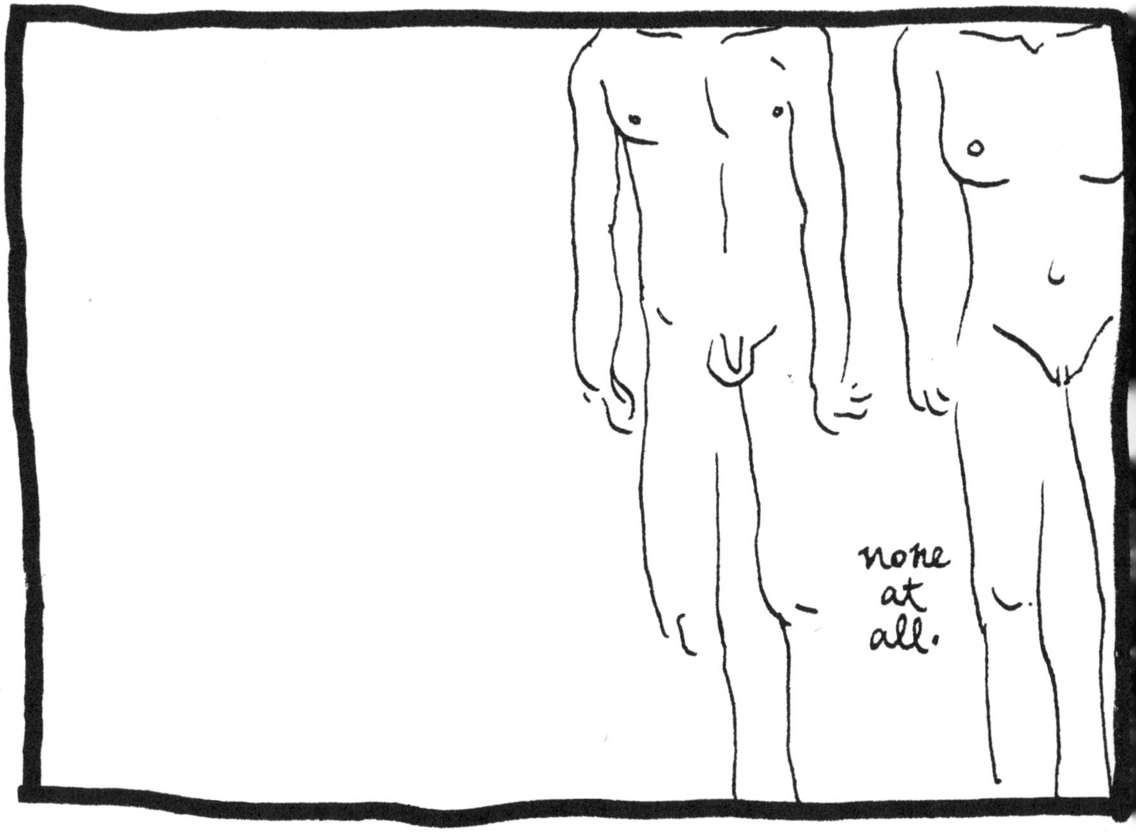
none at all.

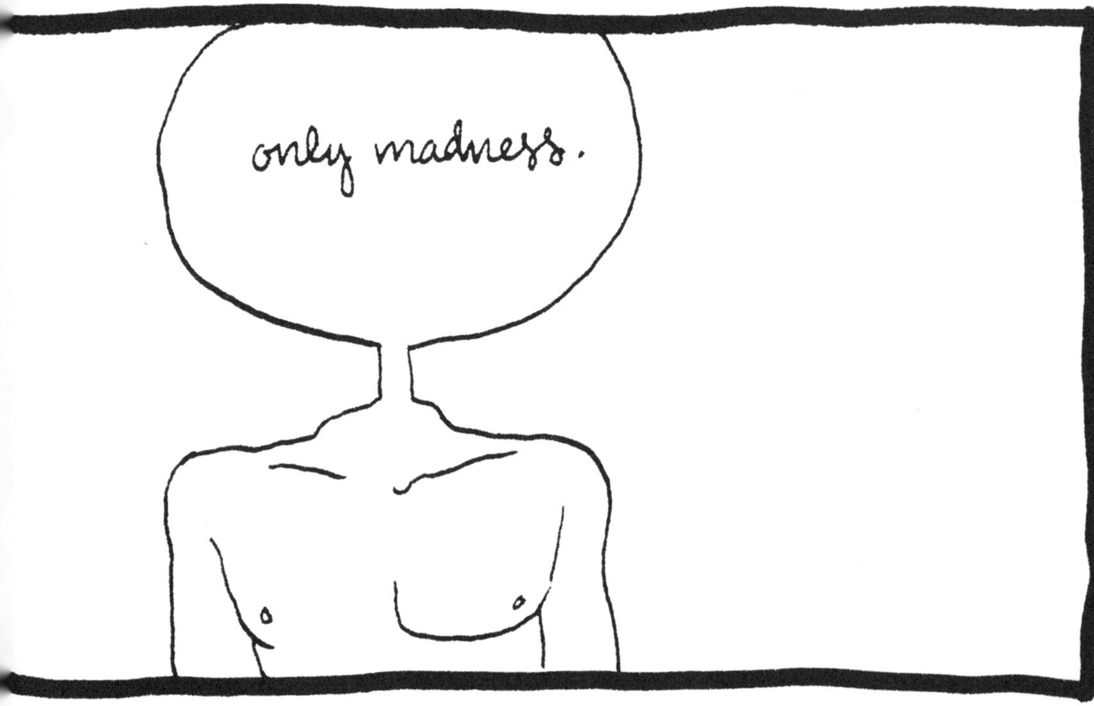
only madness.

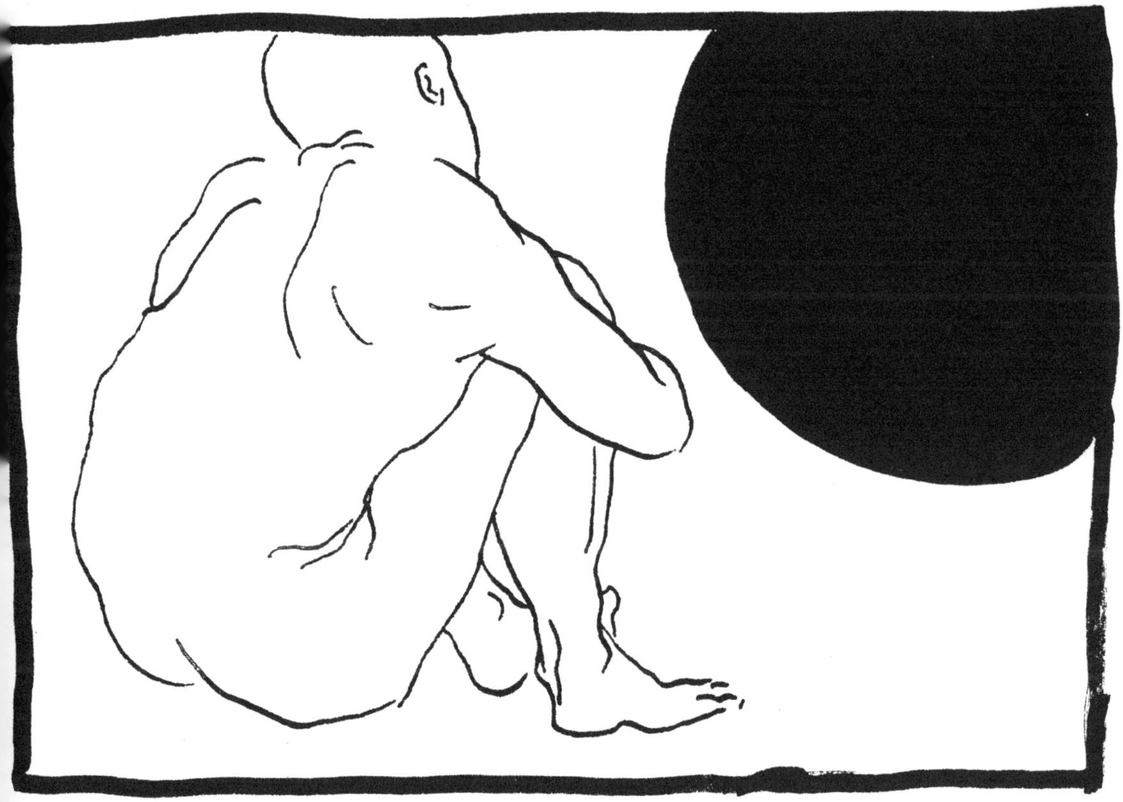

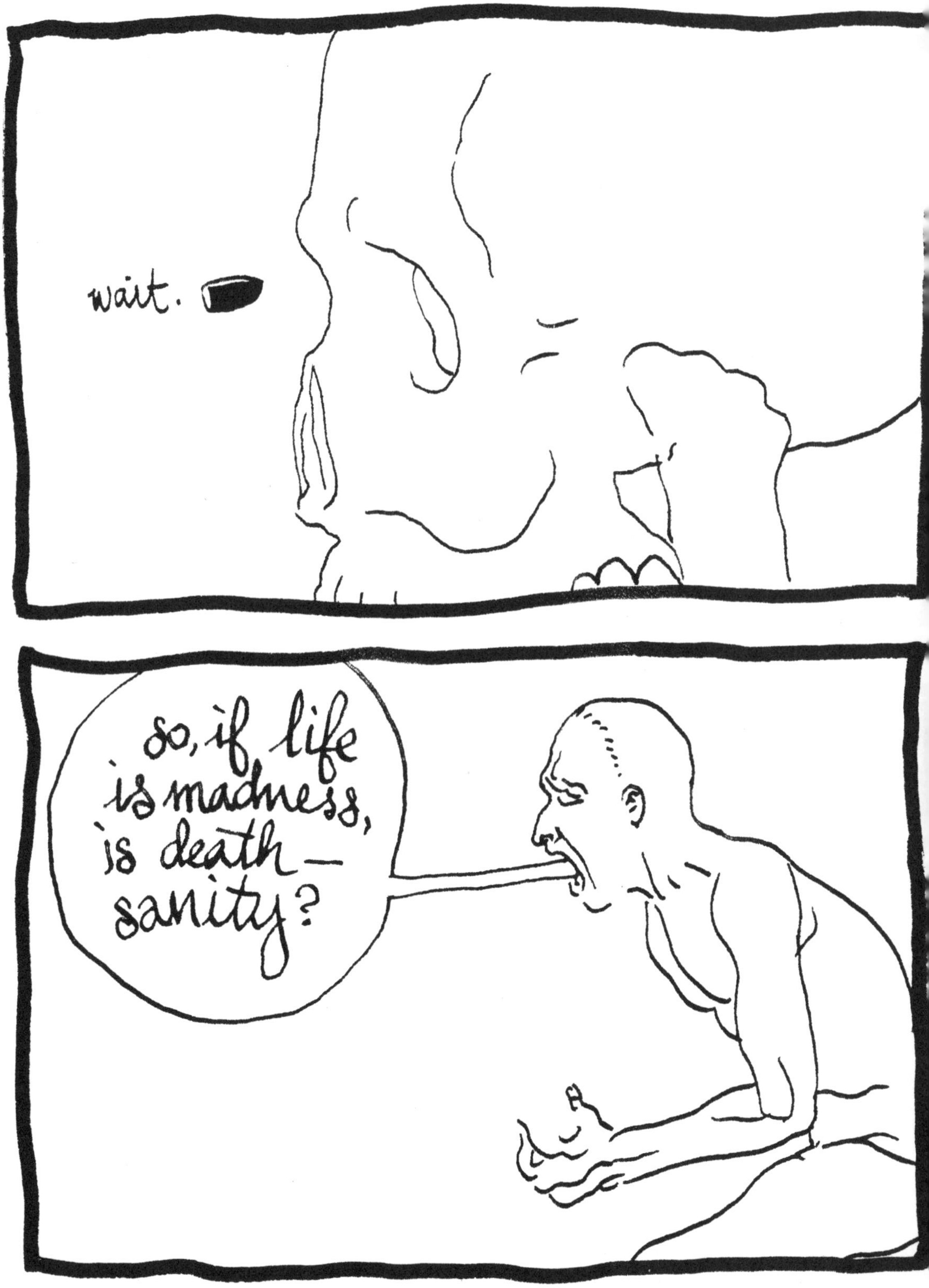
wait.
so, if life is madness, is death— sanity?

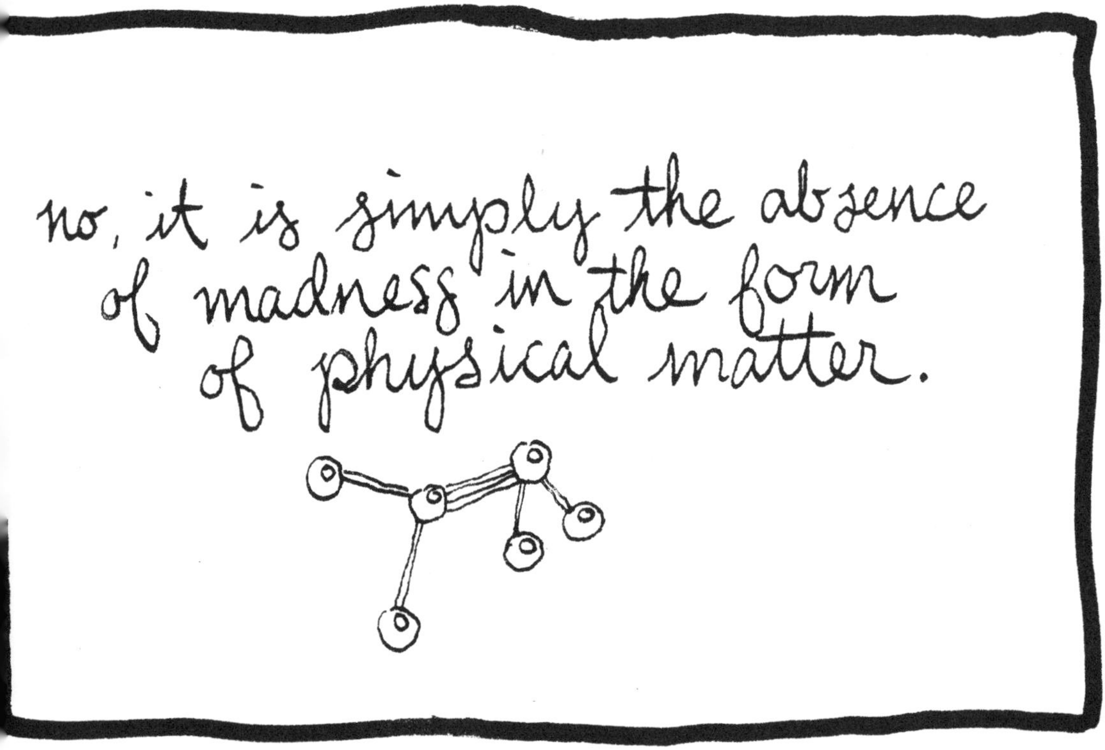
no, it is simply the absence
of madness in the form
of physical matter.

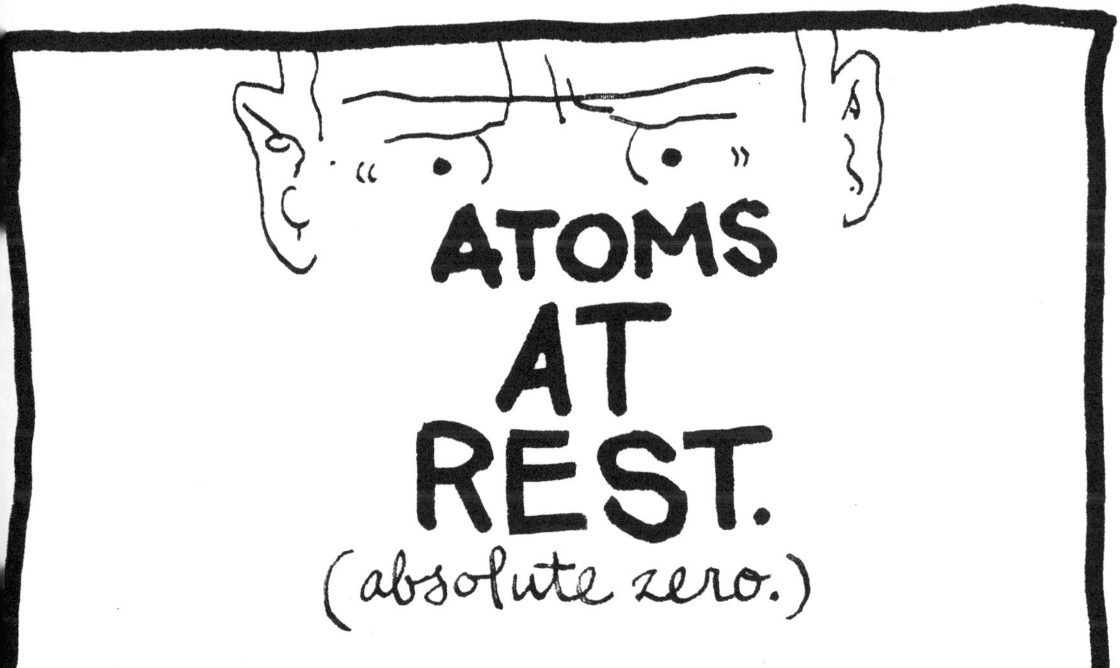
ATOMS
AT
REST.
(absolute zero.)

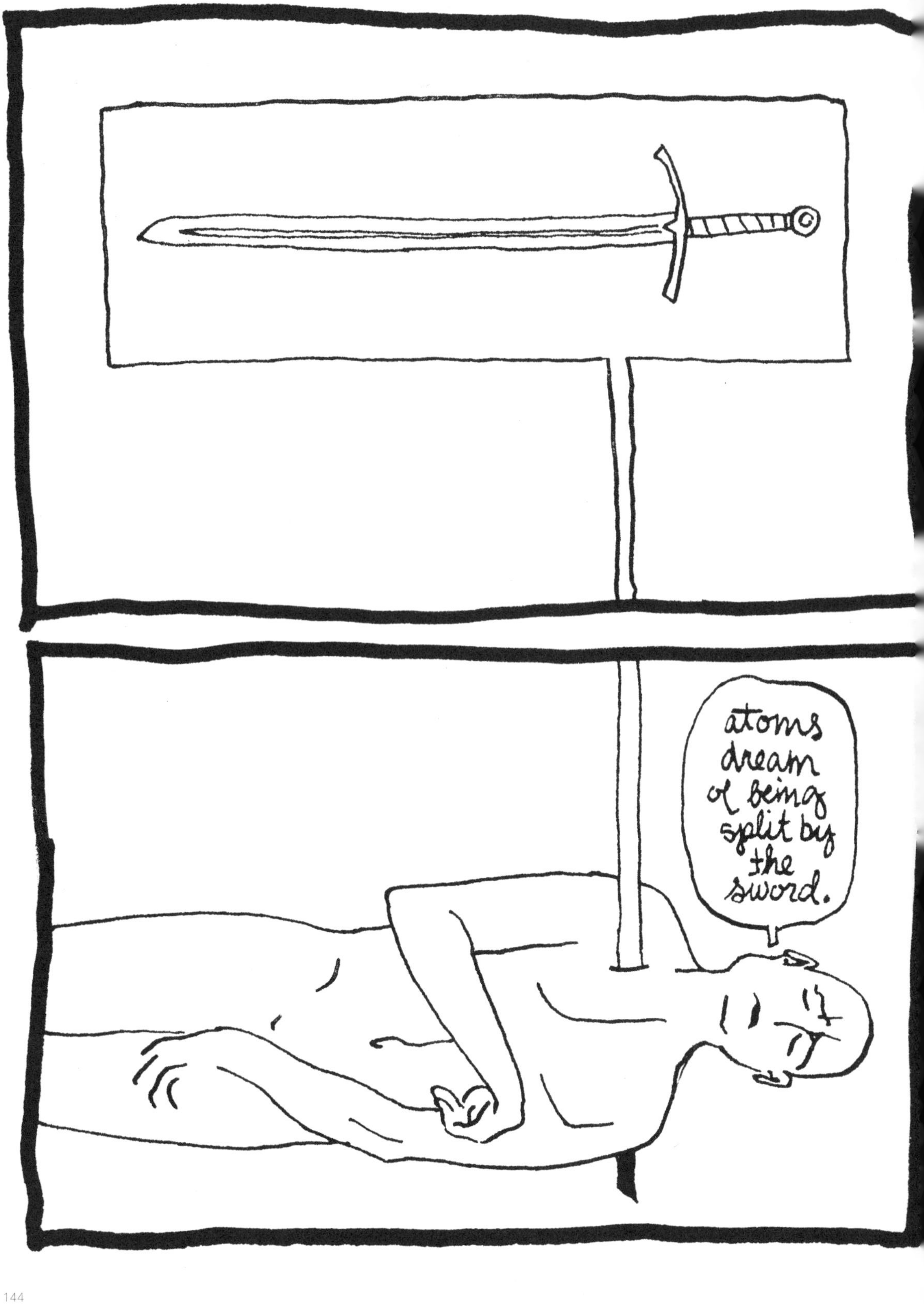
atoms dream of being split by the sword.

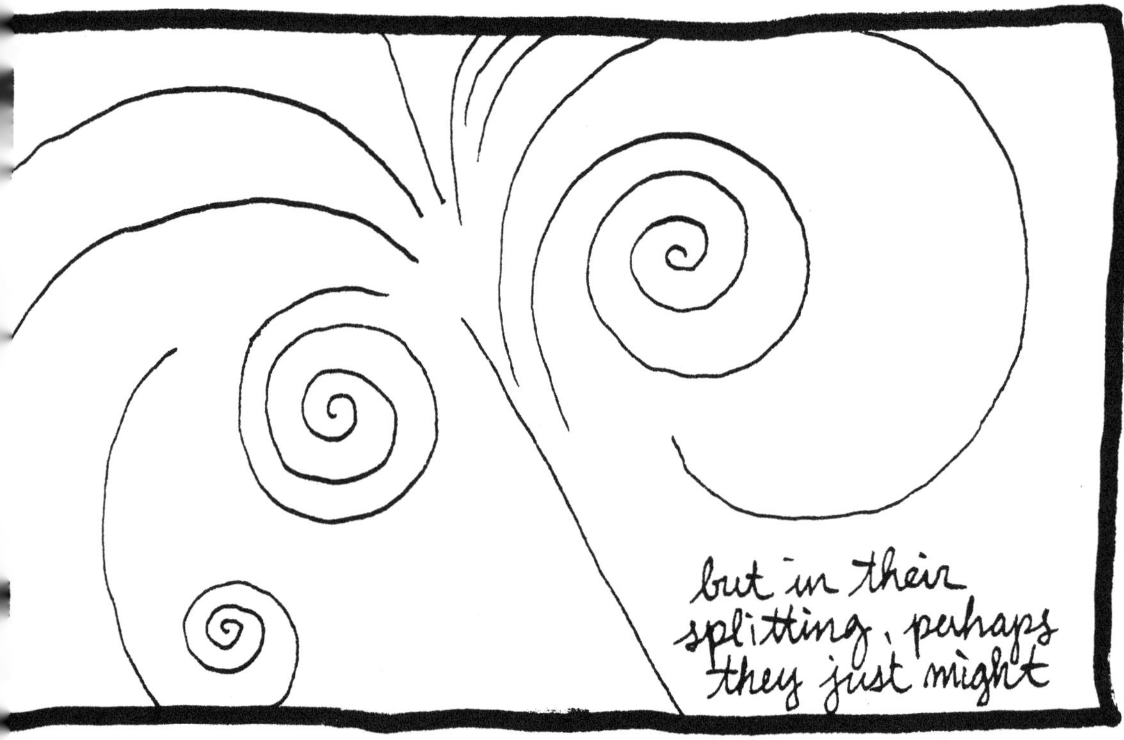
but in their splitting, perhaps they just might

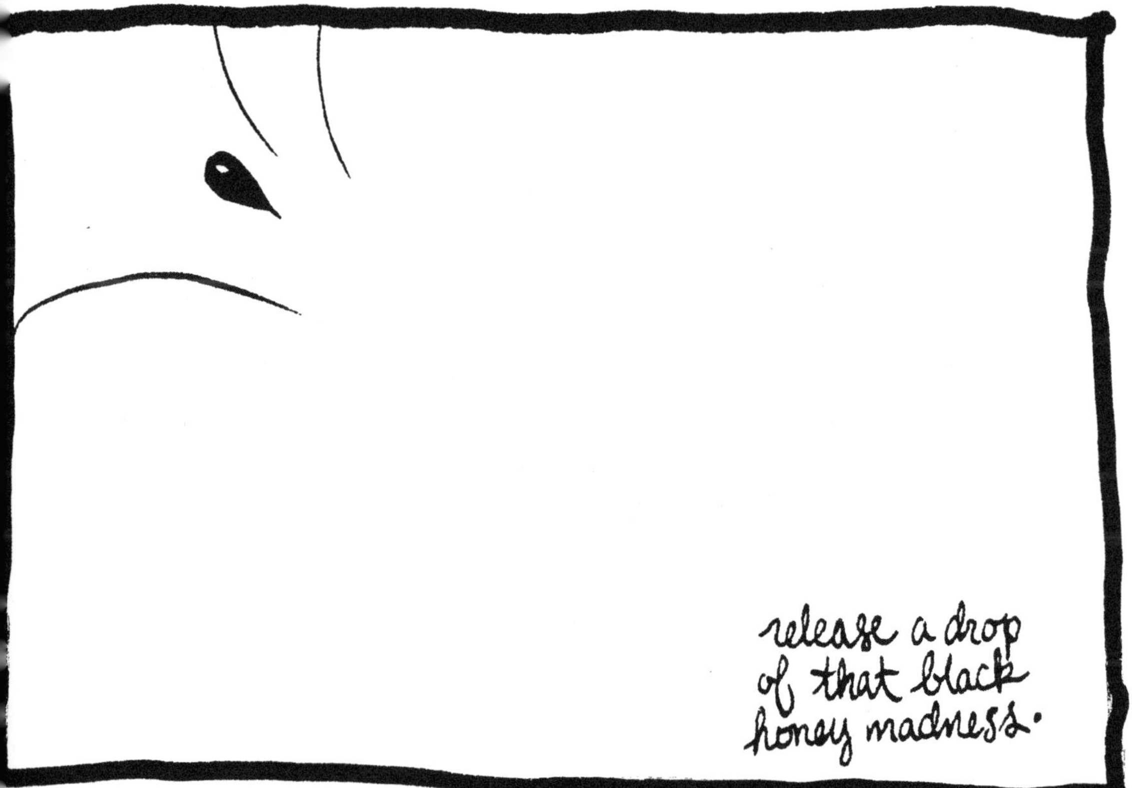
release a drop of that black honey madness.

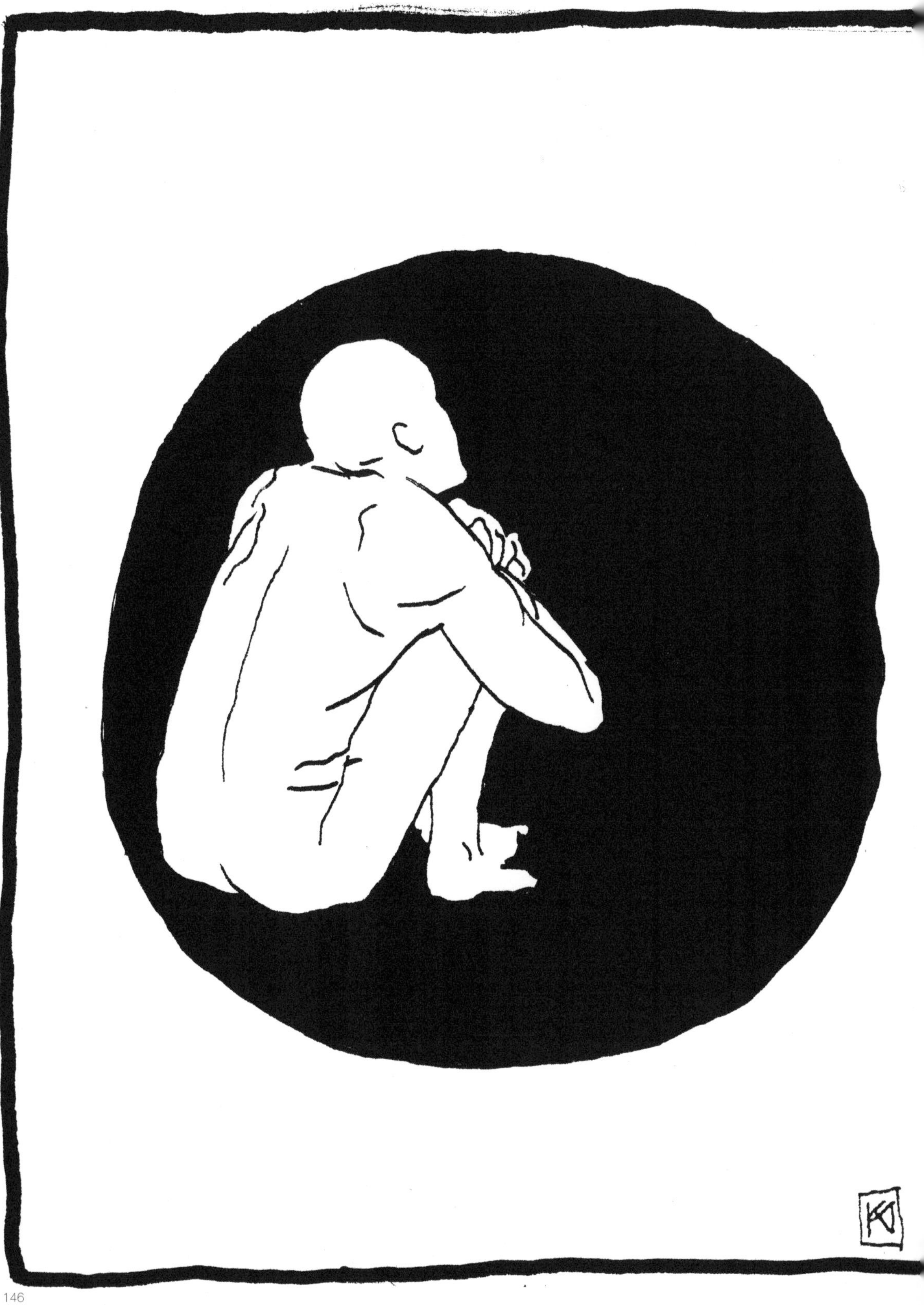

Abstract & Experimental Comics:

Pump, Starbucks, Gluten Free Soap, Parsons Talk, Abstract, People Containing Caffeine, November Nor'easter

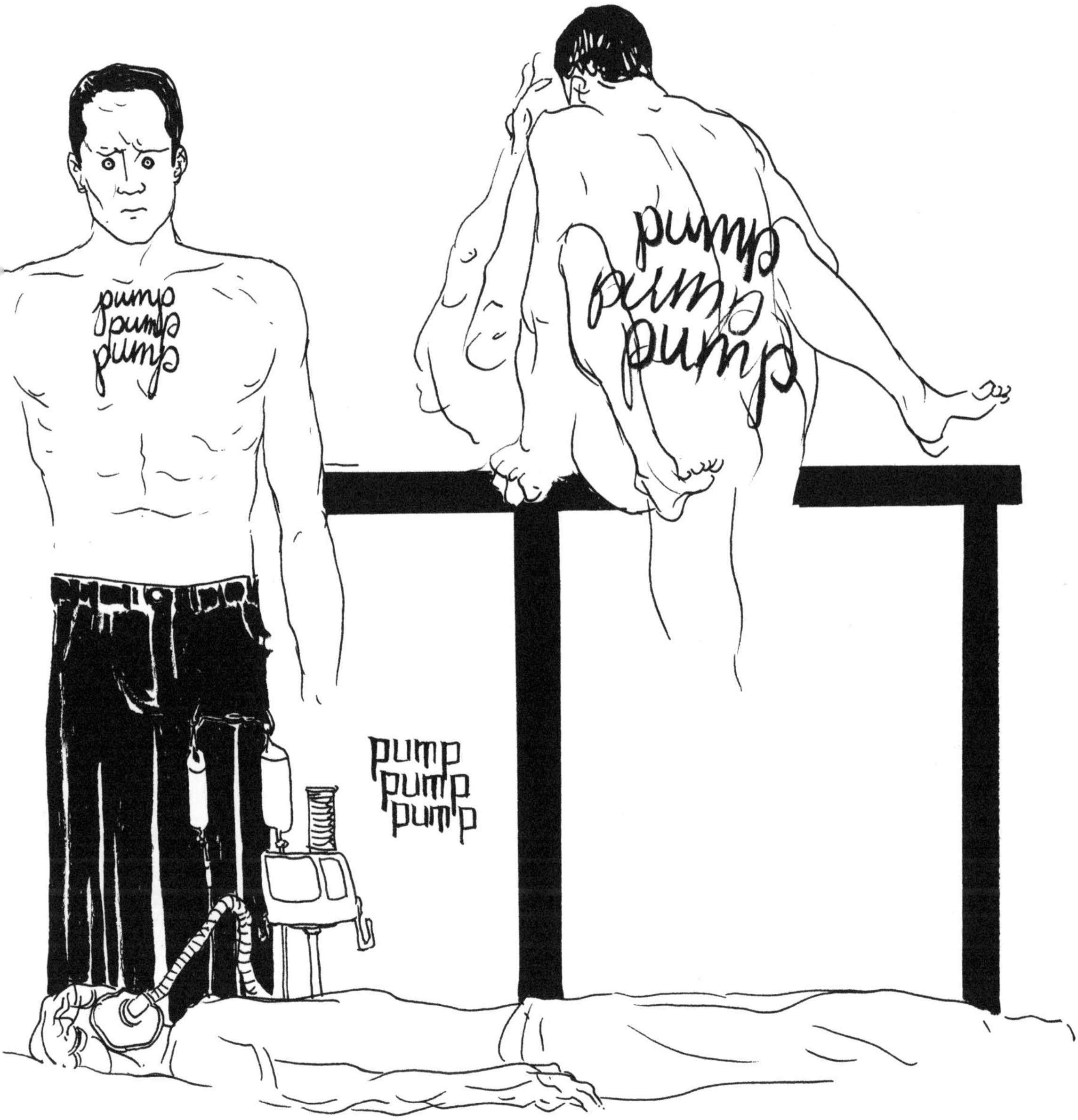
pump
pump
pump
pump
pump
pump
pump
pump
pump

"pump"
2014

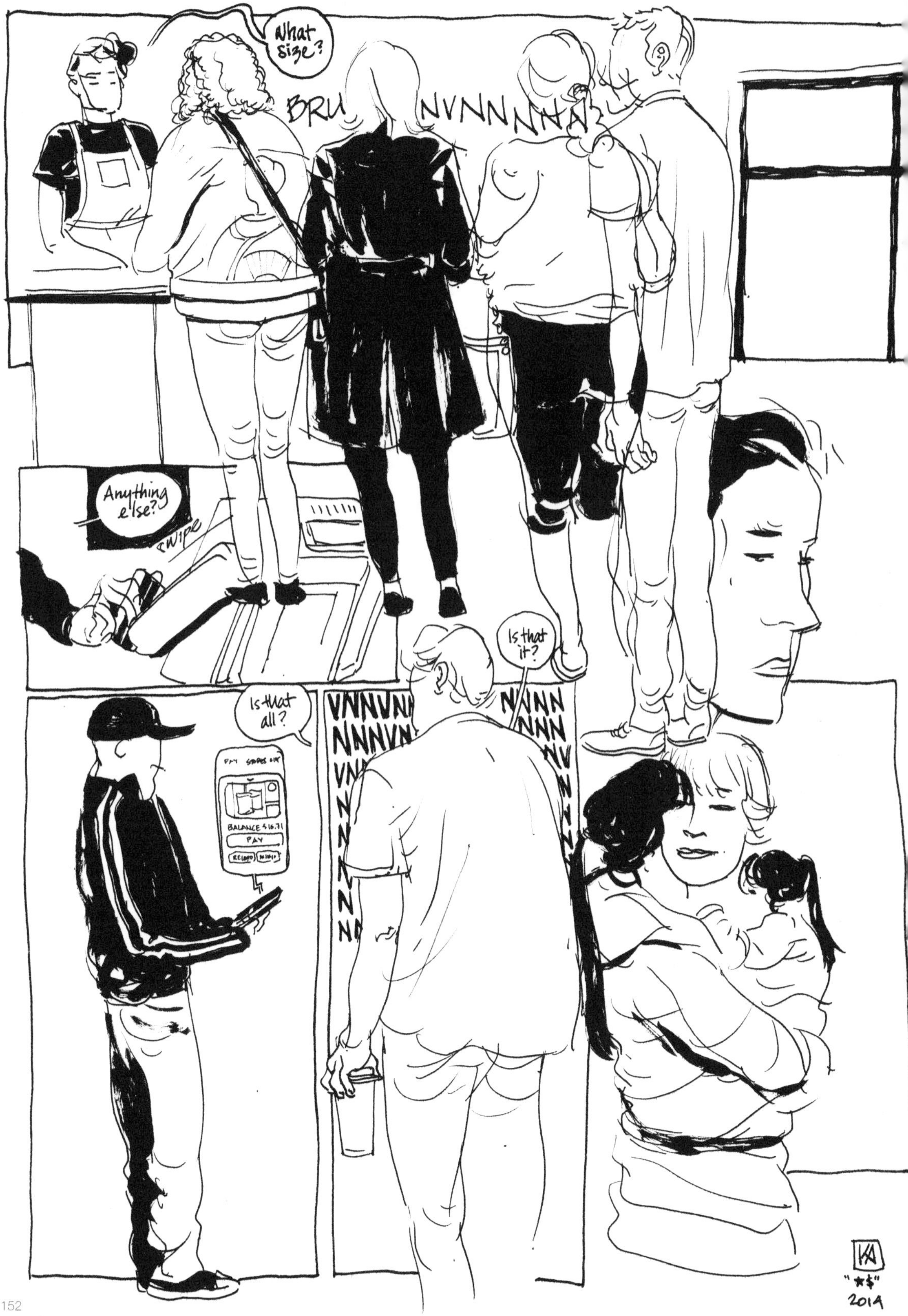
What size?
BRU NVNNNNNA
Anything else?
swipe
Is that it?
Is that all?
BALANCE $16.71
PAY
KA
2014

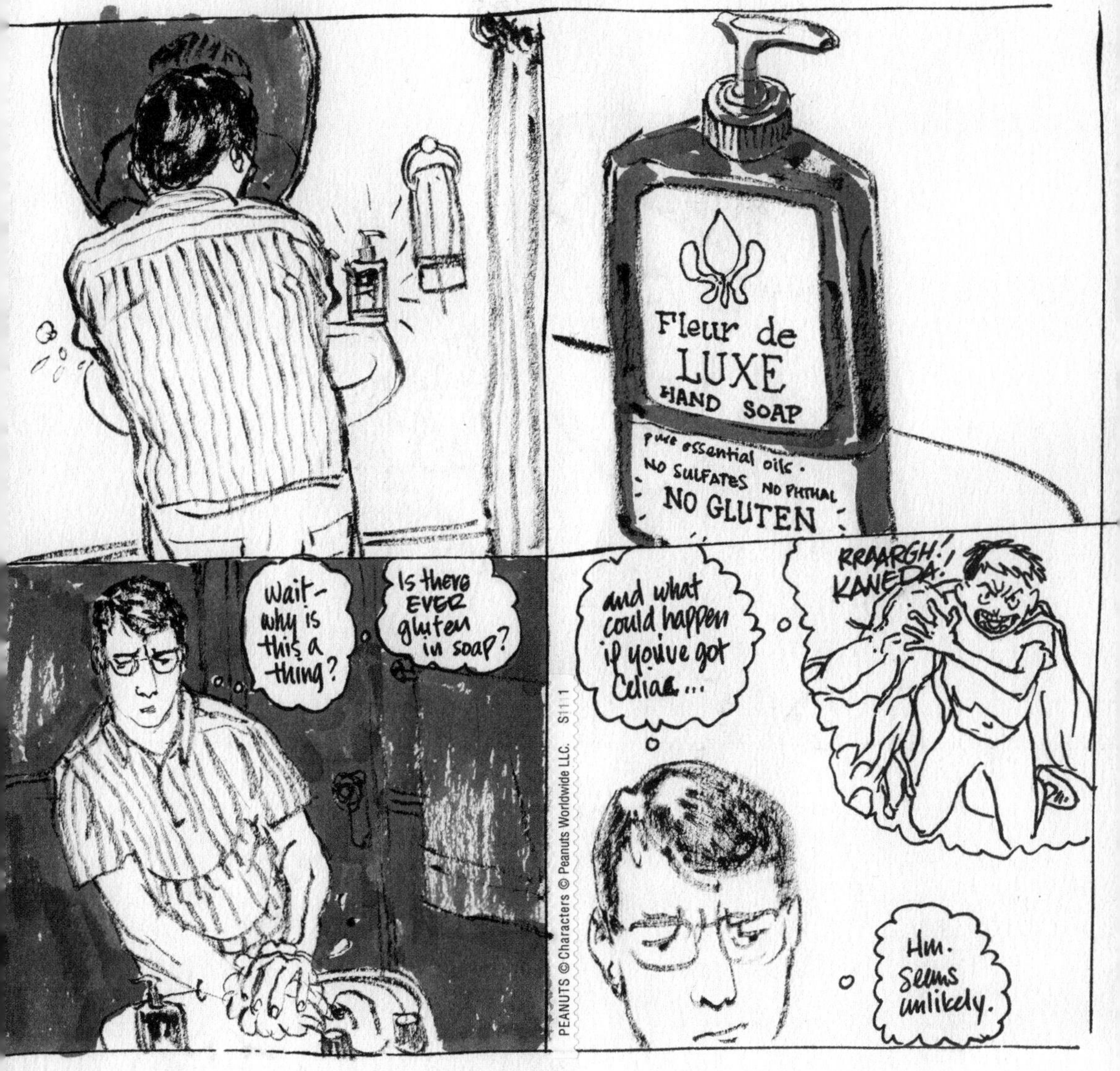
Fleur de LUXE HAND SOAP
pure essential oils.
NO SULFATES NO PHTHAL
NO GLUTEN
Wait- why is this a thing?
Is there EVER gluten in soap?
PEANUTS © Characters © Peanuts Worldwide LLC. S1111
and what could happen if you've got Celiac...
RRAARGH! KANEDA!
Hm. Seems unlikely.

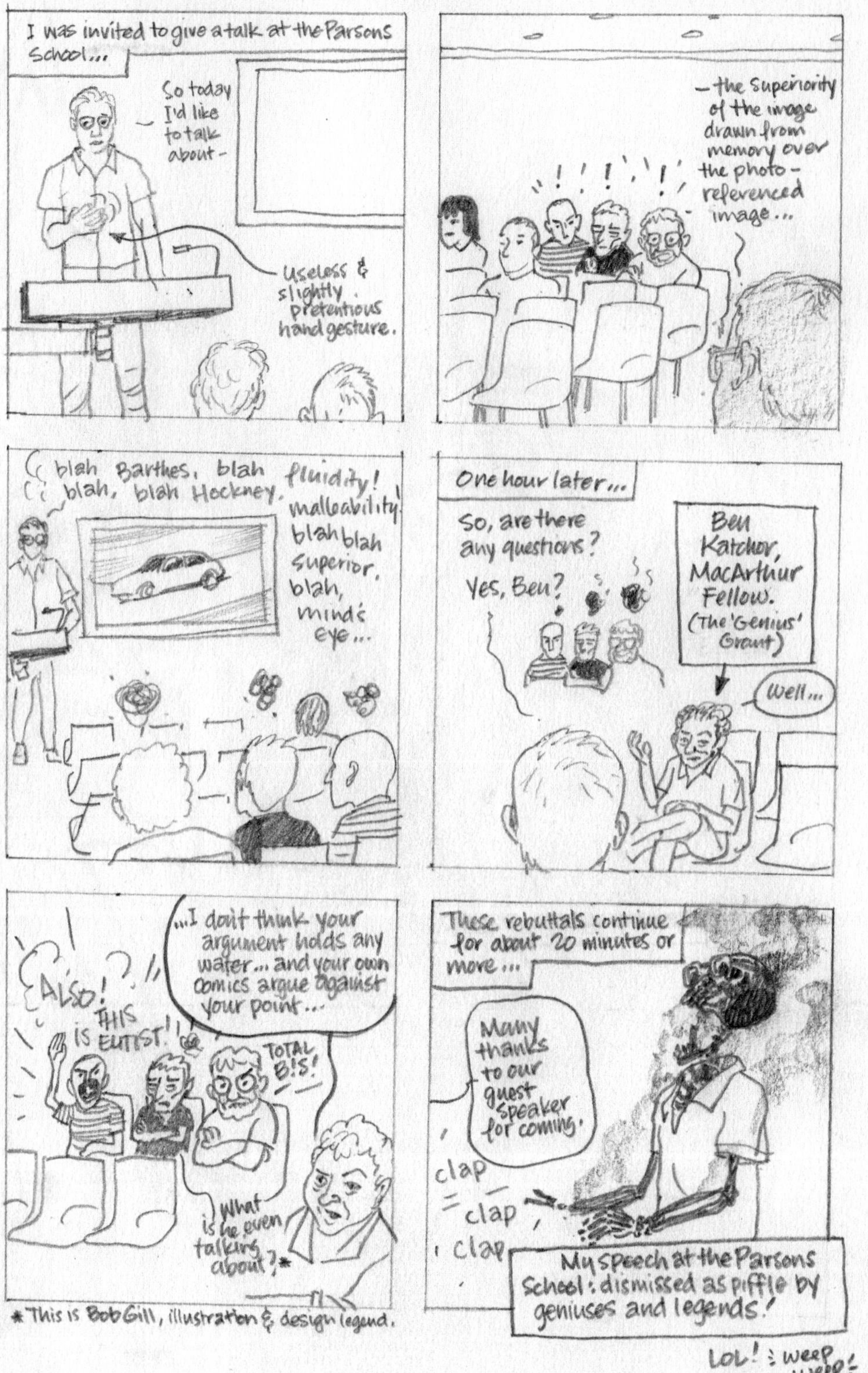
I was invited to give a talk at the Parsons School...
So today I'd like to talk about -
Useless & slightly pretentious hand gesture.
- the superiority of the image drawn from memory over the photo-referenced image...
! ! ! !
blah Barthes, blah blah, blah Hockney.
fluidity! malleability! blah blah superior, blah, mind's eye...
One hour later...
So, are there any questions?
Yes, Ben?
Ben Katchor, MacArthur Fellow. (The 'Genius' Grant)
Well...
...I don't think your argument holds any water... and your own comics argue against your point...
ALSO!
THIS IS ELITIST!
TOTAL B!S!
What is he even talking about?*
These rebuttals continue for about 20 minutes or more...
Many thanks to our guest speaker for coming.
clap
clap
clap
My speech at the Parsons School: dismissed as piffle by geniuses and legends!
* This is Bob Gill, illustration & design legend.
LOL! weep weep
12 OCT 2017

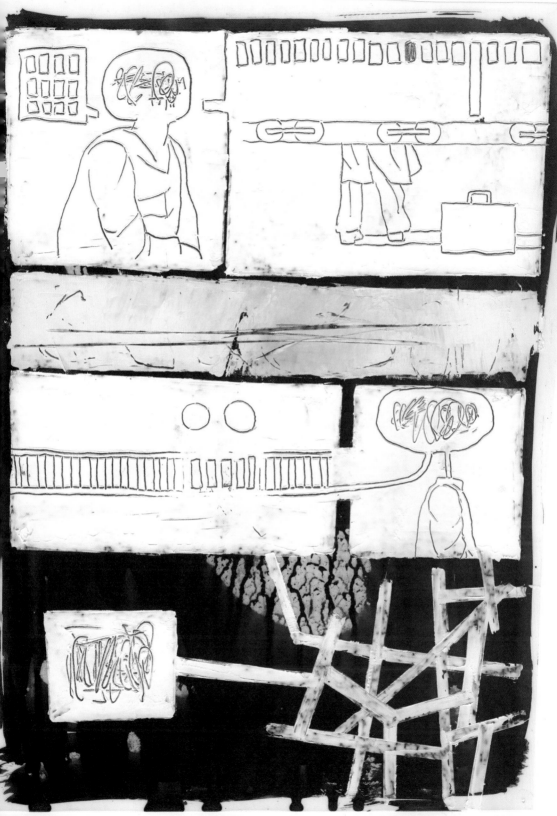

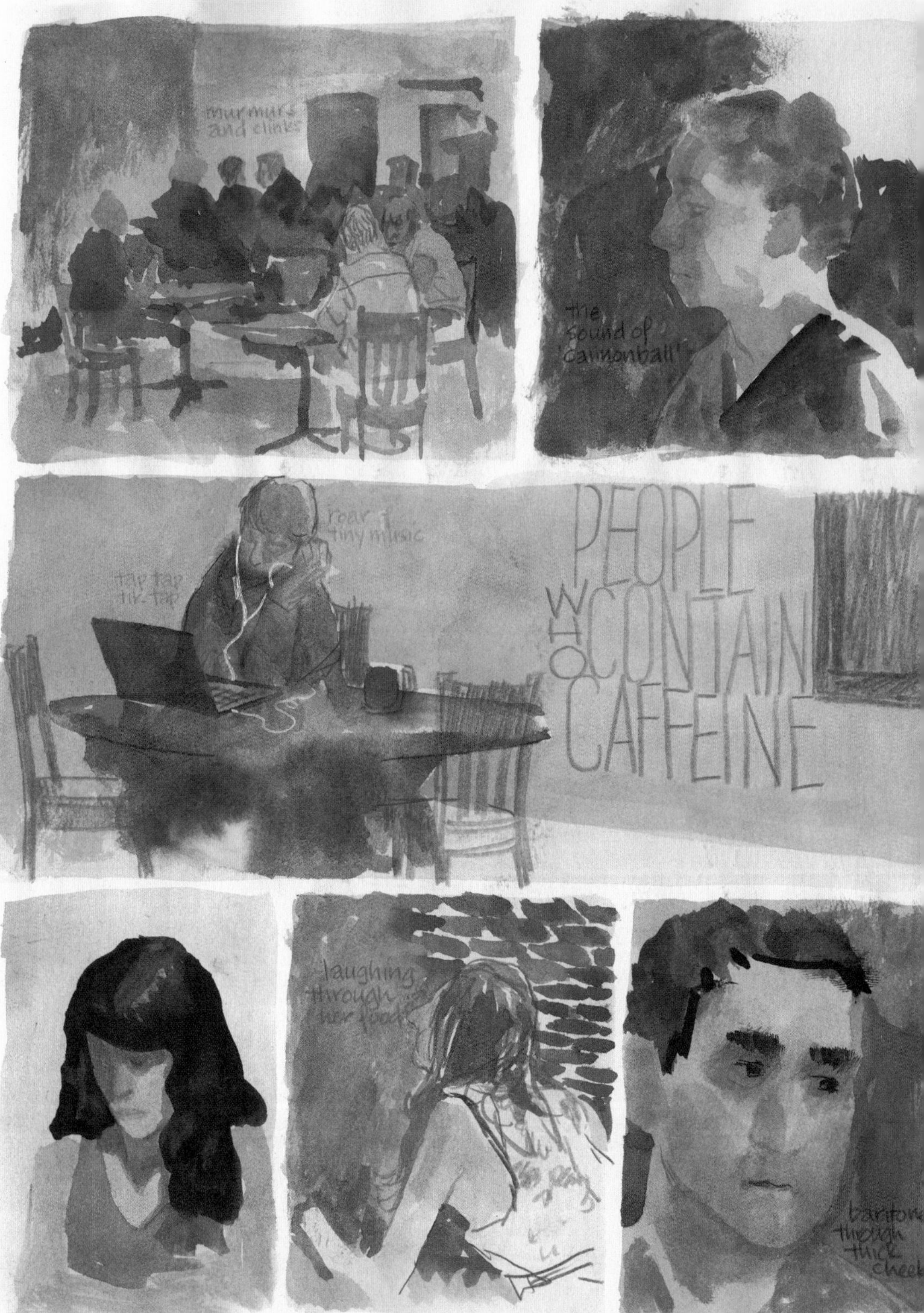
murmurs and clinks
the sound of 'cannonball'
roar of tiny music
tap tap tik tap
PEOPLE WHO CONTAIN CAFFEINE
laughing through her food
barito through thick cheek
2018 23 AUG

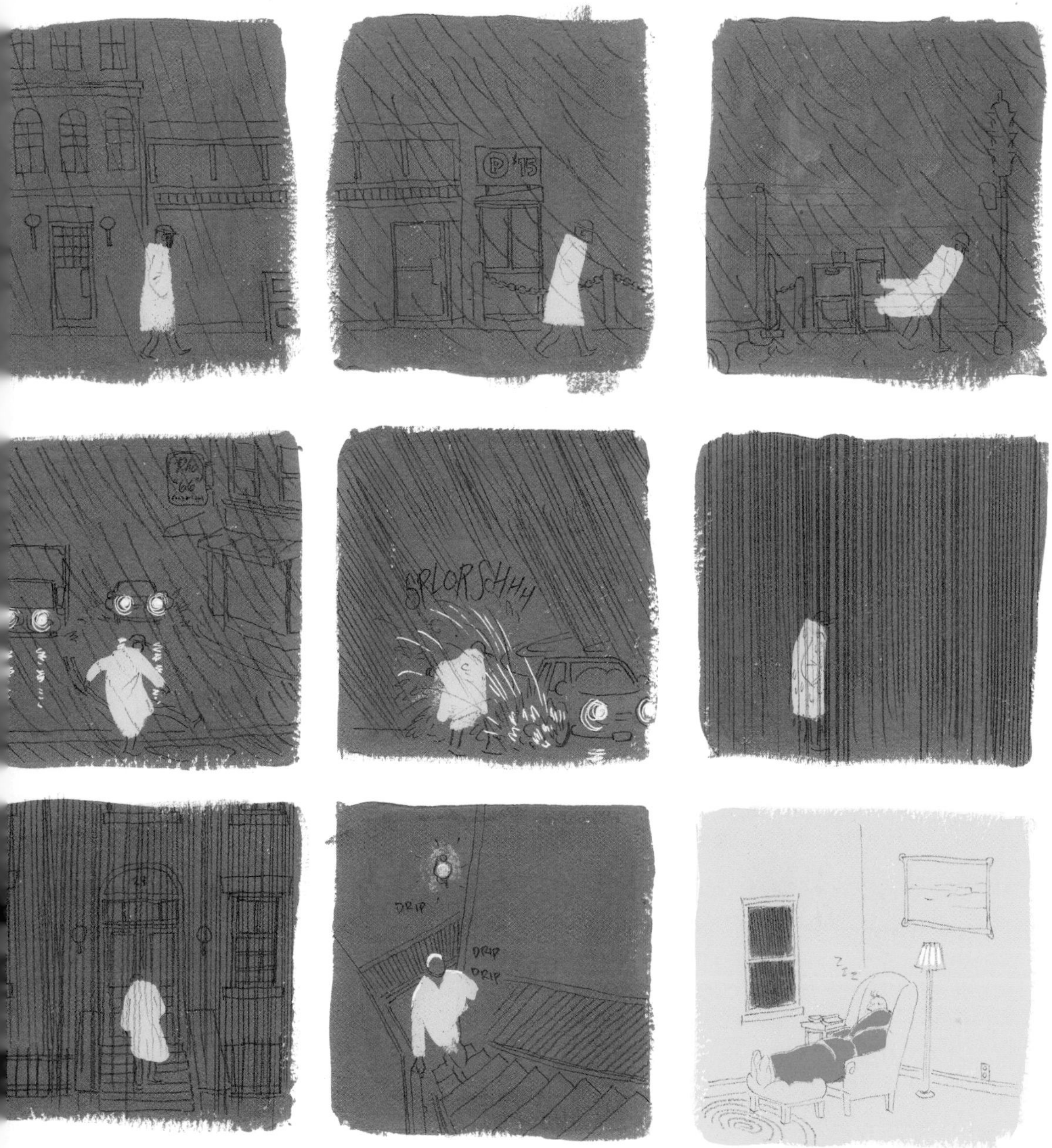
P '15
SPLORSCHHH
DRIP
DRIP
DRIP

"NOVEMBER NOR'EASTER" 2014

The Synthesizer

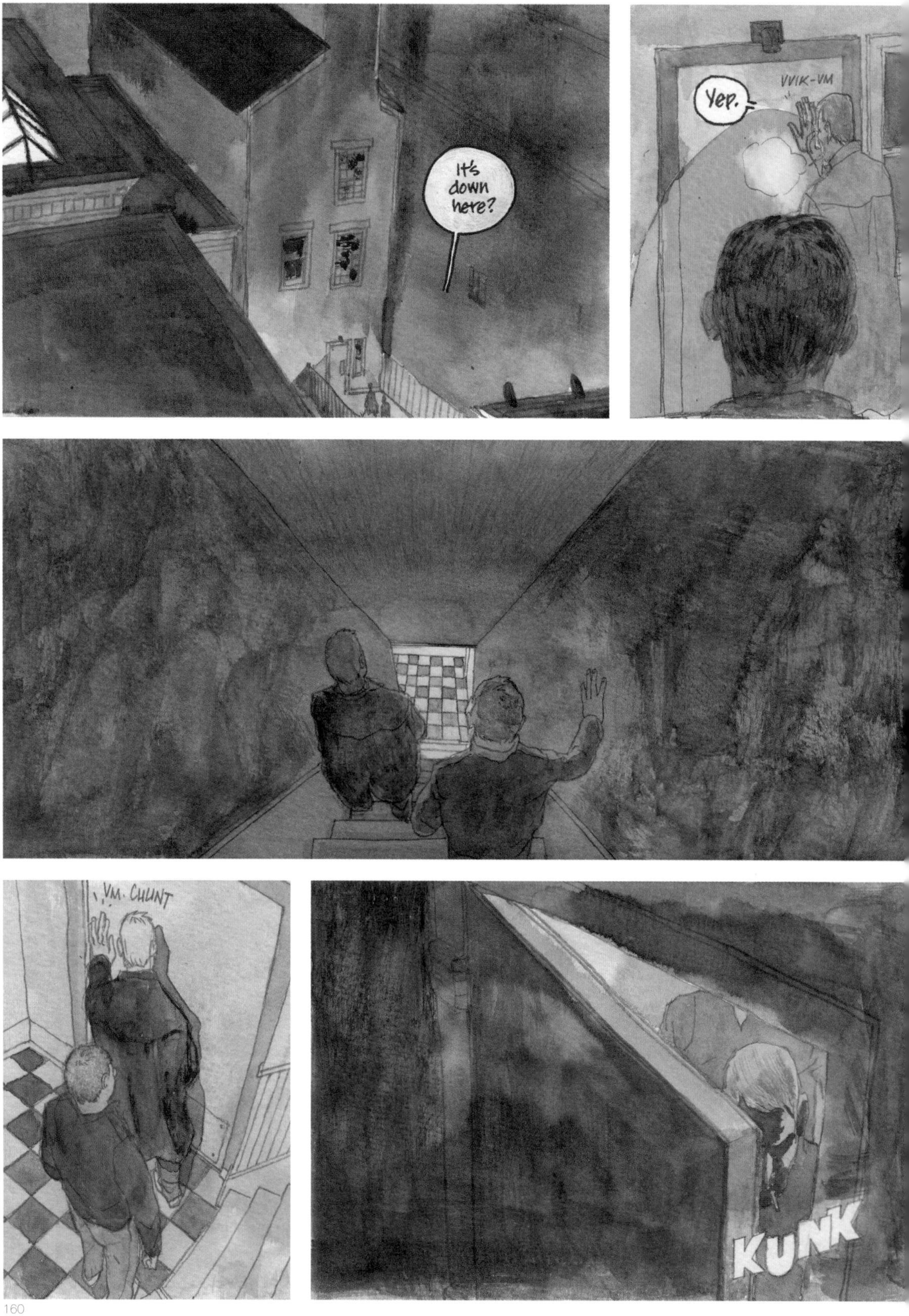
It's down here?
Yep.
VVIK-VM
VM. CHUNT
KUNK

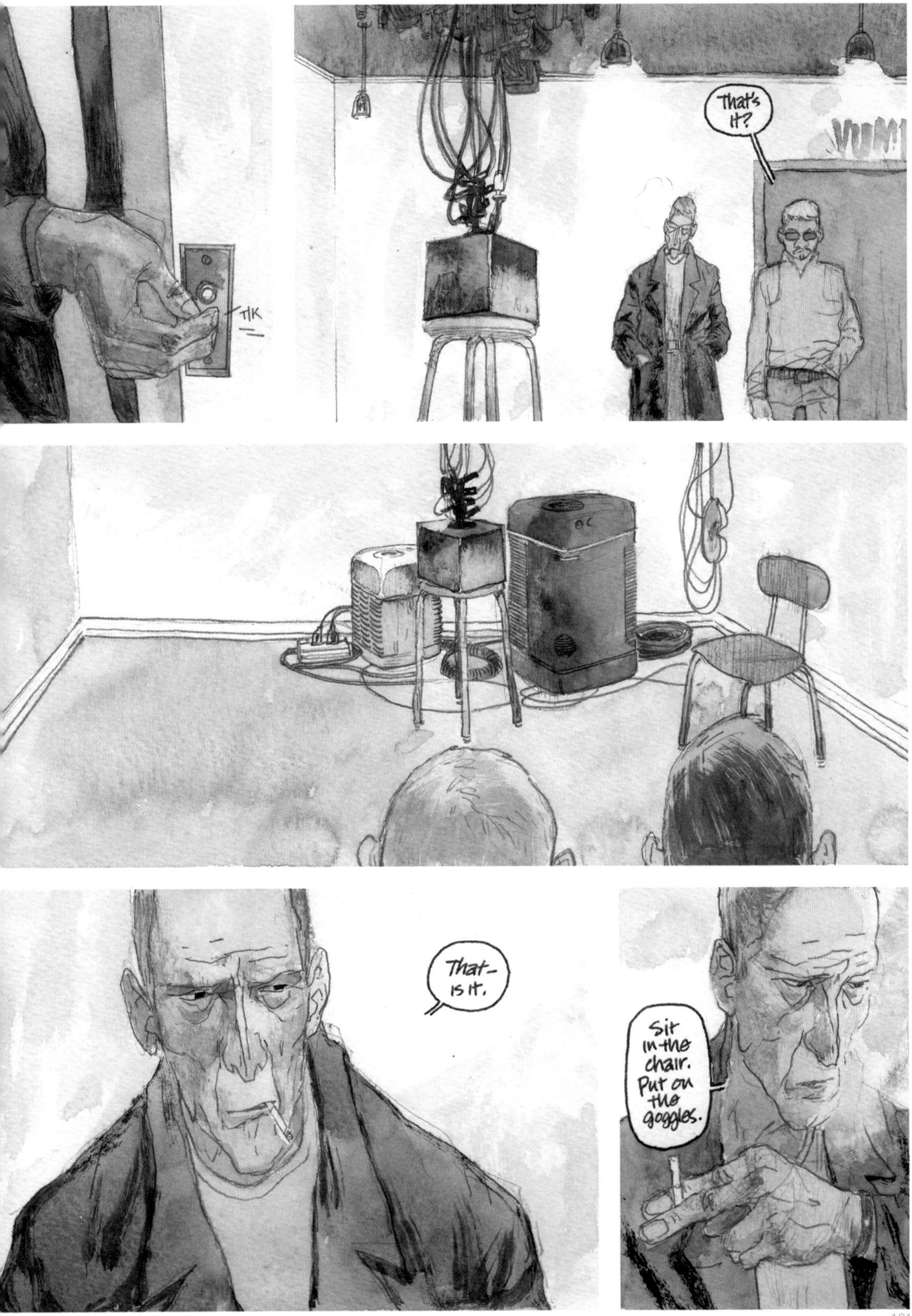
TIK
That's it?
That- is it.
Sit in the chair. Put on the goggles.

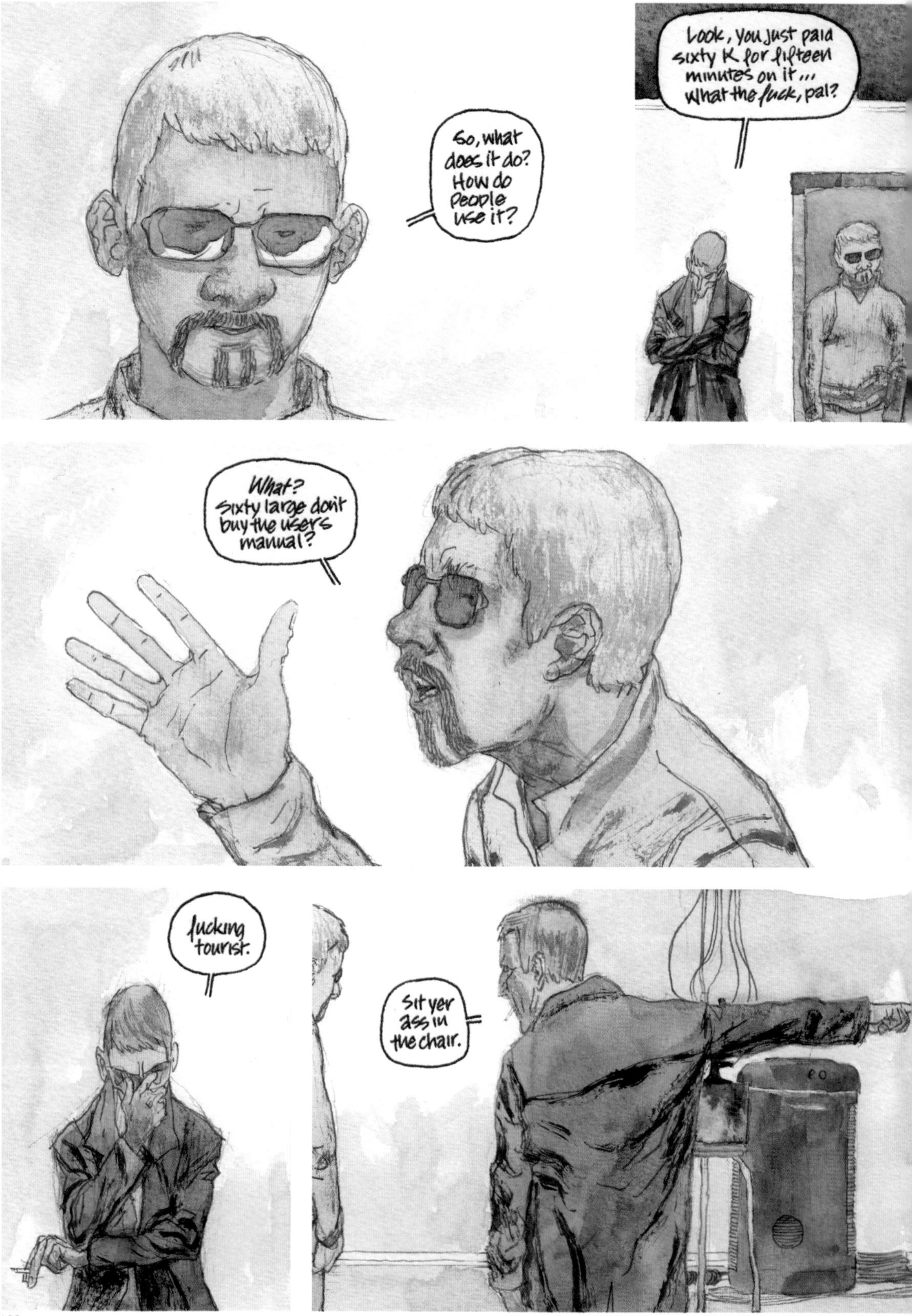
So, what does it do? How do people use it?
Look, you just paid sixty K for fifteen minutes on it... What the *fuck*, pal?
What? Sixty large don't buy the users manual?
fucking tourist.
Sit yer ass in the chair.

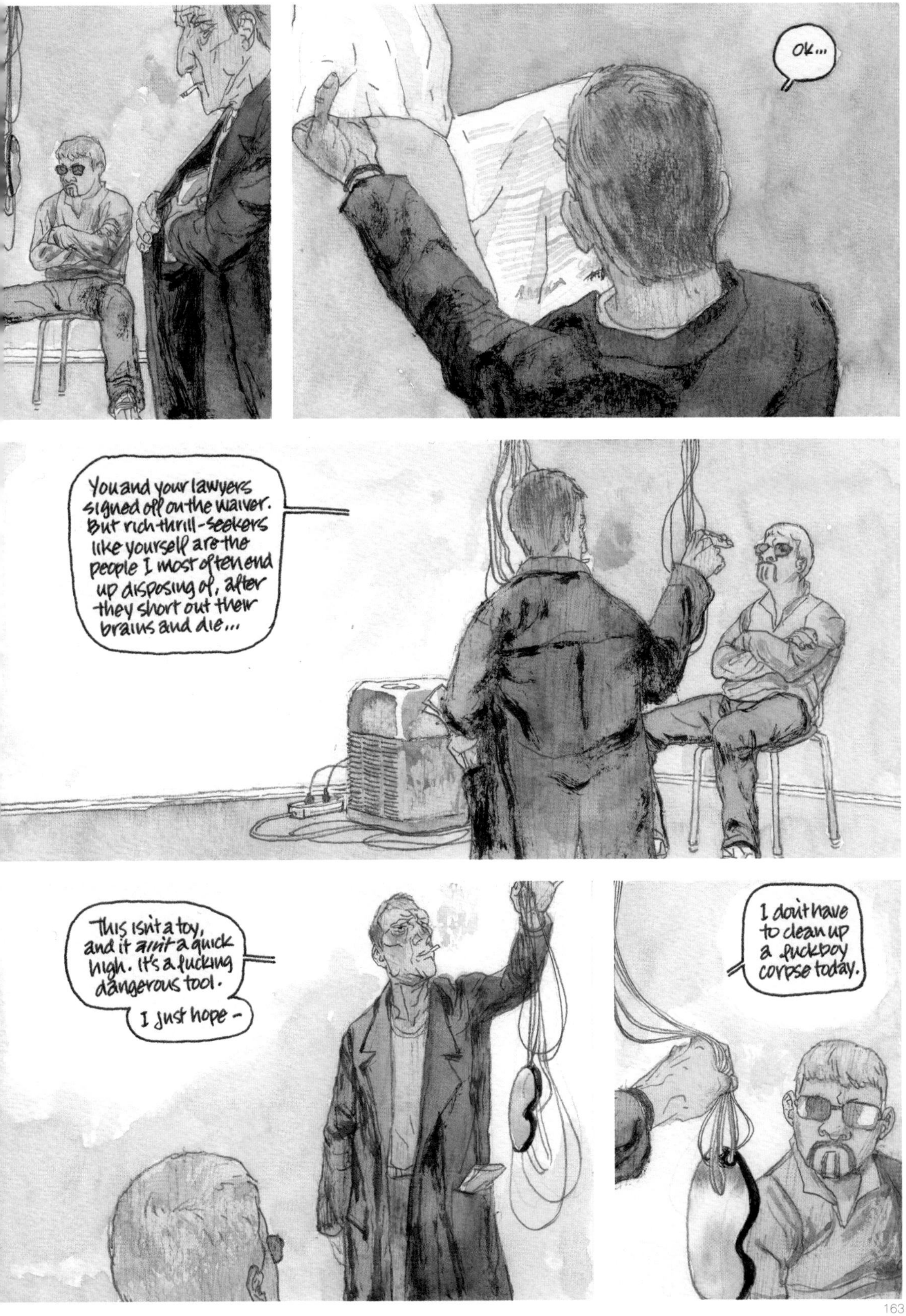

Ok...
You and your lawyers signed off on the waiver. But rich thrill-seekers like yourself are the people I most often end up disposing of, after they short out their brains and die...
This isn't a toy, and it ain't a quick high. It's a fucking dangerous tool.
I just hope -
I don't have to clean up a fuckboy corpse today.

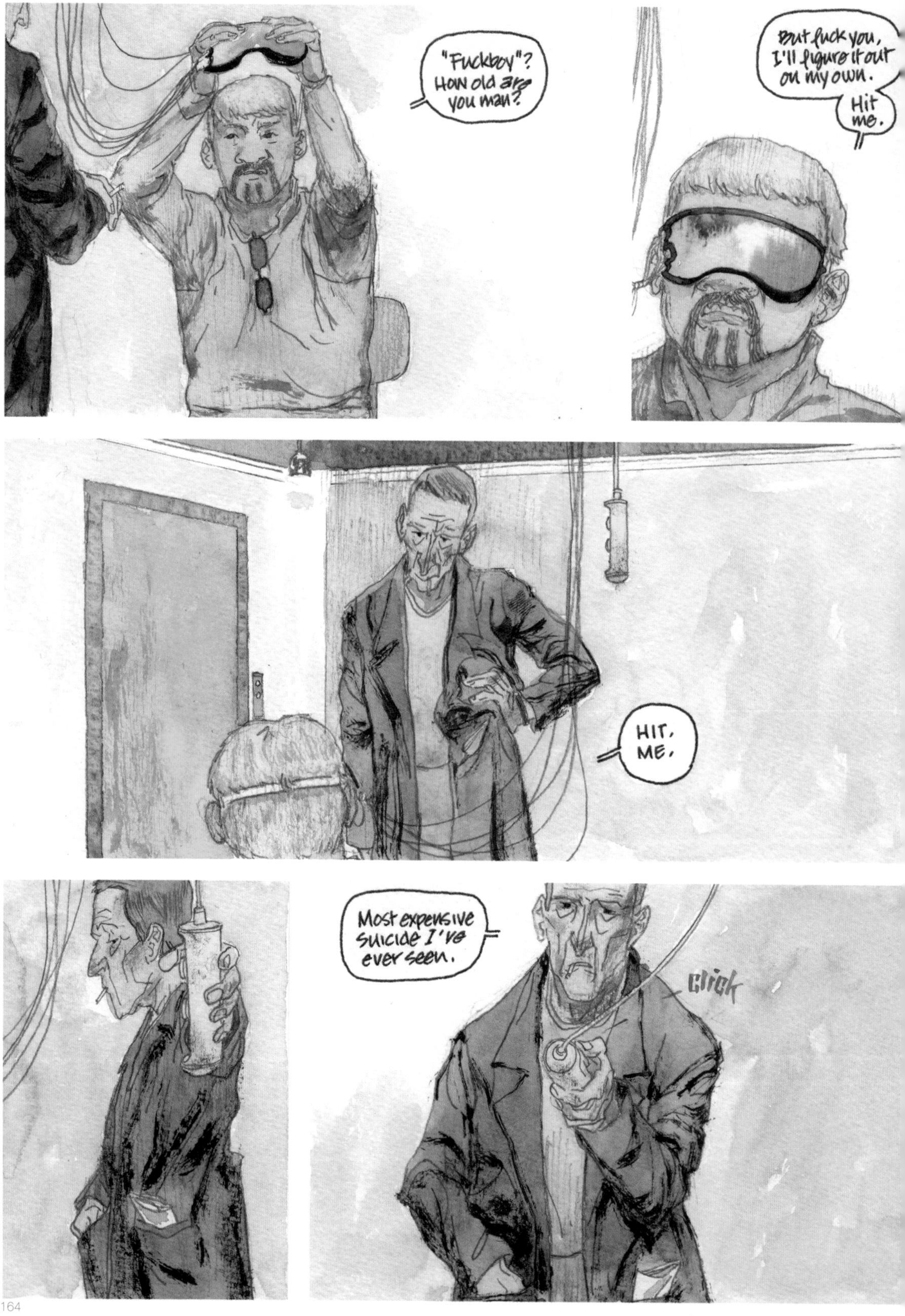
"Fuckboy"? How old are you man?
But fuck you, I'll figure it out on my own.
Hit me.
HIT, ME,
Most expensive suicide I've ever seen.
click

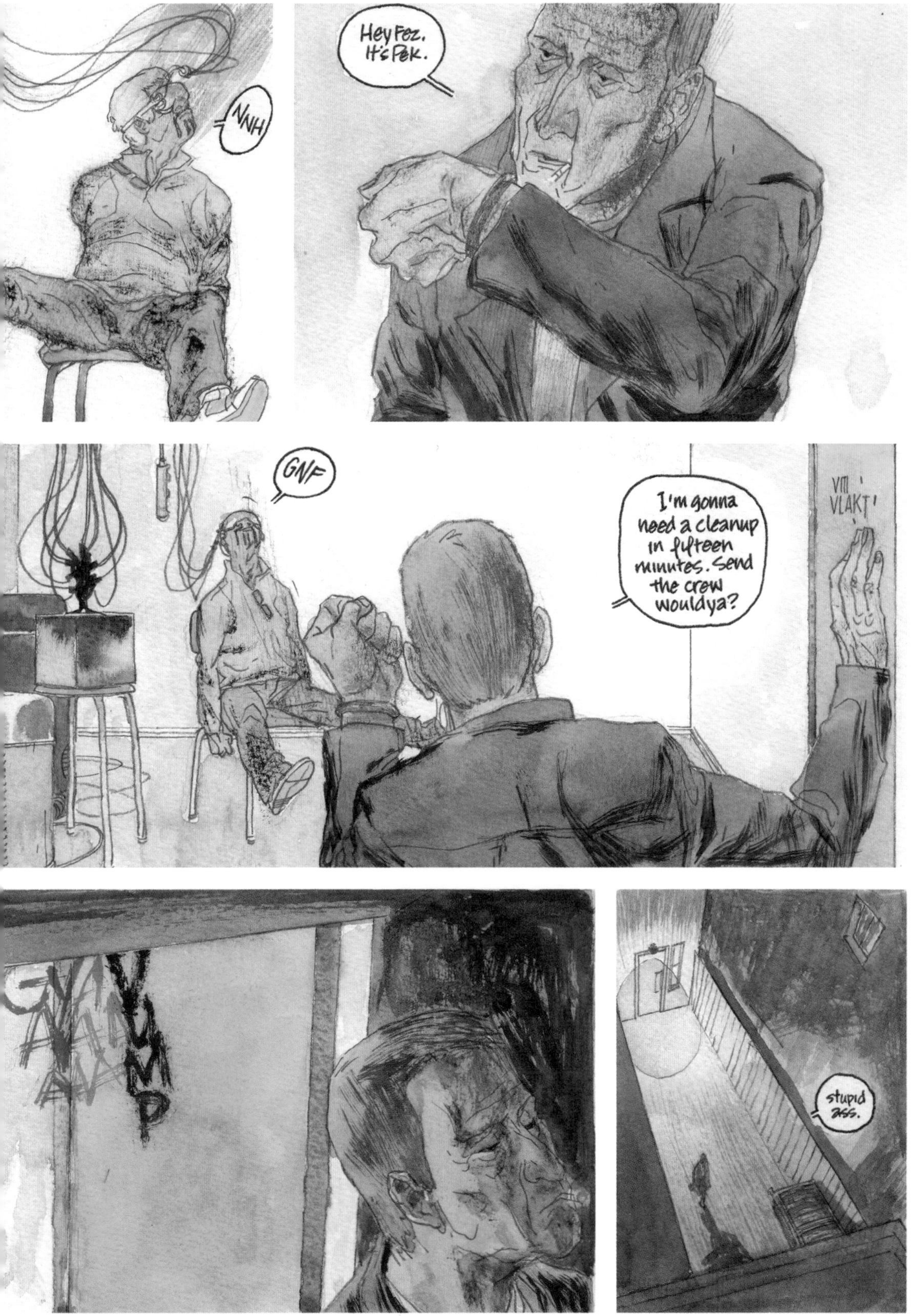
NNH
Hey Fez. It's Pek.
GNF
I'm gonna need a cleanup in fifteen minutes. Send the crew wouldya?
VIII VLAKT
stupid ass.

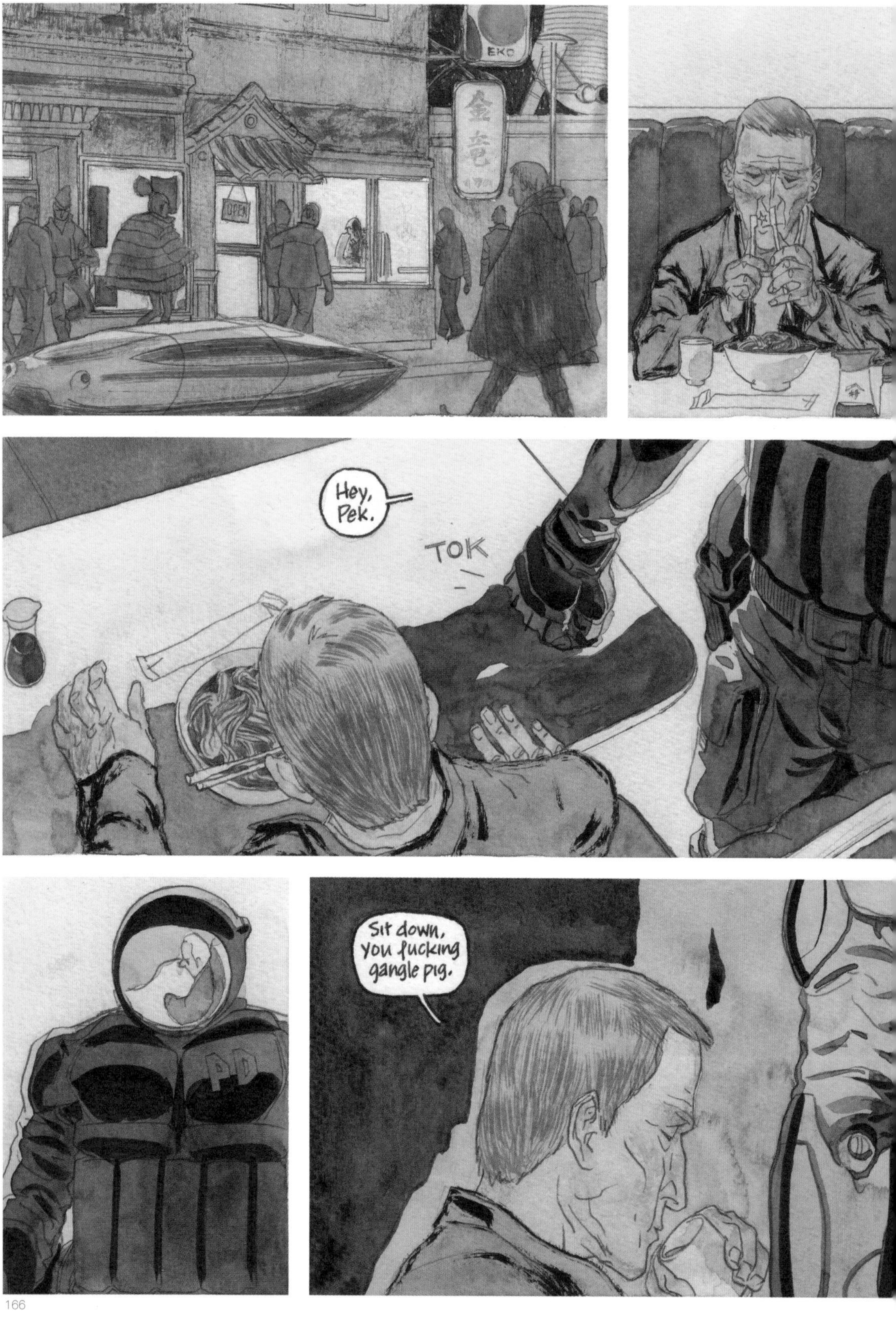
EKO
OPEN
Hey, Pek.
TOK
Sit down, you fucking gangle pig.
PD

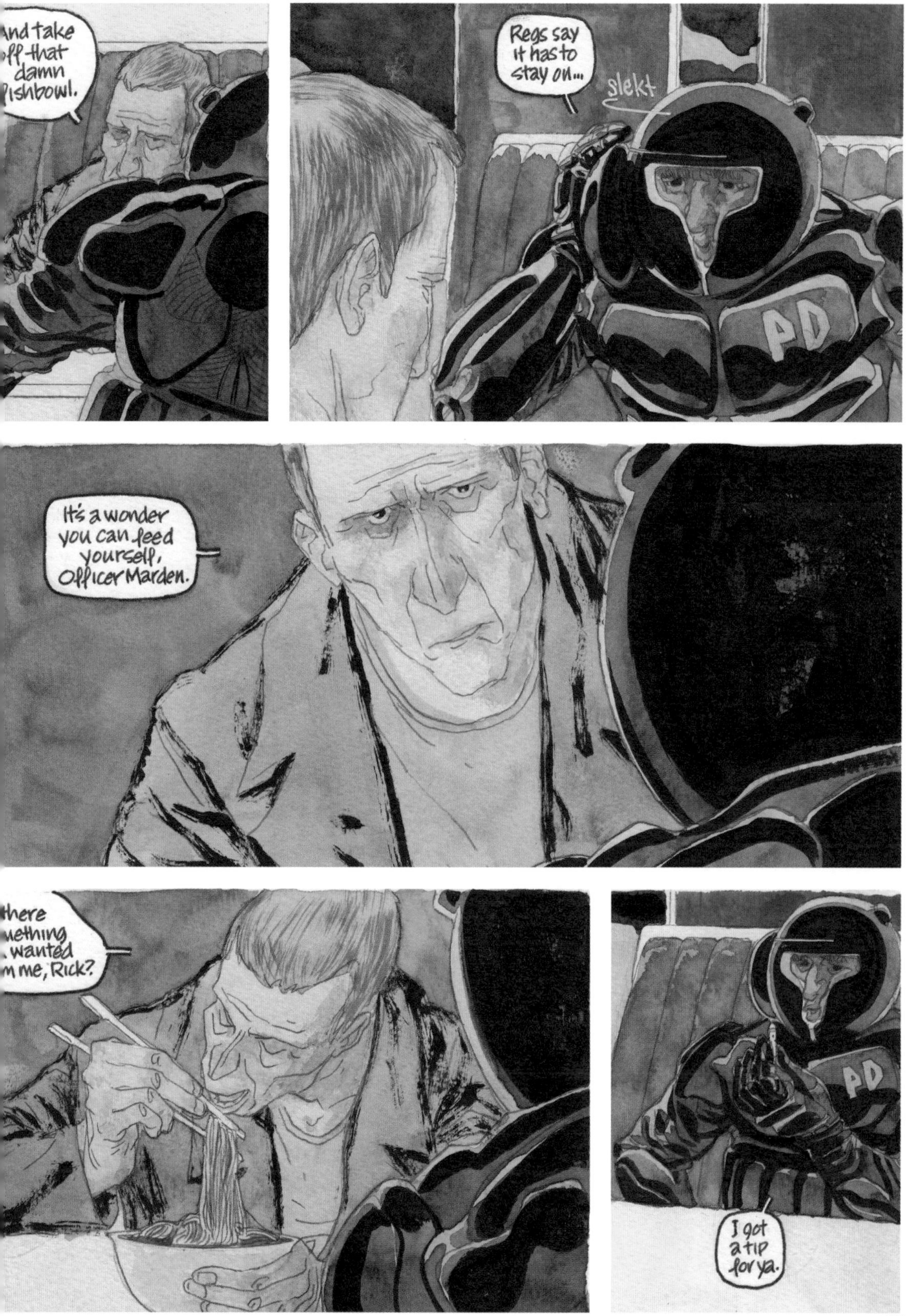

nd take ff that damn ishbowl.
Regs say it has to stay on...
slekt
It's a wonder you can feed yourself, Officer Marden.
there mething wanted m me, Rick?
I got a tip for ya.

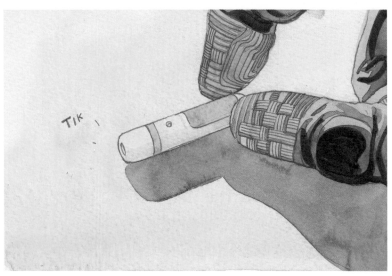

TIK

Who and how much?

A kid. Hunnerd K.

Not another overconfident frat boy. Fez just had to do one earlier this week.

No, no.

A kid.

She's like ...twelve? Gave me the plug herself.

Knew about you.

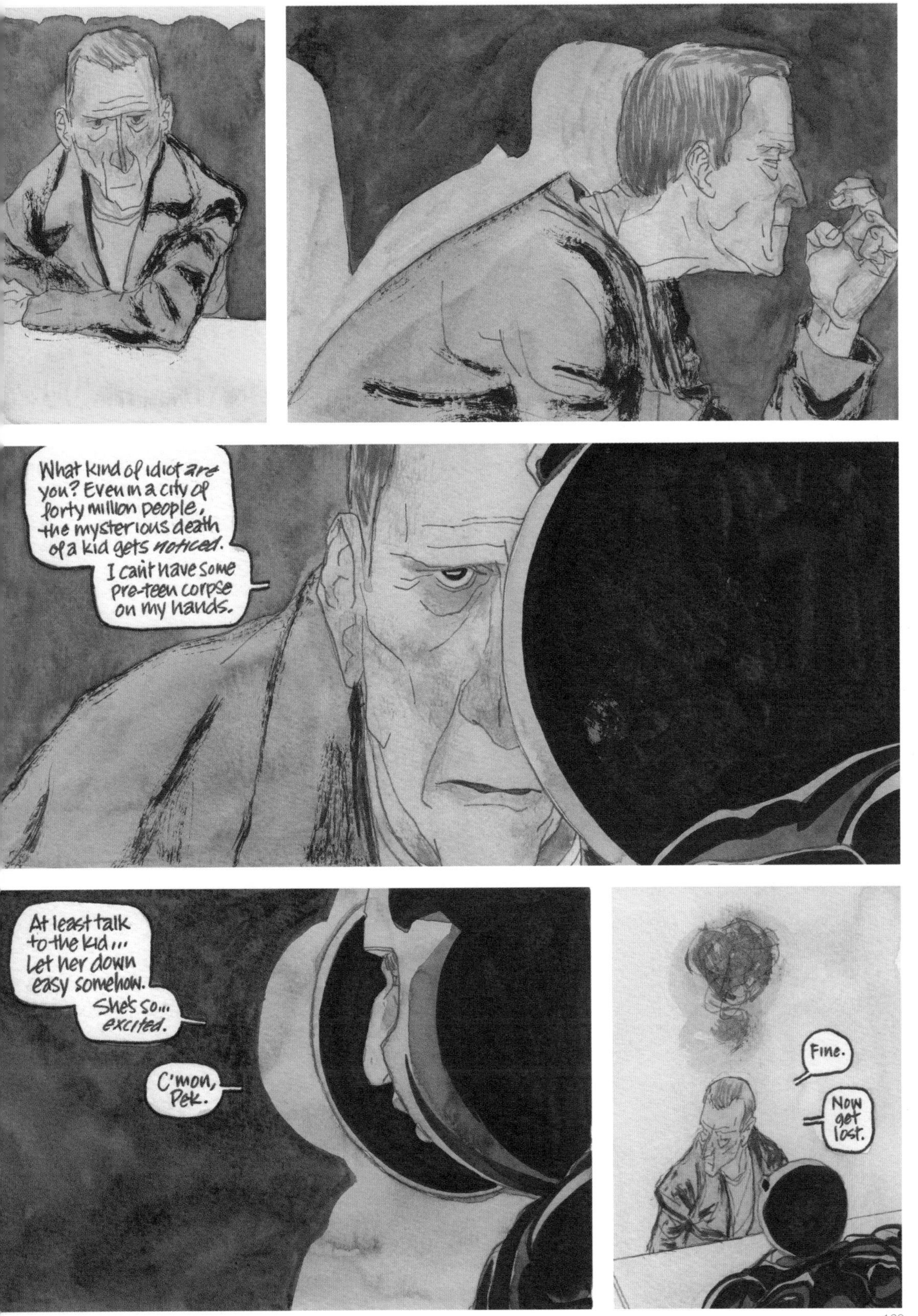
What kind of idiot *are* you? Even in a city of forty million people, the mysterious death of a kid gets *noticed*.
I can't have some pre-teen corpse on my hands.
At least talk to the kid... Let her down easy somehow.
She's so... *excited*.
C'mon, Pek.
Fine.
Now get lost.

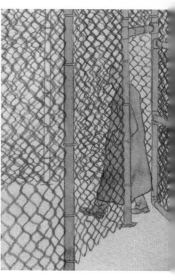

I'm Sofia.

Pek.

So, why'd you want to meet me, Sofia?

Well, I...

I mean, I didn't want to meet you, really, I just wanted to use your machine.

Sorry, that's kind of rude.

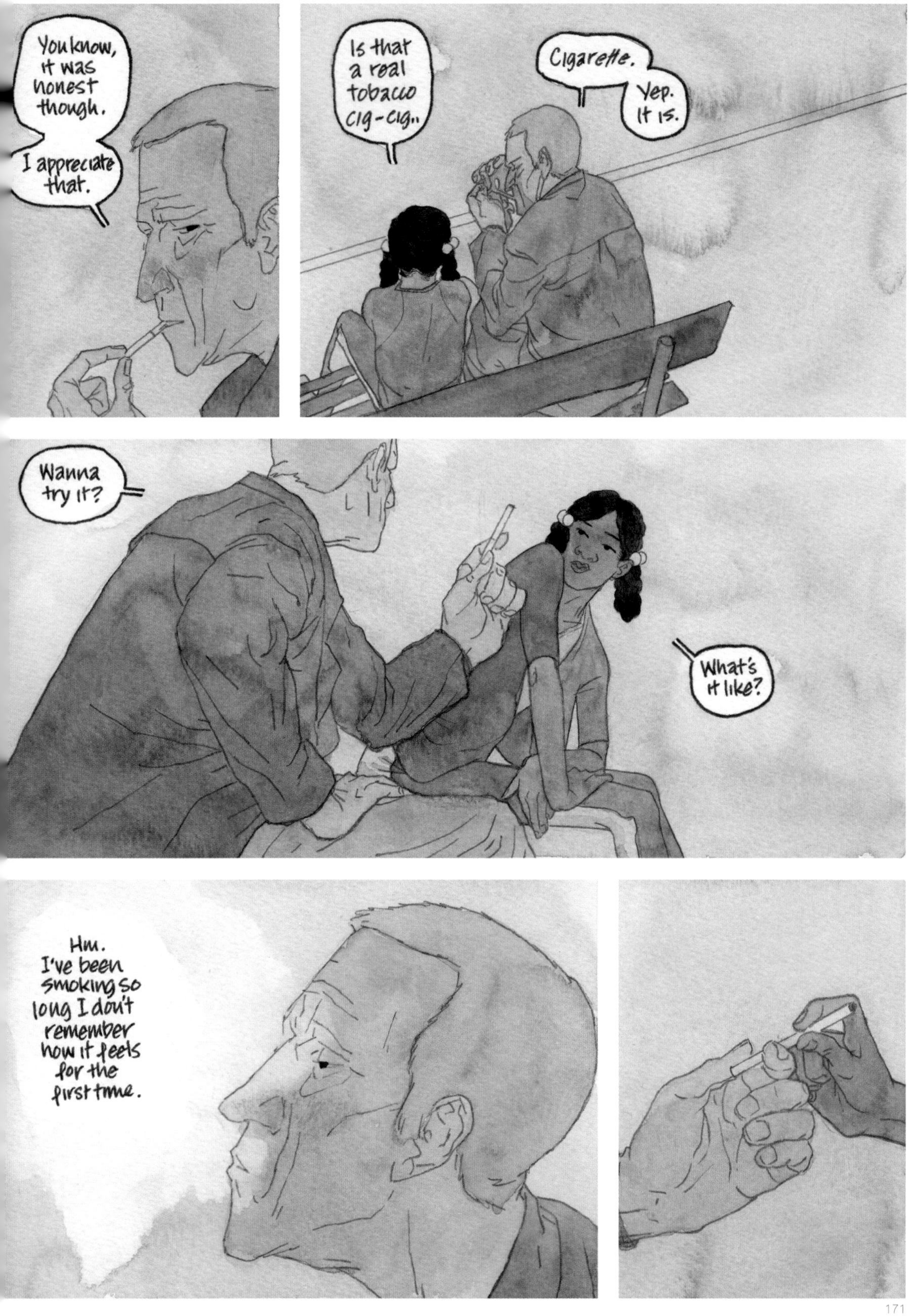
You know, it was honest though.
I appreciate that.
Is that a real tobacco cig-cig..
Cigarette.
Yep. It is.
Wanna try it?
What's it like?
Hm. I've been smoking so long I don't remember how it feels for the first time.

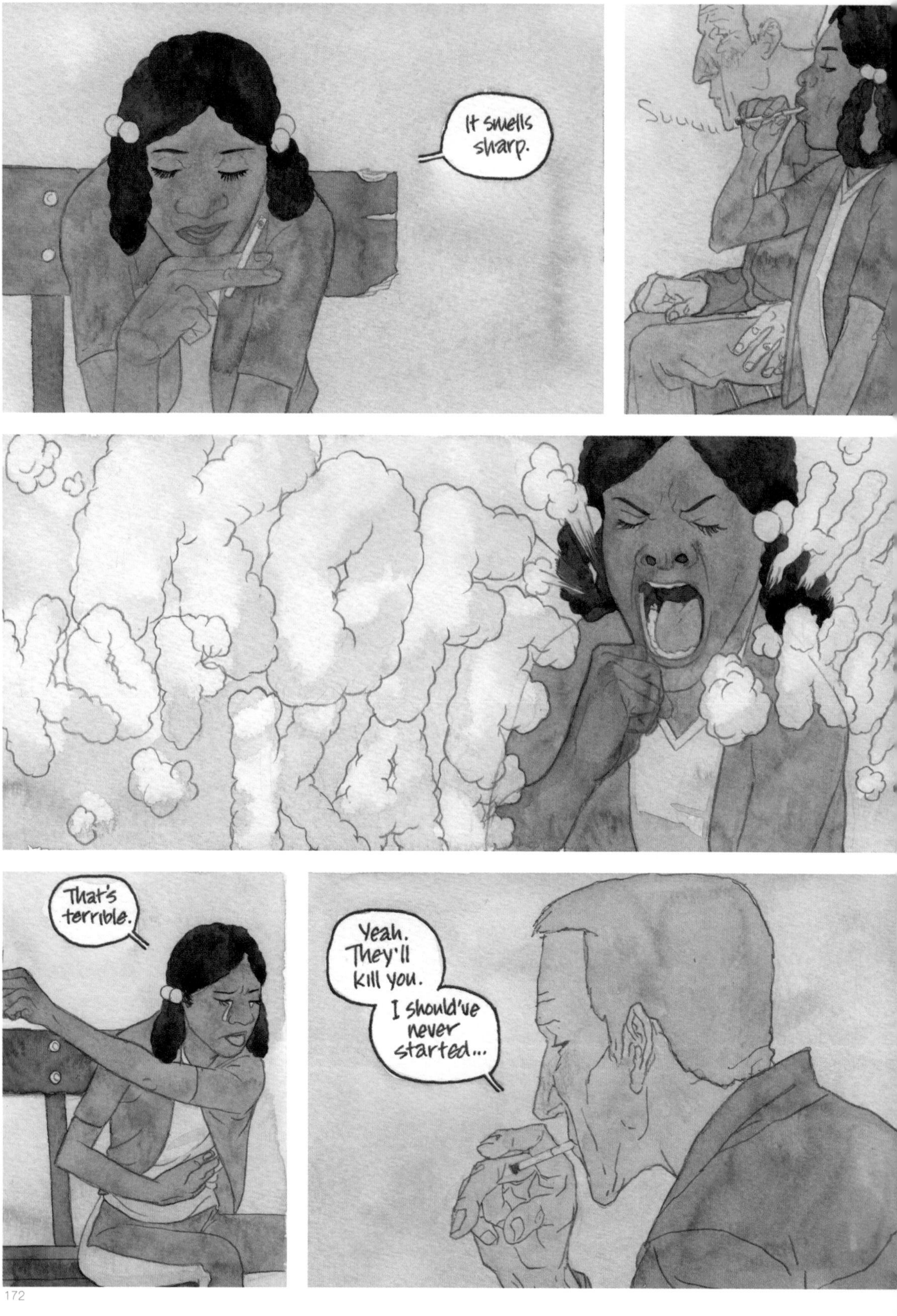
It smells sharp.
Suuuu
That's terrible.
Yeah. They'll kill you.
I should've never started...

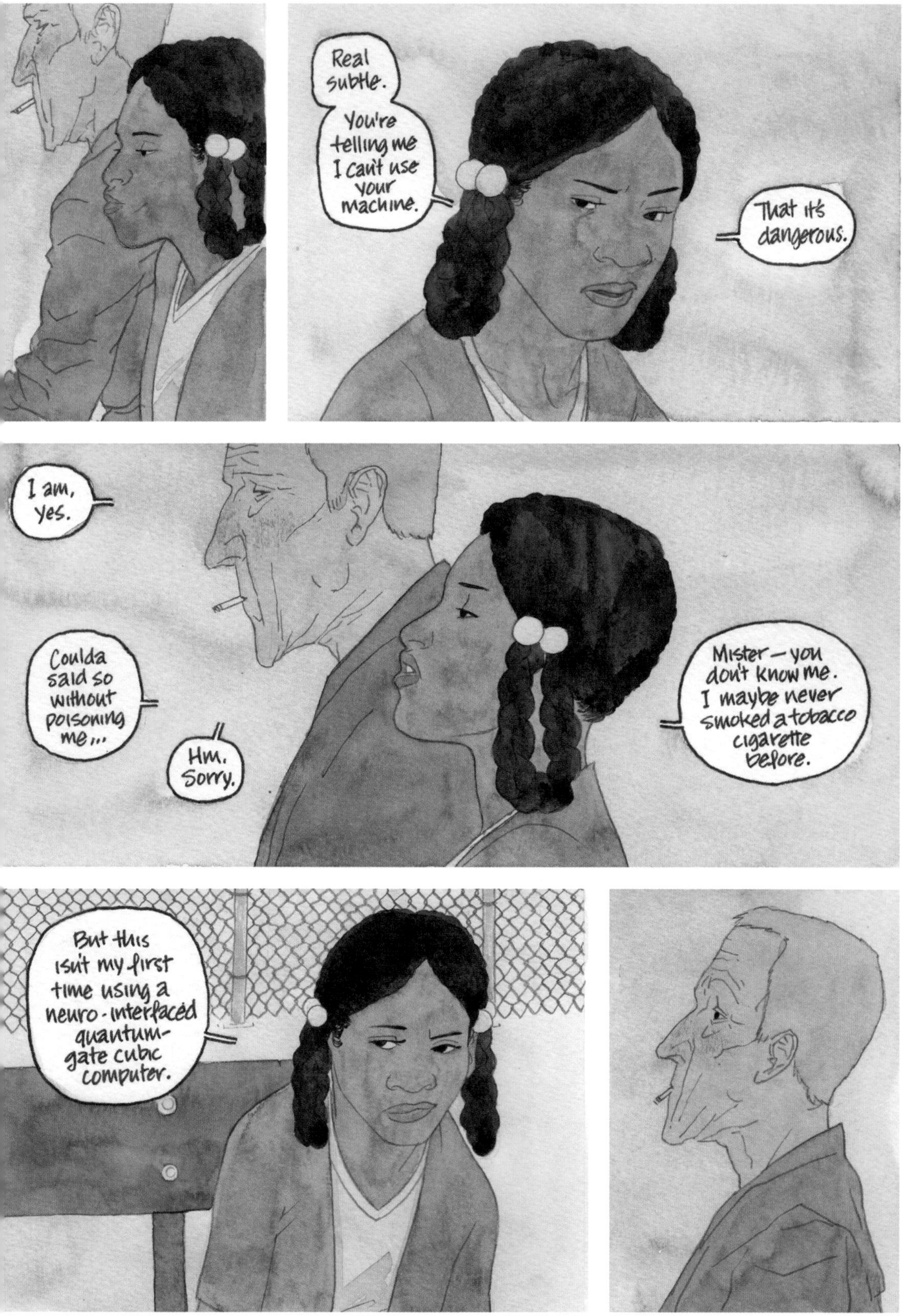
Real subtle.
You're telling me I can't use your machine.
That it's dangerous.
I am, yes.
Coulda said so without poisoning me...
Hm. Sorry.
Mister—you don't know me. I maybe never smoked a tobacco cigarette before.
But this isn't my first time using a neuro-interfaced quantum-gate cubic computer.

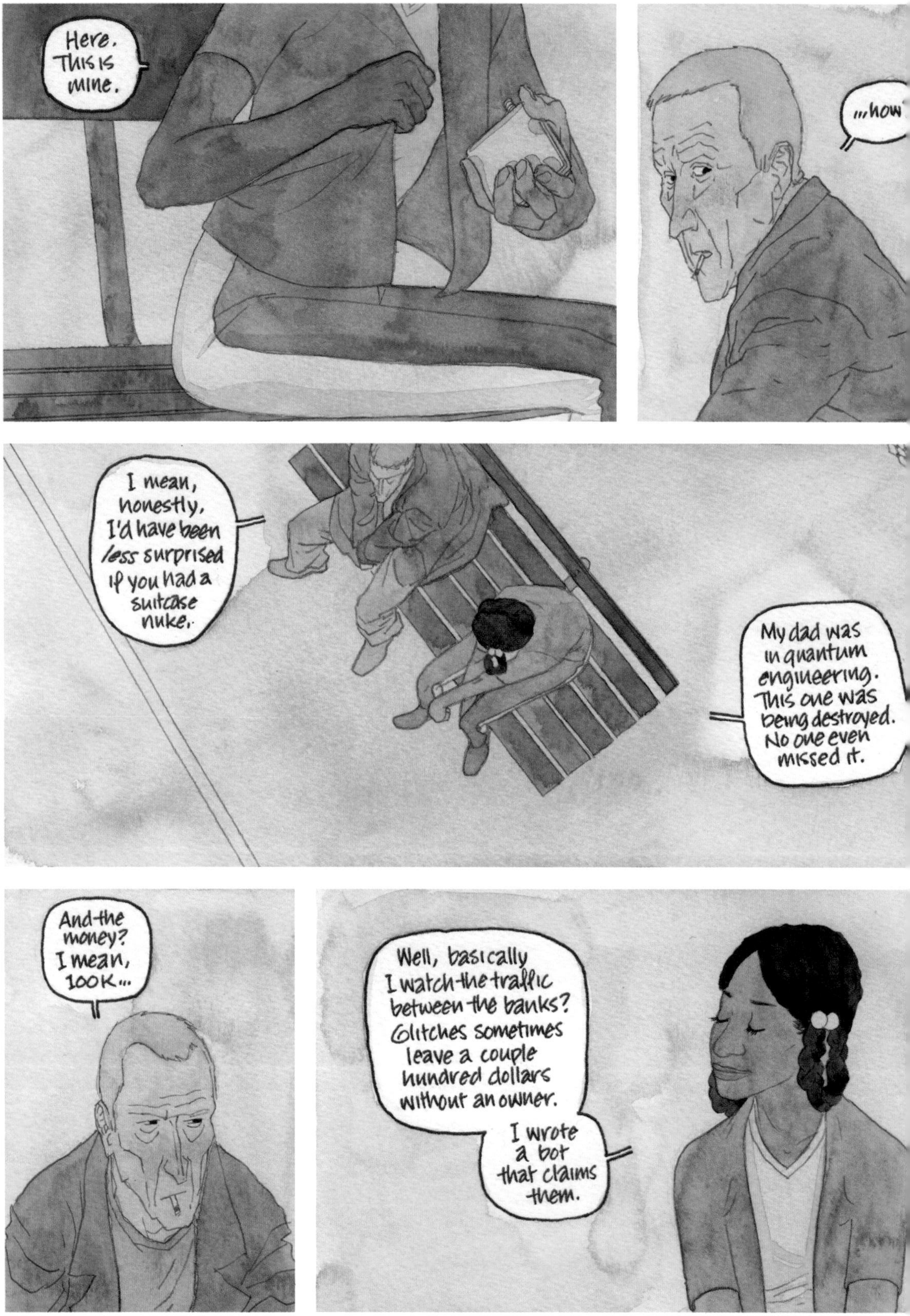
Here. This is mine.
...how
I mean, honestly, I'd have been less surprised if you had a suitcase nuke.
My dad was in quantum engineering. This one was being destroyed. No one even missed it.
And the money? I mean, 100K...
Well, basically I watch the traffic between the banks? Glitches sometimes leave a couple hundred dollars without an owner.
I wrote a bot that claims them.

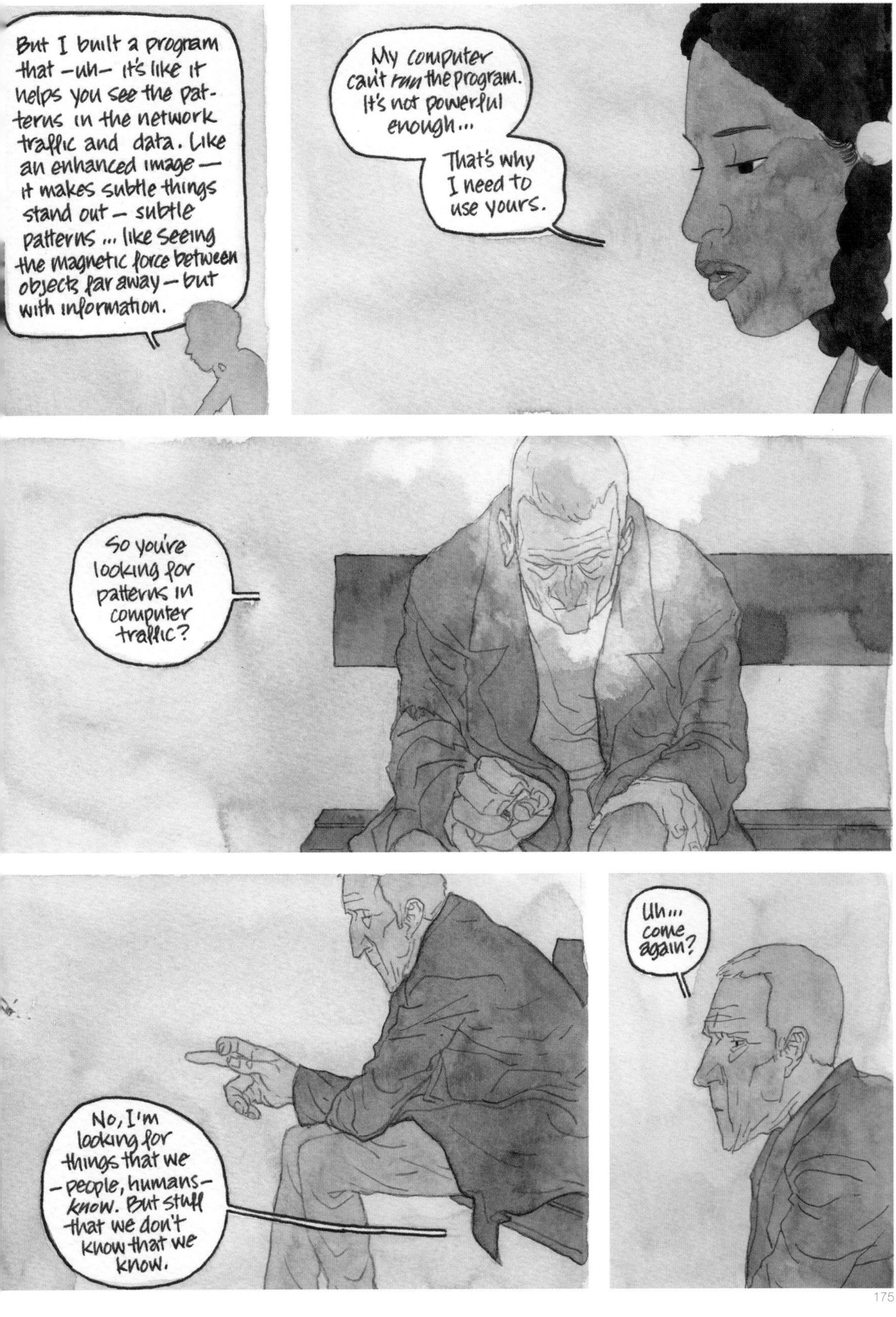
But I built a program that -uh- it's like it helps you see the patterns in the network traffic and data. Like an enhanced image — it makes subtle things stand out — subtle patterns ... like seeing the magnetic force between objects far away — but with information.
My computer can't run the program. It's not powerful enough...
That's why I need to use yours.
So you're looking for patterns in computer traffic?
No, I'm looking for things that we -people, humans- know. But stuff that we don't know that we know.
Uh... come again?

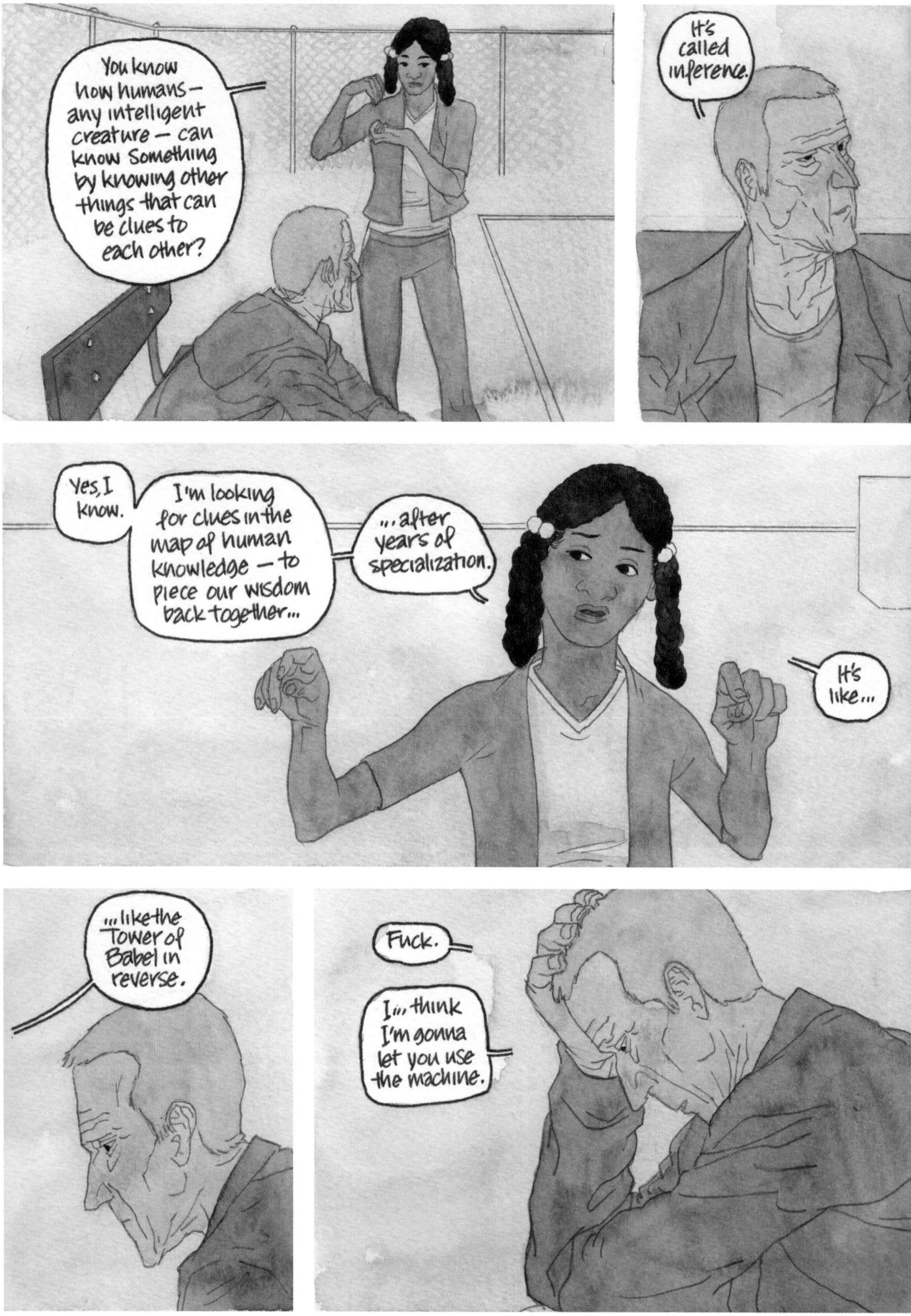
You know how humans— any intelligent creature — can know something by knowing other things that can be clues to each other?
It's called inference.
Yes, I know.
I'm looking for clues in the map of human knowledge — to piece our wisdom back together...
...after years of specialization.
It's like...
...like the Tower of Babel in reverse.
Fuck.
I... think I'm gonna let you use the machine.

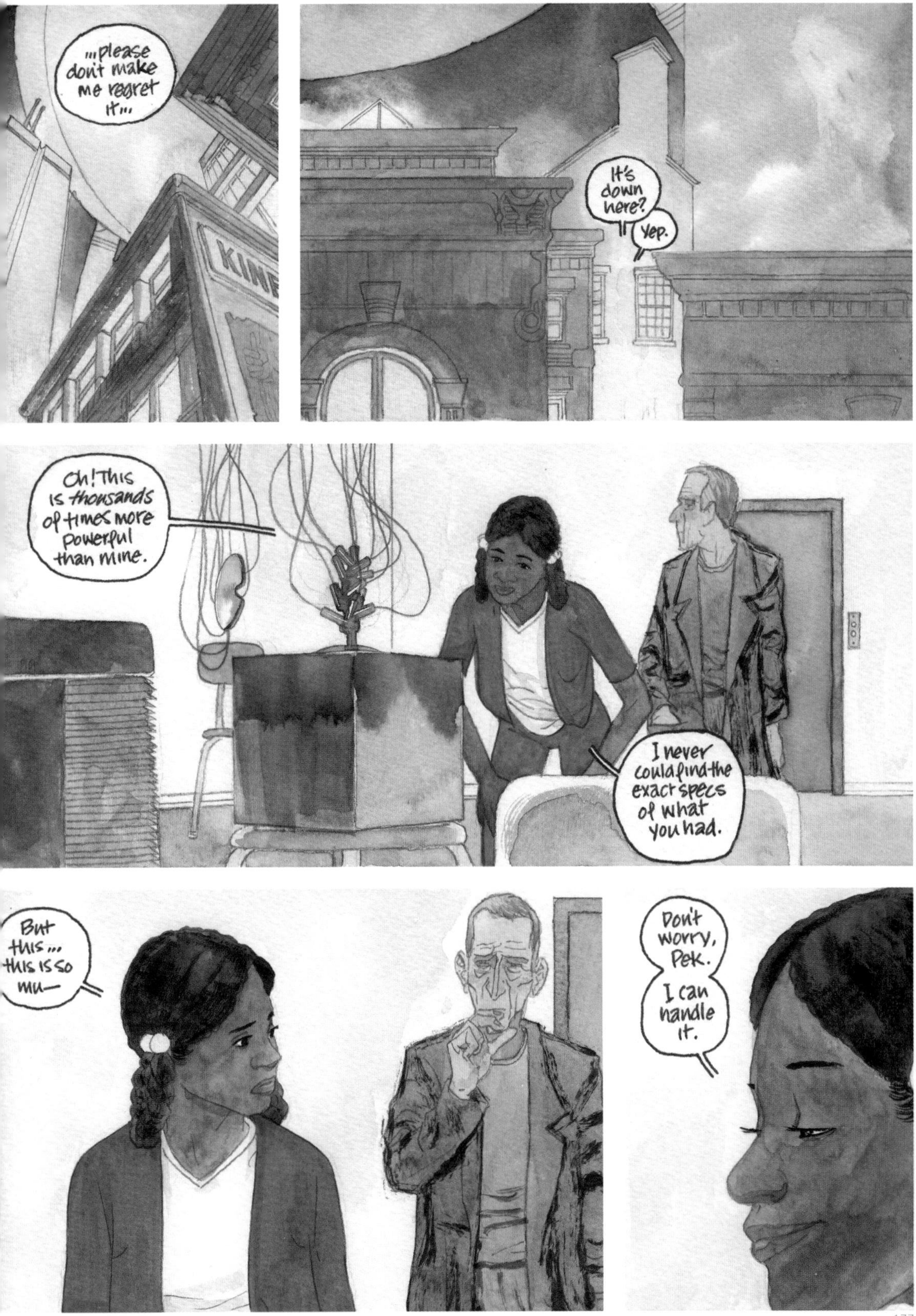
...please don't make me regret it...
It's down here?
Yep.
Oh! This is thousands of times more powerful than mine.
I never could find the exact specs of what you had.
But this... this is so mu—
Don't worry, Pek.
I can handle it.

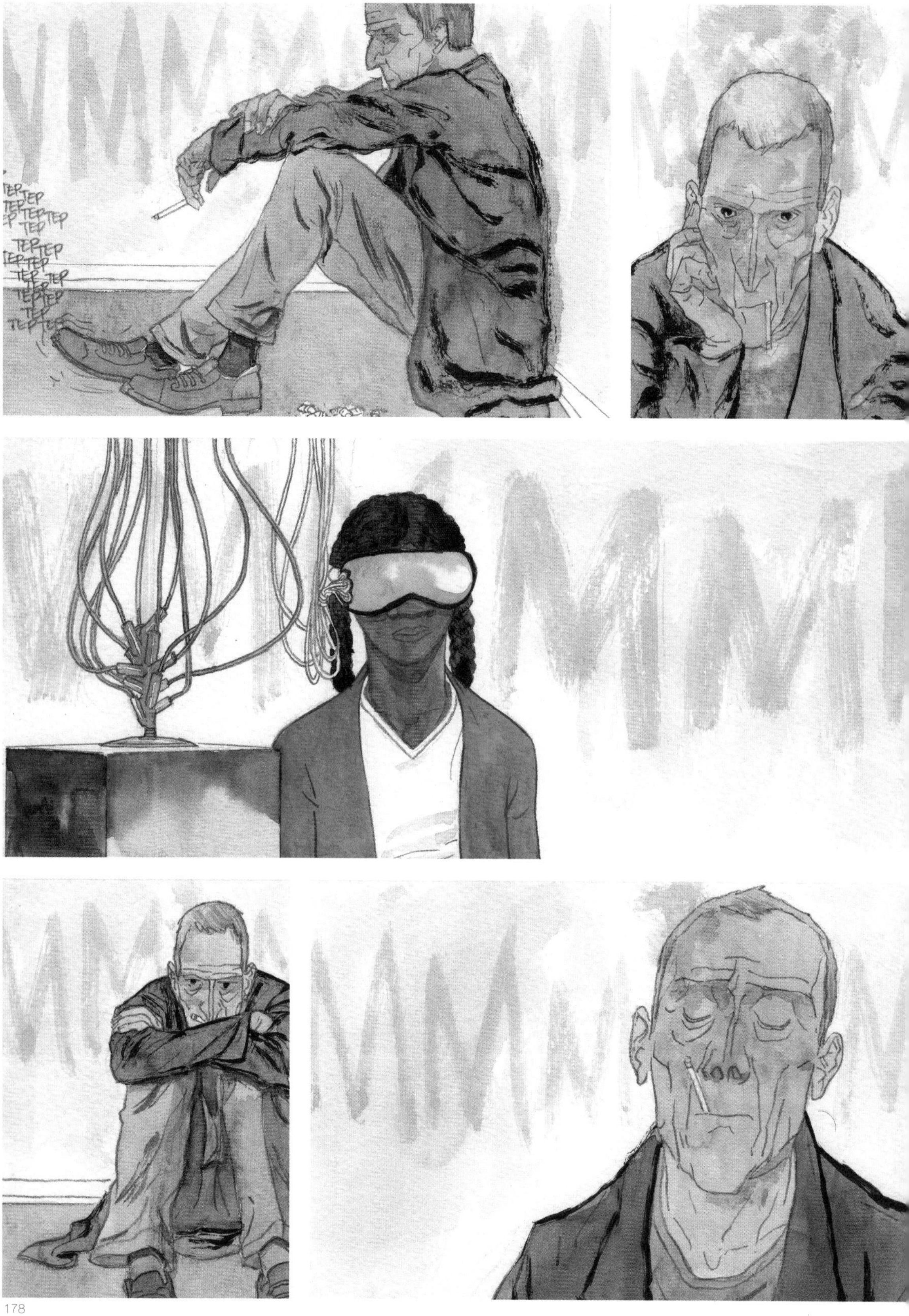
TEP TEP TEP TEP TEP TEP TEP TEP TEP TEP TEP TEP TEP TEP TEP TEP TEP TEP

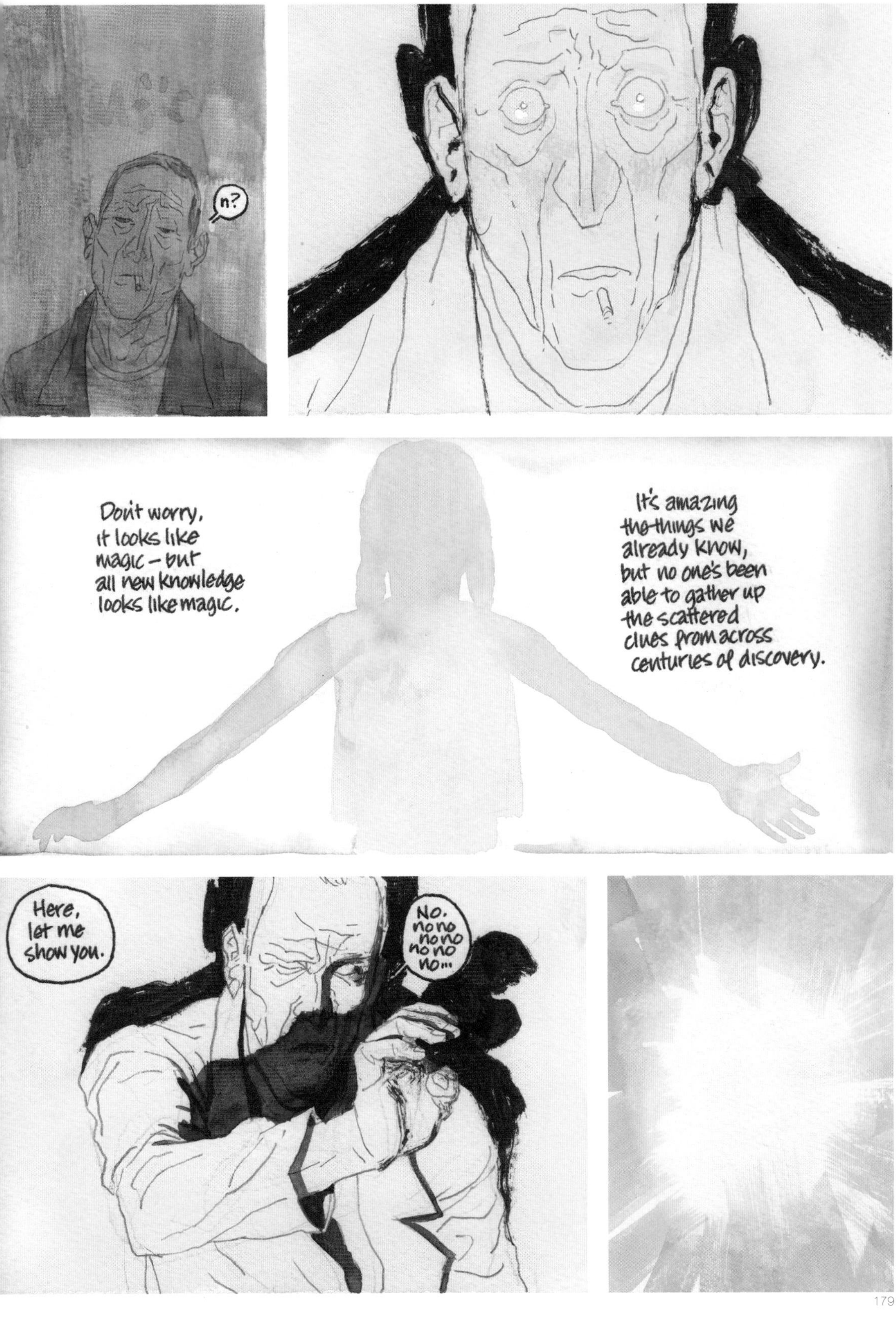
n?
Don't worry, it looks like magic — but all new knowledge looks like magic.
It's amazing the things we already know, but no one's been able to gather up the scattered clues from across centuries of discovery.
Here, let me show you.
No. no no no no no no no...

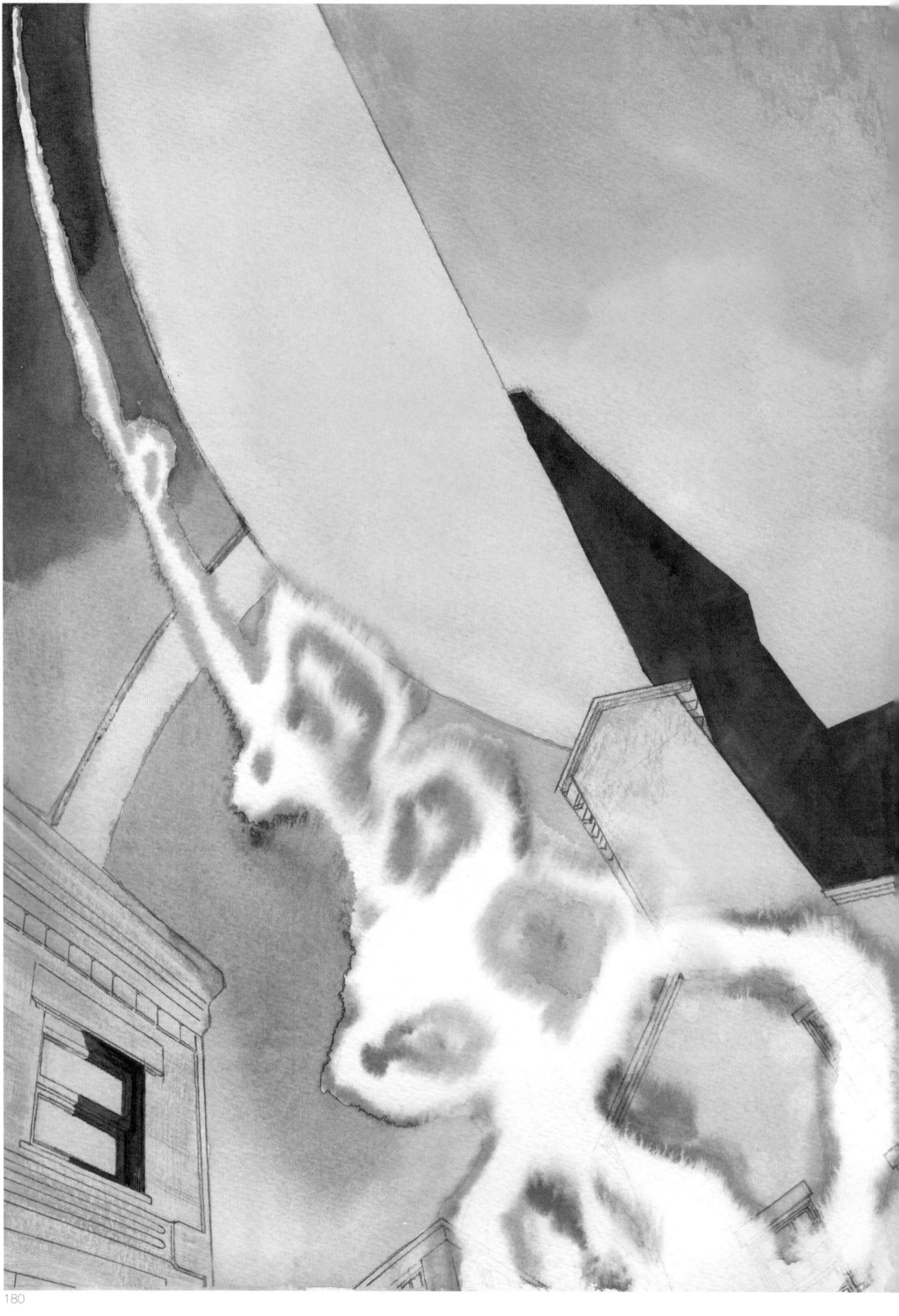

Pleading with Stars
by Kurt Ankeny
& published by AdHouse Books

Library of Congress Control Number: 2019943149
ISBN 1-935233-52-1
ISBN 978-1-935233-52-7
10 9 8 7 6 5 4 3 2 1

Design: Ankeny + Pitzer

AdHouse Books
3905 Brook Road
Richmond, VA 23227 USA
www.adhousebooks.com

First Printing, October 2019

Printed in Malaysia

Cover: 300 gsm Da Dong
Text: 140 gsm Golden Sun uncoated woodfree
Type: Helvetica Neue UltraLight
1 color signature: PMS 280 U

Thanks to my family: Mom & Dad, Kristen, Kyle,
Gladys & Rafael, Cici, Heather, Lander & Loden.
Thanks to those who have taught and supported me:
Cole, Gene, Rob, Frank, Sally, Juan, Caleb,
Bill, Audra, Shelli, Braden, Anthony, Pete, & Meg.
Special thanks to Matt, Whit, Connor, & Ben for
support and opportunity. Thanks to friends and staff
at my 'offices': Gulu, Atomic, & Front Street.

Thanks to Chris for making me part of AdHouse,
it's an honor.

To Jen and Cy: ♥